FATHER AND DAUGHTER

FATHER AND DAUGHTER

Patriarchy, gender and social science

Ann Oakley

First published in Great Britain in 2014 by

Policy Press
University of Bristol
1-9 Old Park Hill
Clifton
Bristol BS2 8BB
UK
t: +44 (0)117 954 5940
pp-info@bristol.ac.uk
www.policypress.co.uk

North America office:
Policy Press
c/o The University of Chicago Press
1427 East 60th Street
Chicago, IL 60637, USA
t: +1 773 702 7700
f: +1 773-702-9756
sales@press.uchicago.edu
www.press.uchicago.edu

© Ann Oakley 2014

British Library Cataloguing in Publication Data
A catalogue record for this book is available from the British Library

Library of Congress Cataloging-in-Publication Data
A catalog record for this book has been requested

ISBN 978 1 44731 810 1 paperback

Cover design by www.thecoverfactory.co.uk
Printed and bound in Great Britain by Hobbs, Southampton
Policy Press uses environmentally responsible print partners

For my children and grandchildren

'The greatest semantic difficulty arises, inevitably, with the word "social". Nor is it made any easier by the fact that so many disciplines, professions and groups claim it as a ... forename. Is it really necessary to drive home so ponderously the fact that all these subjects and groups are concerned in some way with man in society ... Are they not all, in short, emphasizing that man is a social being?'

R.M. Titmuss (1974) *Social policy: An introduction*, p 14.

'Sociology is sexist because it is male-oriented ... it exhibits a focus on ... the interests and activities of men in a gender-differentiated society. The social situations of men and women today are structurally and ideologically discrepant, and the dominant value-system of modern industrialized societies assigns greater importance and prestige to masculine than to feminine roles.'

A. Oakley (1974) *The sociology of housework*, p 2.

'"Now", I said, "comes the season of making up our accounts. Now we have got to collect ourselves; we have got to be one self ... Now is the time of reckoning."'

V. Woolf (1942) 'Evening over Sussex', in
The crowded dance of modern life (1993), p 84.

Contents

List of illustrations

Cover: Richard Titmuss, mid-1960s, Titmuss Papers (AO); Ann Oakley, 1964, photo taken by Robin Oakley.

Key dates

1907	Richard Titmuss born in Bedfordshire
1922	Richard Titmuss leaves school and the family move to London
1926	Richard Titmuss starts work in insurance industry
1937	Richard Titmuss marries Kay Miller
1938	Richard Titmuss publishes his first book, *Poverty and population*
1944	Ann Titmuss born
1950	Richard Titmuss publishes *Problems of social policy* and becomes Professor of Social Administration at the London School of Economics and Political Science
1951	The Titmuss family move to the house in Acton which is commemorated by an English Heritage blue plaque in 2011
1958	Richard Titmuss publishes *Essays on 'the welfare state'*
1962	Ann Titmuss goes to Oxford to study Philosophy, Politics and Economics; Richard Titmuss publishes *Income distribution and social change*
1964	Ann Titmuss marries Robin Oakley
1967	Adam Oakley born
1968	Emily Oakley born; Richard Titmuss publishes *Commitment to welfare*
1970	Richard Titmuss publishes *The gift relationship*
1972	Ann Oakley publishes first book, *Sex, gender and society*
1973	Richard Titmuss dies
1974	Ann Oakley publishes *The sociology of housework* and *Housewife*, and becomes Research Officer at Bedford College, University of London
1977	Laura Oakley born
1984	Ann Oakley publishes a semi-autobiography, *Taking it like a woman*
1987	Kay Titmuss dies
1991	Ann Oakley becomes Professor of Sociology and Social Policy at the Institute of Education, University of London
1996	Ann Oakley publishes *Man and wife: Richard and Kay Titmuss, my parents' early years*

For details of main publications for both Richard Titmuss and Ann Oakley see pp 287-8.

The Titmuss family tree [abbreviated, key names in bold]

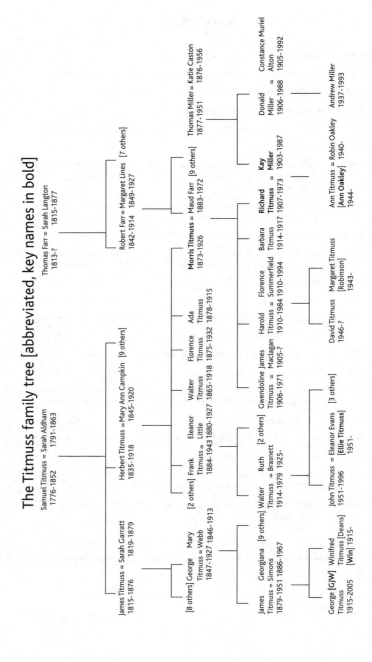

Preface

This book crosses different literary zones and has a foot in different disciplinary camps. For instance, it's neither and both biography and autobiography, neither and both a social history and a history of ideas. Some readers may be disappointed, expecting a more prosaic journey, while others (I hope) will appreciate the book's refusal to fit stereotyped notions of what books ought to be.

One starting point for *Father and daughter* is the familiar notion that the past becomes more important as we age, not only because there's more of it, but because its call for meaning becomes ever more insistent. We feel an intemperate need to assemble life stories that explain who we are and how we got here. No straightforward exercise, this task involves memory, experience, data, interpretation, evidence, context, systematic and non-systematic analysis – in short, all those tools social scientists use to ply their trade. The central task of *Father and daughter* is to draw on these methods in order to investigate two intellectual and social biographies: my own and my father, Richard Titmuss's. I try to show in the book how these biographies are connected and also disconnected, how who he was and what he did intersects with the trajectory of my own work and identity. This story is intensely context-dependent, so there's much in *Father and daughter* about the development of 20th-century social science, that disciplinary universe in which a good part of both our lives have been spent. There's even in it the outline of an alternative history of social science, one in which women's achievements surface from their subterranean rumblings to form a visible part of the historical landscape. The women's story is part of a wider one about how the 'socials' of the 20th century – social work, social policy, sociology, social reform – have variously confronted, competed and coalesced with one another.

Father and daughter is a personal and public story – it's that, perhaps, above all. There are two provisos. The first is that I've chosen not to say much about my own contemporary relationships with men, women, (adult) children and grandchildren. These aren't part of this particular story. The second proviso is that *Father and daughter* is what it says it is: a narrative about the patrimonial inheritance from a father to a daughter. My mother is here, but she appears as a secondary, perplexing figure. This is a tale about patriarchy. Patriarchy is a technical word – 'a system of society or government ruled by men'. The biographies of women like me are irreducibly shaped by the ways in which patriarchy insists on particular forms of gender.

Because of its variegated nature, *Father and daughter* has an episodic quality, and is best read as a series of essays. Its interwoven stories don't follow a straightforward chronology. The focus is on the 1950s and 1960s when Richard Titmuss built up his powerhouse of social policy analysis at the London School of Economics and Political Science (LSE), and his daughter grew up, discovered sociology and gender, and became an academic of her own kind. The history of these years is told mainly in the second half of the book. In the first chapters I explore the legend of who Richard Titmuss was, using documentary and historical materials and also my own experience as his daughter. There isn't much in the book about the later period of my own work from the 1980s on; it seemed more important to give space to the alternative history of women and 'the socials' I uncovered serendipitously while scrutinising the Titmuss legend.

Some names have been changed (these are noted in the text) because their owners are still alive and may not want others to recognise them. I've included a brief timeline and an abbreviated family tree to help readers through the book's interrupted chronology, and to make sense of the complicated kinship structures laid out in Chapters 4 and 8.

The usual disclaimer must be noted: I alone am responsible for the pages that follow. Many people read the manuscript of *Father and daughter*, either in whole or in part, and gave me the benefit of their comments. Thank you so much to: Maureen Beckstette, Tessa Blackstone, Jen Coates, Graham Crow, David Donnison, Karen Dunnell, Sue Fyvel, Howard Glennerster, Tony Gould, Anne Ingold, Tony Lynes, Eileen Munro, Robin Oakley, Roy Parker, Bob Pinker, Penrose Robertson, Hilary Rose, Joy Schaverien, Ian Shaw, Adrian Sinfield, Tytti Solantaus, Ellie Titmuss, and Jane and Felix Wyler. I'm really grateful for all your help, and apologetic about the places where I haven't taken your advice – for example in putting more of my personal experiences in or in taking more of them out; and in failing yet again to rise to Graham Crow's challenge of embarking on a formal social network analysis. One day ...

Many archive and library staff have helped by supplying me with material. I'd particularly like to thank staff in the Bedfordshire and Luton Archives; the British Library of Economic and Political Science at LSE; the Modern Records Centre at the University of Warwick; and, in the USA, the Social Welfare History Archives at the University of Minnesota and the University of Chicago Library, Special Collections Research Center. I'm indebted to Anne Ingold of the Social Science Research Unit for performing invaluable detective-agency services in tracking down some of the characters who appear in Chapters 4 and 10. She in turn was helped by Fiona Wilkie of the World Young Women's Christian Association, by Stefan Dickers of the Bishopsgate Institute, and in Hendon and Surrey by Peter Jerome, Gerrard Roots, David Smith and Hansaben and Vinodrai Patel. We are both grateful to Eugenia Hobday and other members of the Branscombe family for information on Martha Branscombe's life and work used in Chapters 10 and 11. Research for the book was facilitated by financial support from the Titmuss–Meinhardt Fund at LSE, by a Leverhulme Trust Emeritus Fellowship, and by the Institute of Education's continuing tolerance of having a maverick in its midst. I want also to thank those who talked to me about Richard Titmuss for *Father and daughter* – conversations glorified by the term 'interview' in the notes at the end of the book. I recognise, and apologise for, the fact that shortage of space has meant that I haven't been able to do their own careers sufficient justice. I've tried to trace all owners of copyright in the photographs and other material used in the book, and apologise for any I haven't been able to contact.

Writing the book has involved holding back the tide of commitments to family and friends, so I also apologise for the strength of my flood defences, and especially for my derelictions of duty as a grandmother. That isn't why this book is dedicated to my children and grandchildren. The dedication is evidence-based: the material of our childhoods and our parentage is an enduring resource to be alternatively remembered, celebrated, plundered, complained about, investigated, analysed, forgotten, recited and thus endlessly reinvented. Many people said, on reading the manuscript, that it made them think about their own childhoods, to reflect on these, sometimes to consider them in a new light. *Father and daughter* makes, I hope, a contribution to the evolving genre of life-writing, especially as this intersects with the epistemology of social science. But the book can also be read as just a little bit of history for those people I love the most, whose connection with me keeps me rooted, challenged and constantly inspired.

Ann Oakley
Rutland
March 2014

1

Daughter of a Blue Plaque Man

My bedroom is awkwardly-shaped and unfriendly, just as I remember it. Its one window, hung to the side of the room, lets in a mean rectangle of light. Was this absence of light, a feature not shared with any of the other bedrooms in the house, the reason my parents reserved this room for me? When I was first brought here more than 60 years ago, there was brown linoleum and a washed-out green rug on the floor, and my little bed, only slightly wider than a baby's cot, had been sequestered in the room's darkest corner. Even in full daylight you needed a lamp by the bed to read by. I don't remember the decor on the walls then, only, some years later, being allowed to choose a quirky combination of blue-and-white spotted wallpaper and bright red curtains. The colours were completely out of tune with the rest of the house. The rest of the house was composed of matt white surfaces, dull carpets that wouldn't show the dirt and such an economy of decorative items that the eye was mildly shocked to chance on any of them. Muted furniture sat hoping for a more interesting time with guests. There were a few highly polished dark wood tables and chests inherited from my mother's respectable South-East London family, and later some blonde wood constructions, my mother's pride and joy, acquired in the 1960s from new furniture stores such as Habitat.

It was a house bought by my father and made by my mother in a formula rife among the English middle-middle-classes in the 1950s. They bought it from a man who worked in the Ministry of Food and who was delighted to sell it to 'good English folk'.[1] It was a family home for a family that didn't ever really, to me, feel like one. There was her and there was him and there was me. I was their child, planted among their walls and their carpets. It was their life. They wanted a child, or at least my mother did, and the getting of that child had not been easy. My mother was four days away from her 41st birthday when I was born during a general anaesthetic in St Mary's Hospital, Paddington, and a girl instead of the boy they'd already named Adrian. It was wartime and she was, understandably, nervous. Her husband was on his way up from dissecting insurance statistics to worldwide fame as a social scientist and pioneer of the welfare state.

That's why we're here today, to honour him. The occasion of my re-entering the physical domain of childhood is the affixing of a blue plaque to the house where I grew up. *Father and daughter* is a story about two people and about the history and biography of social science. Richard Titmuss and his daughter, Ann Oakley, both social scientists – although of different kinds – are a case-study in how the impulse to understand and change 'the terrible and magnificent world of human society'[2] is driven and shaped by people's place within it. Gender, class, material and intellectual resources, disposition and temperament – all these are important. Beyond the Titmuss–Oakley case-study lie other stories: about the interlocutions of gender and social studies; about the pull and distortions of family relationships; about the twinning of accredited knowledge with power; about the impositions of the academy itself on gender relations and on what counts as knowledge.

Richard Titmuss's writings justly made him famous as the 'premier philosopher and sociologist' of the welfare state.[3] He was an indefatigable pointer-out of errors in the perception and functioning of the welfare system, of the mismatch between people's social needs and the inflexibility of increasingly specialised and bureaucratised welfare services. He used his armouries of facts to contradict those who said 'the welfare state' – a term he always encapsulated in quotation marks because welfare wasn't one system but many – had solved the problem of poverty, and those who said the burden on the better-off meant that it was time to embed welfare in the capitalist system. He said that welfare was about moral relationships as well as economic ones. He opened up discussion of social policy so that it became a subject in its own right, a new way of understanding the logic and consequences of public interventions in private lives. He said many things we still need to hear today. His daughter has used her social science to make different points, but also some of the same ones. The main difference lies in the boundless topography of gender – its prevalence, its injustices, its affront to any kind of democratic morality. The informal welfare of the private world and its effects on public roles lay beyond Richard Titmuss's vision. The similarity between the Titmuss and Oakley brands of social science lies in the marshalling of evidence to understand how social systems work, and a respect for the uses of social science in promoting real-world welfare.

This awkward book – neither biography nor autobiography, neither straightforward history nor standard social science – is a reckoning of a kind. It's my reckoning of how two professional lives, within the broader sweep of social science in the 20th century, have been shaped by their personal and intellectual connections. The book has taken time to write; much more significantly, it has *needed* the perspective of time. The book's purpose is not to settle old accounts or contribute to the sad genus of whistle-blowing memoirs. What I did want to do is take a keener look at the fabrication of legends – formulaic stories told about individuals as ways of explaining who they are and what they did. *Father and daughter* is probably best read as a series of reflections about biography, autobiography and history – about my

father's work and my own in the context of British society and social
science in the 20th century.

Everybody knows that as you age the distant past encroaches more
and more. Anything can set it off: a sight, a scent, a taste, a phrase.
When I first started cycling regularly in my 40s to save the time and
cost of other forms of travel and to strengthen my bones, a journey
through that Proustian land of the senses which recovers and recycles
memory was an unanticipated bonus. Cycling and recycling: the pun
is apt. Random prompts from the external world spark the brain, an
autonomous organ, into its own internal wanderings.

Now, starting here, in the bedroom of the Blue Plaque House, to
which I have kindly been admitted by its current owners, the air's
memory forces me back to what it was like to live here with those
people, my parents, to be moulded by them and by this place, an
uninspiring house on the western edge of London in the British
1950s. I want to say − it is almost obligatory − that mine was a
materially easy childhood, that my needs were met, that my parents
loved and cherished me, that I really have nothing to complain about.
In so many conversations over the years in the social research world
I've inhabited we've talked about class and deprivation. It is said, and
I agree with this, that no one from an advantaged background like
mine can conceivably understand the adversity of those brought up
in poverty and hunger.

We all struggle to understand anyone apart from ourselves. (We
all struggle to understand ourselves.)

I remember one particular night in that angled and by then
blue-and-white spotted bedroom (with the brown linoleum still
covering the floor). I would have been about 11 or 12. I couldn't
sleep. I don't know why I couldn't sleep, but this had been going on
for some days or possibly weeks. Only other insomniacs − for that
is what I later learned to call myself − can appreciate the absolute
awfulness of lying awake when everyone else is safely unconscious.
The unconsciousness of sleep is a really good place to be, unlike other
forms of unconsciousness, which are bad. If the price of existential
awareness is perpetual consciousness, give me a coma every time.

Either I or my mother had suggested moving the furniture around
to help me go to sleep. So my bed had journeyed from its dark

corner to face the parsimonious window. The red curtains were pulled back so I could look at the stars. I lay in bed and looked at the stars. They were bright, really astonishingly bright. There was no risk in those days of confusing them with aeroplanes, and there was probably a good deal less of what we now call light pollution. I stared at the unpolluted sky all night. I interrogated those stars and wondered if alien 11- or 12-year-olds were looking back at me. I thought about time and existence and the immensity of everything, and how, beyond all this, there was absolutely nothing: no world, no reason for being alive, no mind or soul or love; no red curtains or scratchy school uniform or schools; no bird-eaten cherries in the garden, no terror, no loneliness, just absolutely nothing at all. The thought of absolutely nothing is quite terrifying. That night became emblematic of my childhood. The loneliness, the questioning, the panic: the childhood of the daughter of the man whose name is now inscribed on the wall of the house.

The starry sky framed by my bedroom window hovered over a flat roof onto which I could, and sometimes did, lower myself in the daytime by pushing the window right up and sliding down a shiny black drainpipe. From there I could in theory jump some ten feet down onto the hard concrete of the driveway shared with the next-door house. Then in theory I could run away and never be seen again. But I never made that jump. I just used to crouch on the flat roof, out of my bedroom, not in the house, but not anywhere else either. I thought my parents couldn't find me (although the open window must have been a bit of a give-away), but otherwise what had I accomplished except an accentuation of my liminal state? That was, and is, another abiding feature of my remembered childhood: what the anthropologists call liminality. It was the sensation of always being an outsider, an observer (of myself as well as others), of inhabiting a territory that bordered with other territories, but yet was entirely its own, with its own rules and imaginations. I call this a sensation rather than an experience because I felt it physically, in my skin and my nerves and the lining of my stomach and the chambers of my heart.

In the black night of the shining stars I fell victim for the first time to the ultimate insomniac horror: the panic of the thought that one will never sleep again elided gently but relentlessly into the reality of actually staying awake all night. The mind stares at itself, running around in manic circles, becoming one enormous electric seizure, giving up completely the capacity for rational thought. The darkness went: the stars got lost in the dawn. My mother, before she went to their bedroom to sleep herself, promised me that no one ever stayed awake all night. But I did. Her error condemned me to a lasting condition of suspicion. All promises thereafter, so far as I was concerned, were likely to be rhetoric and deceit.

The house in which and on which my father is honoured was the place in which he wrote his books – books which I much admire about healthy social structures and about philosophies of action which make us moral human beings. He wrote these texts here while my mother looked after the house with all the socially approved passion of a 1950s housewife, and while I sat in my bedroom playing or reading or writing or crying or walked up and down the long wide stultifying road to and from my stultifying school. It seems I can't write about my childhood without resorting to these unpleasant epithets. Their insistent negativity surprises me. I think that for a long time I have acceded to a version of my childhood in which I was the fortunate child of two loving and able parents, and especially the very lucky daughter of a famous and charismatic man.

My father left my upbringing largely to my mother, as was the fashion at the time. Because *his* socialism conflicted with *her* desire for upward social mobility, I was sent to fee-paying schools until about the time insomnia set in (there was no causal connection). Then I succeeded in getting a 'free' place through that iniquitous and unsocialist system known as the 'eleven plus' examination. In and out of school my daily care lay in my mother's hands; she didn't work outside the home after I was born. Her child was her labour: her child, her husband's ascent to fame, their joint social diary, and the house they lived in, this one with the blue plaque stuck on the outside wall of what used to be my father's bedroom after they stopped sharing a room sometime in my teens. It's a tiny room, barely big enough for a bed and a small chest and a chair for him to put his clothes on. There was an electric fire cemented into the wall and I would hear the switches being snapped on and off from my bed across the landing. My father suffered from insomnia too, but his remedy was barbiturate sleeping pills. The capsules, which waited in a phial on the small chest by his bed, were coloured a cheering bright sea-green.

In the house's reincarnation overseen by its present owners, that room is now a bathroom. The owners take me and my family on a tour of the house and then allow us, after the delivery of speeches on the steps, to kneel in the bath which is positioned under the window, and so allow our faces to be captured in the same plane as the blue plaque. So there am I looking out, next to my father's circular glazed ceramic memorial, both of us facing the cameras.

Children take their experiences for granted. This is how it is, and it couldn't be any other way. This father who dresses in crisp dark suits and departs for the office every morning with his importantly bulging briefcase, the yellow front door slamming so decisively behind him. This mother bent on attending to the surfaces of her house: everything polished as much as it can be, the silver cleaned, the curtains pressed, all the paintwork and walls washed down every year by the obliging Mr Crawford with his cough and his watery blue eyes, and then by the rather less proletarian Mr Pearce, who talked in such a draining low voice about his invalid wife. My father couldn't change a plug or put a nail in the wall. He wouldn't have known what to do with the blue plaque. He couldn't drive a car or choose his own socks. His dependence on my mother for these necessities was as much a matter of pride to her as the meticulously managed interior of the house. She couldn't have achieved this without an array of helpers – not only the men who washed the walls and put the nails in, but a succession of working-class women who came from the cheap terraced streets of Acton in their pink overalls (I only remember the overalls being pink, just as I only remember my father wearing yellow ties the same colour as the front door) to follow her precise instructions about what had to be done on what day in what order. He was always referred to as 'The Professor'. Shirley or Sharon or whoever it was (they never had surnames like Mr Pearce or Mr Crawford did) had to be especially careful about not disturbing 'The Professor' when he was at work in his study.

What did professional men do in houses in the 1950s? They paid for them. They entered them in the evenings and at weekends, they stored their wives and children, their suits and their shaving equipment in them. I remember stories of R.H. Tawney, he who spattered our immaculate Christmas hearth with golden strands of coltsfoot tobacco. After his wife, Jeanette, died Tawney lived on his own in Bloomsbury, in a tall house in Mecklenburgh Square which smelt of kippers. The house was slightly unhygienic because the loss of a housewife was an irremediable blow for any man. Jeanette was the sister of the man whose famous report established the welfare state. William Beveridge's sister wasn't much lauded for her domestic habits. She's reputed to have personified the acquisitive society while her husband wrote a book about it. Like most such stories, there's bound to be another one lurking here. The politician Richard Crossman, who once tried to teach me the principles of British history, called Tawney's marriage an encumbrance, whereas Titmuss's, he declared, was an inspiration.[4]

An inspirational marriage, what is that? In the small space next to the confrontation of the cooker and the back door in the Blue Plaque House's tiny kitchen, my father used to dry the dishes sometimes, and sometimes he would stand at the sink to peel the potatoes, but that was the extent of his contribution to household labour. There were two steps up from the kitchen to the breakfast room, so the person drying the dishes was higher than the person whose hands were in the sink. He was taller than her anyway, but this elevation exaggerated his dominance. He never looked after me, his only child, or took me out or away, on his own. He never wielded a vacuum cleaner or a brush or a duster; I don't think he even engaged in that most epigenetically masculine of all domestic tasks, emptying the rubbish. He never went out to buy food, not even in a masculine bag-carrying capacity. He never made a bed, rising from his own and returning nightly to its magically straightened embrace. He never washed or ironed his clothes or anybody else's. She organised his wardrobe, forcing him periodically to attend a bespoke tailor's in order to commission a new suit or set of shirts: his arms, she said proudly, were too long for the ordinary ready-made kind. Her husband was not a ready-made man. Thus she was able to eject him from the Blue Plaque House every morning, every inch a well-attired Professor.

This is how I remember them, with their tireless enactment of gendered domestic ideology. At the time it all appeared, of course, simply normal to me. Children begin by assuming that the practices of their own families are universal, and then spend the rest of their lives discovering, sometimes happily, sometimes not, that this is not so. Deviation may be the norm, but the emotional potency of those early impressions sticks with us.

Time changes the bodies and faces of our parents, yet in our memories they tend to be fixed in one particular era and style. It is some time in my teenage years, probably the late 1950s. They stand side by side with air in between them. He stoops slightly, as though wishing to accommodate himself to her, as in the drying-dishes-by-the-kitchen-sink position. Her hair is grey and pulled back off her face, which is comfortably creased. Her blue-grey eyes have acquired a watery tinge. Her back is rounded, another reason for his inclining position. That tailor-made suit hangs off him as though the tailor got his measurements wrong. My father's body is thin, it always was, as though the attributed poverty of his childhood meant that he never had enough to eat. When he was dying of cancer my mother bought him double cream – the doctor told her she should – but food never made much impression on him. His great dark eyes look at me, unreadable in their depths: the face is structured by bone, not flesh. Dark hair, almost black, and very straight, is combed back from his face. I learnt early from my father that adage about men's discomfort at the rituals of bathing. Her daily bath was a ritual but his was to wash himself gingerly in the sink of his special room, his not-to-be-disturbed-in room, 'the Shaving Room' we called it, because he did shave in it, in the old-fashioned sink in its corner, but he also wrote his books in it, gazing out over the tidy suburban garden, with his pride and joy, the greenhouse, tucked away in the corner.

His image is stronger than hers – the black hair, the dark eyes, the dark suit, the height, the dissembling posture. Beside him she's a misty grey, a paler, blander, more ordinary set of contours. I knew by the time of those locked images that I featured as 'one d.' in *Who's who*. I realised that my father was important enough to have his own entries in publications about famous people. My mother fell on these with the eagerness of a playwright reading the first West End reviews, but, with traces of normal teenagery alienation, I didn't pay them very much attention. I do remember one, though, an *Observer* profile from 1959 headed 'Welfare Professor' which made a point about my father's modest private life with his wife and daughter in Ealing and his main worry being whether he should allow his daughter to leave school at 15 in order to play the flute.[5] I don't remember this premature departure from education ever being discussed, because where on earth would one go at 15 to play the flute?

Between his work and hers lay mine: to do well at school, to look pretty and accomplished when visitors came, and not to get in the way the rest of the time. When my parents had dinner parties for important political figures or their socialist friends, I would slip away from the dinner table after the main course and play the piano in the next room. Between the dining room and the sitting room there was an old-fashioned 'hatch' through which clean sherry glasses passed one way and my Grade Seven piano pieces the other.

There were other occasions I can remember with affection, helped by documentary evidence. A fuzzy black-and-white photograph shows my father and me (I am about eight or nine) sitting in the garden reading on a summer afternoon. I am squinting (I had bad eyesight and the sun was shining directly at me). My father's shirt is open to the sun. Our garden backed onto playing fields owned by the North Thames Gas Board, a nationalised industry. 'They'll never be built on,' pronounced my father confidently of these green fields. They never have been, although the current owners of the house have grown Leylandii to screen the garden from the oafish behaviour of the men who play on them now.

That photograph captures the stillness of the day: I can feel the touch of butterfly wings, I can sense the scent and colour of the flowers my mother was good at growing. There I am, a happy child.

Memory plays tricks. It's striking that I remember few occasions like the one in the garden. I don't remember us having fun as a family – the kind of fun I had with my own children and that they now have with theirs. Did we have fun and have I simply forgotten?

We did go to the cinema sometimes, on the bus to Acton, and occasionally to a restaurant called The Lantern, going the other way, towards Ealing Common. We visited relatives who ran a farm in Bedfordshire growing peas for Birds Eye, and these were for me episodes of delight, as I had three other little girls to play with and boss around (I was the oldest by two years). I thought they were a happy family, although I later found out that they weren't. And my parents and I had an annual holiday, often by the sea in Devon or Cornwall, in the early years accompanied by both my grandmothers who were exact opposites of one another: one fat and passive, the other thin and sprightly. I only had grandmothers. The grandfathers were dead. My parents spent a lot of time complaining about these grandmothers: I gained the sense early on that having an ageing parent is a terrible burden. It was only recently that I worked out exactly how old they actually were in those shared summers by the sea – one was the same age as I am now and the other a few years younger. Yet neither of them ever took me anywhere or did anything with me; I never stayed a single night with either of them, or even went to the park with them. When I enjoy the company of my own grandchildren now – and enjoy is an understatement – I'm suffused with sadness for what these women missed.

Like childhood, grandparenthood changes with the years. But there's enough social history on this for me to see that in some respects my childhood was distinctly odd. It was odd, then, to be an 'only' child – a term redolent with misery – of a mother in her forties; it was odd to live in a household that was so determinedly un-child-oriented. A small outward sign of this was that I was never allowed to have any of my toys or books in the living room or anywhere downstairs – they all had to be kept in my bedroom. Perhaps the confinement of childhood to its own space goes hand-in-hand with the 'onlyness' of some childhoods – as the sociologist Norbert Elias said, it is never in this sense good to be an 'only' child: 'just as astronomers have discovered that the whole universe is full of the radiation noise from the Big Bang, so people carry with them a background feeling about their existence that stems from their early days in their family'.[6] My parents were very wrapped up in each other. They had a deep psychological involvement which is sometimes known as love. I was not then, and am not now, any kind of expert on love – although I've had more than my fair share of it, and am grateful for that – but this love seemed to me in some strange way unkind. It seemed devoid of tenderness, and laced with anger. When my parents had been out for the evening they would often come back and, having dispatched the babysitter (usually a Mavis without-a-surname who made me my favourite meal of egg and chips), they would stand arguing in the room under my bedroom. The substance of the argument, now forgotten, if I ever knew it, was less important than its impact on the atmosphere. They would both smoke energetically throughout, so the smoke flew up with the words through the brown lino of my bedroom floor. They were heavy smokers all their adult lives, and my mother had a smoker's cough which was brought on by emotion.

Of their sexual lives I as their child knew little. I never saw them kiss or caught them in bed together. I never remember wandering into their room at night as small children usually do. I would see my mother naked in the bath, but I never saw my father without his clothes on. This prurience was quite probably commonplace then. Sex itself was never mentioned: when asked direct questions about the 'facts of life' my mother was unhelpfully coy. It would not have occurred to me to discuss such matters with my father. I grew up sensing a divorce between love and sexual passion which has haunted me all my life.

My parents' obsession with each other was a problem for me. Sometimes I felt they would only notice me if I did something deliberately bad. I remember intentionally wetting a chair when I was three or four years old and being pleased that this was the first thing my mother told my father when he came home at the end of the day. She wasn't angry with me, believing it to have been an accident, but I knew better. Much later, I walked out of school and joined various political movements – the National Campaign for the Abolition of Capital Punishment, the Campaign for Nuclear Disarmament, the Committee of 100 – all of which successfully embarrassed them, but for most of my childhood I couldn't work out how to get them to notice the person who was really me. When, as an adult, I read in a book about 'The Family' by a psychotherapist that the greatest failing of families is not to provide children with enough physical affection,[7] this statement rang true of my own life. The childcare manuals in use when I was little specified leaving even newborn babies alone in a cot or a pram to sleep for four hours between feeds, and never picking up a crying baby unless to change or feed him (the babies in these books were always male) for fear of something called 'spoiling'. These mechanical angels slept long hours at night and had discarded their nappies by the age of one: it was all about the control to be achieved through the physical separation of mother and child. My mother was proud of what a textbook baby I was. But I have never met a baby who wanted to be on her own in a cot, who didn't relax and flourish through bodily contact with her mother and other people.

Another thing I remember about my childhood is constantly feeling cold. I think this was also a common experience, and it probably strengthened our immune systems. Sometime in the late 1950s our house acquired night storage heaters – great heavy concrete things which stored cheaper electricity at night and gave it out sparingly in the daytime. When my mother bought these – she made all such arrangements in our household – my room was the only one that didn't get one. I had a small one-bar electric fire to which I used to sit dangerously close. It was glacially cold in that room in the winters, with the rest of the house only edged into the lukewarm range by those insensitive storage so-called heaters. My room never sprouted the fitted carpets that, as my parents' financial circumstances prospered, appeared elsewhere.

An episode watching my mother skin a rabbit in the late 1940s turned me into a (more or less) lifelong vegetarian. I have an abiding image of her back to me, holding the rabbit dripping blood into the sink with one hand, and a knife with the other. My aversion to meat might be one reason I often felt hungry, since my mother's concession to vegetarianism was to provide me with a small cube of cheddar cheese instead of the joints of roast meat or grilled lamb chops or butcher's sausages that my parents ate. Many years later, when I talked to my father's colleague Brian Abel-Smith about my parents, he recalled that at dinner parties in the Blue Plaque House he and his colleagues were served such small portions by my mother that they always went away hungry. 'Experience of rationing in the War seemed to have left its mark on the drab organisation of the house and even its utensils,' noted Peter Townsend, another colleague.[8] 'They were intensely puritanical,' remembers Marina Vaizey, the wife of a third colleague, John Vaizey. '[The house] was immaculate and extremely austere.'[9] Meals were very English: meat and two veg, the green sort generally overcooked. We never ate pasta and only occasionally rice, with fish, which was also occasional. We always had baked or steamed puddings, often with custard. There was very little salad or fresh fruit. Toast dripping with butter accompanied our Saturday teas, when my father, and thus my mother and me too, listened to the football results on the radio. That voice droning on about West Bromwich Albion and Tottenham Hotspur and Wolverhampton Wanderers and, above all, Luton Town – the only sensible name in the list, and my father's favourite – always prompts the memory of thick white toast and melted butter.

The impact of this kind of diet on one's insides was compounded by the fact that after breakfast every morning my father would take *The Times* to the upstairs toilet and my mother *The News Chronicle* to the downstairs one. I had to go to school. Anyway, both my parents smoked while defaecating, so neither toilet was a very pleasant place to be. Like insomnia, constipation became for me an acquired defect.

Did we ever talk about such things? I suppose not. The simplest explanation for my childhood unhappiness was that neither of my parents really knew very much about children or parenting, and neither it nor I were the centre of their lives. They left no record of how their parents brought them up, so that formative experience is beyond knowing. Since parenting is the most difficult job in the world, it's virtually impossible not to make any mistakes (I know I've made many of my own). Perhaps the best idea is for children to be surrounded by many people who love and care for them, so that one person's omissions or commissions have much less opportunity for impact. This is certainly how most children world-wide have been, and are, brought up, and the absence of such a custom is one of many ways in which the model of families in late capitalist societies is culturally very odd.

I find it hard simply to probe the texture and intensity of the experience without dissecting and analysing it. What I want to say about my parents, about my childhood, is that the nourishing little children must have in order to be happy isn't only a question of meeting their material needs. They must *feel* love, in the air around them, through their senses, in their nerves, in the contact of skin against skin. They must know that those who care for and about them are obsessed with their welfare, that somehow they come first. I also want to say that, despite the complaining tone of my narrative, I value the experience of having been my parents' only child. Without it, obviously I wouldn't be who I am, and there's much in my life that has been tremendously positive and worthwhile. If I recall with such clarity the night of insomnia in the awkwardly shaped room, it's partly because I've learnt to manage this condition, which I now accept as part of me (although if I had my life again I'd definitely try to change it). If I remember my parents' arguments seeping up through the uncarpeted floorboards of my bedroom, this may have something to do with my lifelong understanding that love between men and women is a difficult thing.

Some years ago, I went to see an internationally renowned medium. I was curious about this man's reputed powers, which I had heard about from two scientific friends who, like me, preserve an open mind about methods of accessing past and future. Bill practises in a small Swiss town, in a heavy many-storied house in a street of spectacular ordinariness. One of the friends who had recommended him took me there. It was snowing; I was a little afraid, I thought of the icy conditions (which in a different country had caused me a bad arm fracture a few years earlier), but probably also of what Bill would do with or to me. I asked, as my friend had suggested, for a tape recording of the encounter to take away with me.

We sat, Bill and I, in a sort of conservatory attached to the back room of the house. There were teddy bears and dolls – he specialises in helping parents whose child has died. A box of tissues lay waiting on the table. A little way into the session, Bill claimed to encounter the spirit of my father, whom he described as 'a little bit complicated' and as having had particular difficulties with boundaries. 'He must a number of times have overstepped the boundaries with you.' Bill went on to tell me some things about my life that were true and which he couldn't possibly have known from any other source. There was another disturbing feature about this story. Like many insomniacs, one of the remedies I tried once was hypnosis. In a hypnotised state I had experienced the apparent memory of an incident that dated from my earliest years: I was in the bath, aged perhaps two or three, and my father and another man, a historian colleague of his, were in the bathroom with me. I was very frightened. I called for my mother, but when she came, she merely stood in the doorway smiling, the customary cigarette protruding from her lips.

'Traumatic remembering' is the hallmark of many modern autobiographies.[10] It's a way of unravelling the mythologies of 'nostalgic remembering', which used to dominate the autobiographical tradition. Interestingly, I can't remember now what I did feel about my father while I was growing up, only what I felt about my mother. She tried to be a good mother and I tried to be a good child. 'The essence of being a good child is taking on the perspective of those who are more powerful than you.'[11] Richard Titmuss was a Freudian father, distant and symbolic, a closed creature whose eruptions remained internal, unlike my mother, who was prone to florid displays of them. What to make of my father's problem with boundaries? He was, as the medium declared, a complicated man. I regret now that I didn't know him better, but the only time he opened himself up to me was a few weeks before he died of lung cancer aged 65 in 1973. Then he told me, in the prosaic location of The Lantern restaurant in Ealing Common, something of his difficulties in having 'normal' heterosexual relationships, and of how he felt confined by my mother's intensely dependent love for him. By this point his cancer was terminal and causing him extreme pain. He would have wished the relief of death, he said, but this wasn't possible because of her. His disclosure reminded me of another, a decade or so earlier, from my mother this time. It was rendered during an Oxford Street shopping trip (memories always come packaged with their locations). In the busy street, with shoppers milling past, she had suddenly turned to me in a very distressed state, her face shining with tears, and had told me about my father's habit of dressing up in women's clothes. He kept a box of such things in his Shaving Room, she said. She said she was trying to get him to destroy them. That's all she said.

The past haunts us, as much for what we don't understand as for what we do.

The period in which I had the greatest difficulty relating to both my father and my mother was in the late 1960s when I was married with two small children. Exhaustion because of those trials of solitary motherhood I had noticed in my own mother had been diagnosed in me as postnatal depression. This was (is) a particular cultural interpretation of women's distress, fuelled, as I now know, by the pharmaceutical industry in league with elements within the medical profession who stand to gain much from the invention of new illnesses requiring chemical remedies. At a time when I needed my parents' support they seemed somehow embarrassed by my predicament, even apologising to my husband for having landed him with such an imperfect wife. This period of difficulty coincided with my father's move to the political right in the student demonstrations of 1968, and in other matters. I told them both I had nothing more to say to them. I felt angry and hurt. It must have been terrible for them too. But instead of hanging on in there and trying to keep the channels of communication open (a rule I've always tried to practise with my own children), they rejected me completely. Many years later, my mother told me how my father had spoken to their friends quite venomously during this period about his ungrateful daughter. According to her, he said he wanted nothing more to do with me and would leave me nothing in his will.

It was a very sad time. It was a long time ago. It's never productive to wallow in the agonies of the past. Yet there are legacies.

In that house – in this one which boasts its sparkling new blue plaque – I learnt to be the child of a Blue Plaque Man and his wife. I also learnt about gender. Man and wife: I wrote a book called that. Sex, gender and society: I wrote a book about that, too. What puzzled me as a child was why my mother seemed so frustrated (this is an adult adjective, I would probably as a child just have called it very cross), and why I felt closer emotionally and later intellectually to my father. There were other layers to this enigma. I learnt to share her impatience at having to listen to his recitation at the end of each day, when the yellow front door opened again, of the events of the external world – his world, the world of men at work, of important university business, of public affairs. My mother and I lived in the realm of the private: we were *his* private world. Yet both she and I knew our world was more than that. I was the one who (later) was able to analyse this, to talk and write about it, to insist (along with many others) that what is private, the life of the home and of children and women, is also a matter of great public importance.

When I wrote a biography of a university colleague of my father's, Barbara Wootton – a social scientist of much intelligence and insight, and a woman of strong radical persuasion – I was surprised at how little space the politics of gender occupied in her frame of reference. She saw that social and economic divisions by class and ethnicity were endemic in Britain but, despite many episodes of unfair treatment she had personally experienced from the 1920s through practically to her death in 1988, she failed to perceive these inequalities as structural – as rooted in the historical domination by men of the capitalist economic system. My father, similarly, took a socialist view of inequality, but one which excluded gender. So gender-blindness, which produces gender-obscuring,[12] was a habit of the time. It was less remarkable in him, because he was a man. But perhaps there was, or even is, something about academia that protected them both from an uninterrupted vision of gender.

My own discovery of gender politics came at the end of that sad period of the falling out between myself and my parents: indeed, it was the remedy, what for me brought that period to a close. But it didn't endear me to my parents. I was very proud of my first book, its shiny red and black and white cover sporting a half-naked hippie couple with flowers painted on them. I didn't like the image much, but it was appropriate, and publishers nearly always have the upper hand when it comes to the business of book covers. I gave the first copy to my father. He said nothing: he looked at it, then laid it to one side and embarked on another conversation. The book was my baby – although I had also by that time had two of those as well, his grandson and the first of his two granddaughters. Was he not proud of me? There I was, being the dutiful daughter, and what was my reward? It didn't matter – I had to make it not matter.

By the time my next book on housework was being written, my father was terminally ill, and this seemed to change his attitude, for he read the manuscript and we talked about it. He found my choice of subject uncongenial – those very private spaces of the house and intimate life which he, like most other men of his class, gender and generation, was used to keeping hidden. They were certainly not a proper subject for policy discussions. The nearest you could politely get to them was in talking about 'The Family', how relations between 'The Family' and 'The State' had changed, and so forth. My occupation of the more overtly political territory of gender seemed no less troubling for my mother, whose deep conventionality led her to disassociate herself from most of my strikes for independence. Conventionality can be a considered political choice, or a refuge for the anxious. For her it was the latter. I think my parents would have liked me to marry a civil servant or a doctor or perhaps a left-wing lawyer or MP, have two children three years apart, and become in due course a teacher of some kind with plenty of time to devote to community activities. I should have been safely Mrs So-and-So ('Mrs Robin Oakley' as my father referred to me in the acknowledgements section of one of his books) with political interests that didn't stand out from the crowd.

It's a long time since I've given my childhood such concentrated thought. It was the occasion of the blue plaque that brought it on. On the day of the little unveiling ceremony we held, with speeches on the steps in front of the no-longer-yellow door, and three of the great-grandchildren pulling the cord which drew the pleated red velvet curtain away from the blue plaque, I took the underground all the way from North London to Ealing Common and walked down the Uxbridge Road, a journey I hadn't taken in that way for many years. The Lantern Restaurant was still there, although it had changed its culinary nature. My school had become Japanese. The house where a woman called Mrs Knopps taught me to play the piano looked much the same – I thought for a moment I could see Mrs Knopps inside with her curled hair and anaemic blue jumper bent over the open lid of the piano.

It was raining lightly: images of the coloured umbrellas in a French film slid into my mind as we assembled in front of the house. I felt enormously moved by the blue plaque event. It wasn't just that my father deserved the honour, that public life in Britain today needs a strong dose of all he stood for; it wasn't just my pleasure in having helped to arrange the event, and seeing so many friends and family there, although all of that was true. It was the whole of my childhood that rested on my shoulders under the umbrellas in the lightly falling rain: the room of awkward angles and interrogative night, the sunlit garden of flowers and butterflies, the awareness of division and difference, the dissonance between the real and the imagined.

2

Falling into the bog of history

My instructions are to take the right diagonal from the station ticket barriers. The concourse is full of people: I scan the figures more than, at this distance, the faces. No, that one is too short, that one's clothes look too young, bright blonde hair isn't how I remember her. But she could have changed. We haven't met for nearly 50 years. When we first set eyes on each other it was 1955 and we were both 11 and wearing the stiff green uniform of that stifling school in Acton where I learnt the rules which govern apostrophes ('Haberdashers'', because there were lots of them, 'Aske's' because there was only one Robert Aske) and the inappropriateness of disliking Jane Austen. The school's regimentary attitude announces itself in all the formal photographs we had to have taken: rows of uniformed girls with ironed hair-ribbons. The person I'm now searching for at Birmingham station was my best friend; we clung to each other in what for both of us was a rather alien environment, and we left the school together at 16. She married even before I did and went to live in Canada. Now she has come to England for a holiday, to stay with another friend in Birmingham.

Suddenly she springs out of the crowd and I see the face that I met in 1955: smooth, open, friendly. We hug each other tightly. The years fall away: we aren't nearly 70-year-old grandmothers, but girls again, pristine, guileless, unsullied, pawns in our parents' and teachers' hands. One day our class teacher asked us to hold our feet above our desks; it was one rule among many that our shoes should always be freshly polished, so here we were being checked up on. Her shoes, the Start-rite sandals of the advertisement, with a T-strap and little holes in the toes, gleamed orange-brown in the sharp sunlight of the classroom. They were much the shiniest in the class and certainly a lot shinier than mine. The teacher congratulated her, but I knew it was really her father and not her who had buffed those shoes to such a congratulatory sheen.

I wonder why that memory has lasted when others haven't. Did I enjoy the easy deception of the teacher into thinking of my friend as the arch shoe-polisher? Perhaps I wished I had a father like hers, a proper father who immersed himself in family life sufficiently to cherish his daughter's shoes. That's an interesting footnote on the domestic division of labour: according to a forgotten female colleague of my father's, the social researcher Pearl Jephcott, fathers in working-class homes used to clean their children's shoes.[1] Each recall of the shoe-inspection moment brings with it for me a keen sense of failure which is in no way lessened by the passage of 57 years – indeed, the sense of failure is stronger now than it was then: *my* failure to be the shiny-shoed person I was supposed to be.

Do you remember, she asks later, over lunch in a pleasant country house away from the busy city centre, accompanied by her friend, do you remember how they made us kneel so they could measure our tunics, which had to be exactly an inch above our knees? No, I don't, and I don't remember whether the sin was having skirts which were too long or skirts which were too short. We liked them long, she says, because we thought it made us look grown up. I don't remember anything about the length of skirts at all. I remember, she says, when I came to lunch in your house for the first time, my mother was worried I wouldn't know which cutlery to use when, but it was alright because when I went home I said Ann's mummy put the saucepans on the table. I learnt about social class from her, from the differences between our mothers and our fathers and the houses we lived in. I liked going to her house: it was an exciting bus ride away (I wasn't often allowed to travel on my own), and it was full of little dark rooms, so different from the insipid white spaces of my own house. Some of the rooms in her house were let to lodgers, which made it even more interesting. Her father, a solid kind man with a deep velvet voice, protectively insisted on taking me to the bus stop when I went home. He had an occupation, running a photography shop, which was far more tangible than my own father's daily disappearances from the Blue Plaque House. Her mother, like mine, didn't have a job, and hadn't, like mine, since her only child, like me, was born. There was less money in that household than in mine, but another thing I didn't remember was that all my old uniform ended up in her house due to her being a size smaller than me. The uniform had to be bought from a special uniform shop called Fosters in Ealing Broadway, and it cost a packet.

Her mother was unlike mine in this uniform-affording respect, but there were parallels I didn't grasp at the time. It seems she was frustrated at having no separate occupation of her own (although the lodgers must have taken some managing), and consequently she required her daughter to be good and behave well and achieve and stay close to her, just as mine did. Social class seemed to make more difference to men than it did to women. Why was that? Anyway, all of that was one reason why her daughter went to live in Canada with a German husband. I wasn't brave enough for that; alternatively, it could be said that I found other ways of being subversive.

The house where we eat lunch, an Edwardian Arts and Crafts splendour, has beautiful gardens, and we manage a walk before the unseasonable weather produces hailstones the size of mothballs. For a few moments, the sun shines on our joint past. It's late spring, so there's a reasonable riot of colour in the garden: pink rhododendrons and blue lupins and camomile roses. She wants to take a photograph, and points to a little grotto where stones curve round in front of a rhododendron bush: it should make a nice picture. I put my bag down and take a step towards the stones in front of the flowers. But what I had read as a gravel surface transpires to be a dense scattering of blossom fragments floating on a stagnant pond: the blossom is exactly the same colour as the gravel paths either side. At first I don't understand what's happened, and then the shock of the cold black pungent water round my feet sets in. I have to carry with me for the rest of the day a thick wet covering of smelly black mud on and in my shoes and my socks and the bottoms of my trousers. I scrape some of it off in the toilet of the beautiful Arts and Crafts house, but I really need a bath. Later it dries and isn't too uncomfortable, but on the train going back to London I am horribly conscious of the smell.

It's the symbolism that arrests me more. I have fallen into a bog. I am immersed in the stationary water of history. It clings to my garments and penetrates my skin and resists all attempts to be scrubbed or washed away. Because I reek of it, I am propelled on a series of expeditions into what can be recovered of the happenings preceding my own story: the couplings and the fallouts, the passions and the rages; the making of homes and the planting of gardens; the accumulation and disposal of wealth; the production of people and objects and food and disappointment; but, most of all, the interminable succession of ordinary days and hours and minutes of which lives are made.

3

Memory and identity

On my *curriculum vitae* there are lists of books I've written or edited on my own or with other people. A c.v. is an autobiographical act, a life composed and presented according to certain conventions, a story designed to hide, exaggerate, downplay or boast about aspects selected from the immense and muddled curriculum of one's whole life.

Because I've mostly made my living as an academic, my c.v. is dominated by publications, presentations, lists of research grants, committees and so on. It doesn't tell the story behind these lists. For example, behind each of the books is a story of why it came to be written and how, in what order its chapters got themselves assembled and juggled about, how much agonising and rethinking and reworking went on, whose advice was taken (or not taken) on the path to its final form. Writing a book, whatever it's about, always meshes the personal and the professional. The 'I' is always there: the difference is between the unvarnished admission of its legitimate presence, on the one hand, and the reluctance to acknowledge its refusal to be banished, on the other. No view of the world, of knowledge, of the imagination, is possible from any vantage point other than one's own.

The writing of *this* book is explicitly in that place where personal and professional co-exist. Its credo (or theory) is that only through the lives of individuals are we really able to get a hold on all those complexities of experience and motivation which make up human history. The more we probe this word 'autobiography', and try to settle its differences from other words like 'biography', 'life writing', 'fact' and 'fiction', the less definite we're able to be. What runs through them all is 'the authority of experience'.[1] My heroine, the social scientist Barbara Wootton, once pointed out that: 'Life stories are never easily told, even when their authors are genuinely concerned more with accuracy than with self-exculpation; and the biographies of those who defy the standards of their own society are doubly difficult to get straight'.[2] Biography and autobiography are vehicles for exhibiting an age; they help us to understand processes of social change through the medium of individual lives.

Father and daughter is about me, but it's also about him and about them, the family that lived in the Blue Plaque House. It's about how girls like me grew up in the Britain of the 1950s and '60s and became angry or complacent young women, and then fifty shades of greying older women. It's about the historic constitution of family life and gender identities.

The mnemonic of the Blue Plaque House comes first because the springboard of *Father and daughter* is my father's intellectual work and its social context. I wanted to focus on this for three reasons. The first is because in my 70th year I'm engaged in that excoriating business of summing up my life, a common affliction (or, more positively, prize) of ageing. Like my father, I'm an academic social scientist;

because of the way these proclivities are passed on in families, at least some of what I think and believe and do is likely to have come from him. But my work and interests are also massively different from his. I see oppression and patriarchal domination where he saw progressively declining inequalities and the normal relationships of men and women. What to me is a major research question and the cause of considerable personal distress was to him nothing much to be wondered at, or even possibly merely the hysterical response of unbalanced women.

When my mother died in 1987, 14 years after my father, her will named me as my father's literary executor. A second reason for this book is that my acquaintance with the nature and impact of my father's writings and with the various commentaries that have appeared over the years suggests to me the creation and perpetuation of a legend about who Richard Titmuss was, the background he came from, and the purposes to which he put it. Thirdly, there is this interesting muddle of terms: sociology, social science, social administration, social policy, social work. How are these various formulations of the social related to one another? And how do these, individually and together, speak to the issue of gender?

Young children in modern society often have only vague ideas about what their parents actually do to earn a living. They don't usually see them do it – the only salient matter for them, which is quite enough, is the parental absence from home. All I knew about my father's work when I was a small child was that it took place somewhere called 'LSE'. For a long time I thought 'LSE' was 'LSC'. The air of the Blue Plaque House was laced with acronyms: SBC, UGC, SSRC, MRC, PEP – LSE was just one among many. It appeared for me out of the acronymic mist once a year in December. What happened at LSE in December was a Christmas party for the children of staff. Father Christmas was impersonated by the Director, then Alexander Carr-Saunders, softly spoken demographer and fellow member with Richard Titmuss, and many others among the great and the good, of the Eugenics Society. I know now that Carr-Saunders, unlike his successors among LSE's Directors, had a real interest in social science and its social work roots, an interest which is definitely germane to the story told later in this book. But in 1950 he was just

Father Christmas. I remember his daughter, Flora Carr-Saunders, helping to hand out the presents which were piled underneath the enormous Christmas tree. The tree was hoisted up to the top floor of LSE, to the rather elegant Shaw Library, named after one of LSE's founders. That precious infant – the institution which Sidney Webb considered would turn everyone into socialists because no intelligent person could possibly be anything else – was for me as a child the place where only one person (who was never me) got the fairy off the top of the Christmas tree.

My father, it seemed to me, went to LSE nearly every day of the year. When he came home he was always full of tales which he was bursting to tell my mother and me of extraordinarily boring things that happened there, mostly involving elderly ladies with strange names who taught social work and were given to bouts of hysteria. At the time I took these narratives at face value: these women were obviously enemies. For a little girl, a man's only child, the disposition is for the father to be seen as incapable of doing wrong. 'The life of the father has a mysterious prestige,' wrote Simone de Beauvoir, authoritatively and rather middle-classly, in *The second sex*, 'it is through him that the family communicates with the rest of the world: he incarnates that … world of adventure; he personifies transcendence, he is God'.[3] On the days when he didn't go to LSE, my father worked at home; he shut himself up and wrote lectures, articles and books. The books were known familiarly as 'Essays' (*Essays on 'the welfare state'*), 'Alice (in the Board of Inland Revenue)' (*Income distribution and social change*), 'Blood' (*The gift relationship*) and so on. As soon I was able, he conscripted me to read proofs with him. For example, my diary for 1959 when I was 15 notes that on one April Saturday, 'After lunch I checked a 12-page lecture with Daddy'. In those days books came in two sets of proofs: the galleys – long strips of print, like academic toilet paper (good for drawing on afterwards) – and page proofs. Both had to be done. He insisted that they had to be read aloud. So one of us sat there with the proofs and the other with the typescript and we took it in turns to read. Absolutely everything had to be pronounced, including the punctuation. I developed a tremendous facility for doing this very fast ('op stop cit stop p stop one two three stop'), which I tried to elicit in my own children once I had my own proofs to check, but they were much less compliant than I was.

The punctilious proof-reading was one dimension of a peculiar childhood. Other girls would be out with their friends, while I was reading, although not understanding, social policy texts. I was impressed, not by the substance of his writing, but by its textual quality: the long words, the page-long paragraphs, the diligent footnotes, the mysterious 'Cmd' ('Command') numbers attached to official publications, the liberal use of the royal 'we'. Sometimes I would look round, but there was only him in the room. Those texts and their audible versions, read by him in the slow, pedantic tones which were his hallmark, drew me ineluctably into the tight circle of his intellectual life.

Later, I learnt the persuasiveness of his argument. The development of welfare was a lesson in the corruption attendant on power, he said – the power of some people to determine the fate of many. It was a lesson in how, in the absence of systematic evidence-based policy-making, all sorts of irrationalities and unfairnesses could and would develop. 'What is a social service?', he asked, typically, in his much-quoted 1955 lecture on 'The social division of welfare', possibly the most influential piece he ever wrote.[4] When he turned to official Treasury definitions, he noted that approved schools and remand homes were considered social services, whereas the probation service was not; war pensions were social services, while industrial health services were not; university education was a social service, but the training of domestic workers was not.[5] He campaigned vigorously in his writing for people to have rights that transcended these absurdities and abuses of power. He was spectacularly good at thinking laterally, crossing disciplinary boundaries, and making connections. I learnt from him that what matters is not the title of your expertise (economist, sociologist, politician) but the question (What is welfare? How do different ways of providing health services measure up in terms of efficiency, effectiveness, and satisfaction? How do policy decisions impact on ordinary people's lives?). Behind and around all this, a position more or less consistently argued in his writings from the 1940s through to his death in 1973, lay a framework of moral principles, the kind that is normally a side-effect of religious belief. A number of people wrote to me after he died to gnaw away at this: surely for such a man, who himself personified God, there must have been a greater one somewhere? Where else did he get his morality from?

Richard Titmuss's morality is traceable to a species of nineteenth-century ethical socialism, and it drew also on a concept of the ideal organic solidarity of human society theorised by the early European sociologists. He was a voracious and catholic self-educator, dipping in and out of sociology, anthropology, economics, philosophy, psychology and literature to abstract ideas and phrases that made sense to him, or which were useful in his delineation of a new meaning of the social – the study and application of what was at first called social administration. Social administration meant the study of how public sector services work, but he made it mean much more than this.

In *Taking it like a woman* – a volume of semi-autobiography published in 1984 – and in *Man and wife* – a book written a decade later with, and because of, an archive my mother left me in a small brown suitcase – I examined, remembered and puzzled over the nature of my father's presence in my life and in other people's lives, and in the disciplinary world of the social. In patriarchal culture, where gender is imbibed first in The Family, daughters have particular reasons for wanting to find their real fathers. They have reasons, too, for wishing to get to the bottom of their mothers' lives, but these reasons are different. Germaine Greer's *Daddy, we hardly knew you* chronicles a wretched search for an arch-strategist and deceiver, a man who seemingly didn't wish to be known by anyone. Alexandra Styron wrote about her father William, the Pulitzer Prize-winning author of *Sophie's choice* (a story whose final twist leads us into the worst horrors of maternal misogyny). William Styron was brilliant, alcoholic, egotistical, a typical 'monomaniacal' male artist.[6] He was also prone to depression, about which he wrote eloquently in a personal memoir called *Darkness visible*. At the centre of his life was his often-thwarted creativity, but he loved his children and his wife who, at the end of a long day filled with domestic duties, before the children would wake her, but not her husband, at dawn, would sit and listen to William reading out loud whatever it was that he had written that day. She was a wife 'without whom', as the standard acknowledgement goes. Alexandra grew up with one taken-for-granted certainty – that her father was a great man. He must, she assumed, have been born great. At the age of four or five she would slip up to his closet and take out his honorary degree hoods – crimson, azure, emerald – and would rub their silk and velvet against her cheek. She was deeply attached to her identity as her father's daughter, invested in this myth of his special celebrity: 'it conferred something special upon me'.[7]

It was, I suppose, the same for me. Yet in my case it's hard to distinguish this sense of being special from the others – the only child-ness, the ambiguity of class, the socialist child in the right-wing private school. I was matter-out-of-place in that cultural definition which assigns hygiene only to wanted objects.[8] As a child and a teenager, I never queried the story of my father's unsullied greatness, except that I could see the price my mother paid to uphold it. However, even this insight felt wrong, as though I shouldn't have it, because I couldn't do anything with or about it, and it was an act of disloyalty to draw attention to the fact that Professor Titmuss's wife didn't seem as happy as she ought to be.

Virginia Woolf met Freud in the autumn of 1939, he gave her a narcissus and she observed that he was, 'A screwed up shrunk very old man: with a monkeys [sic] light eyes'.[9] After that she began her tantalisingly brief 'Sketch of the past' in which she recalls life with another publicly important father, Leslie Stephen. Following his wife's death, Virginia and her sister Vanessa bore the brunt of this tyrannical man's bad moods. Men's bad tempers, observed Woolf, are rarely displayed in front of other men, but there's no shame in exposing them to women, who are expected always to be angels of sympathy.[10] Because the exposures are hidden from other men, women's accounts of them tend not to be believed. The veracity of women's accounts has traditionally been open to question: what the less powerful say never possesses quite the same ring of truth as the utterances of the more powerful. I wrote about my father's 'bad moods' in my teenage diary. On one such day, my parents decided to go out to lunch. We drove to Virginia Water, a pleasure spot on the fringes of London, but our search for a suitable restaurant only made his bad mood worse. I recorded feeling sick. Here was a man, then, who inflicted his displeasures and negativities on his loyal family in the secure expectation that they would indulge him. He brought home both the small battles and the big ones – those with the lady almoners in the early years at LSE, and later ones with a number of people whom he counted as close colleagues and friends. I wonder now whether that altruistic human community of which he wrote so passionately, especially in his last book *The gift relationship*, wasn't partly how he himself would have liked to have been. He understood so well that the ability to give is created by the condition of first having been given to: reciprocity is at the heart of good human relationships.

I didn't finger his honorary degree robes as Alexandra Styron did, but I went with both my parents to fetch his CBE in 1966 from Buckingham Palace, across worn red carpets with a squeaky band playing 'The Donkey Serenade'. There we are outside the Palace, on a sunny day, me clutching unworn gloves below the slight bulge of Richard Titmuss's grandson, my mother nursing the CBE box under her arm, my father less posed and more apparently at home in royal circles than either of us. I knew about his honorary degrees, about the adoration of students who trooped out to Acton for an exposure to suburban domestic happiness and Mrs Titmuss's carefully judged hospitality. I respected Barbara Wootton for not attending his memorial service at St Martin-in-the-Fields in 1973 on the grounds that he wasn't religious (whose idea was it to have a *church* event?), but I had to go and sit next to my mother and sing 'Jerusalem' and listen to Brian Abel-Smith reading from Corinthians about people who lack charity. Brian's voice was no stranger to the activity of Bible-reading in great churches. I wore a long black flowered skirt and a hand-crocheted black poncho in the middle-class hippie style of the era. It wasn't considered appropriate for my children to attend the service, so they were at school, not in the church. Afterwards someone took photographs of the children and my mother and me and my father's son-in-law in the summer garden of the Blue Plaque House.

'Professor Titmuss is dead; long live Professor Titmuss.'[11] 'Over 1,000 pay last respects to Prof. Titmuss,' said *The Acton Gazette*. In the list of attendees I appear as 'Mr and Mrs Robin Oakley, son-in-law and daughter'.[12] That was the formula at the time, as it was when we were included in the acknowledgements of my father's books.

When I wrote those earlier volumes, *Taking it like a woman* and *Man and wife*, I had trawled through the post-death letters to my mother, letters and telegrams of fulsome praise from such personages as Julius Nyerere, President of Tanzania; Queen Margrethe of Denmark; Sir Keith Joseph of the British Conservative and Unionist Party and Sir Seewoosagur Ramgoolam, the Prime Minister of Mauritius. I read the obituaries, which are striking for their religious imagery. My father was a saint, 'the welfare saint', the 'quiet saint',[13] the 'high priest of the welfare state';[14] he spoke 'with the eloquent force of an old Testament prophet';[15] he was an 'ascetic divine', an El Greco figure,[16] a Gandhi look-alike,[17] a man of 'ascetic incorruptibility' and 'fastidious emotion' possessed of a poetic, metaphysical vision.[18] Even Barbara Wootton, in a letter to my mother, approvingly quoted her fellow economist at LSE Lionel Robbins, who said to her that 'Richard is really a saint'.[19] For the politician Richard Crossman, my father was simply 'not like other men ... his disciples called him God'.[20]

Did they really, or was it a joke? It isn't easy to be the daughter of God. Charismatic authority, as famously defined by Max Weber, involves notions of sanctity and divine, or at least superhuman, qualities.[21] My father had charisma. His speech was ponderous and thoughtful, so that people hung onto his words partly because of the gaps between them; he gave the appearance of listening even if, in later years, this was possibly because his hearing aid was turned off. He was, according to a colleague, 'a very tall, distinguished but rather ill-looking professor ... who when he began to speak was a magician. He took the dry stuff of social policy & filled it with scholarship, compassion & sociological imagination, & transformed it into a field of compelling interest'.[22] You always thought he knew more than he was willing or able to say about everything. That, in fact, he *did* know everything.

This resurrection of the past we embark on in our later years is a final effort after meaning. We mean to discover the recipe that made us rise or burn or fall apart. They call it 'narrative gerontology'.[23] I prefer Sartre's description of his own autobiography as 'a true novel'.[24] Memory, the main text, is a process, not an act. The object – memory – is indistinguishable from the activity – remembering. Yet, as with biography, the raw material of any life story isn't just what we think we remember, but what is stored in archives, in suitcases, in dusty files, in tucked-away letters and in torn, inscrutable diaries. There is a science of memory. One neuroscientist who has studied it, Steven Rose, who shares his life with the sociologist Hilary Rose who described her colleague Richard Titmuss as a magician, wrote at the end of his book *The making of memory*, 'Memories are public records of past events, more or less transformed to meet current ideological needs'.[25]

My current ideological need is to gain a better (fuller, more detailed, more honest, less legendary) understanding of the interaction of two lives, mine and my father's, in the context of the British social science and policy world, that world in which the public parts of our lives have been played out. It is to grapple (again) with the way the public and the private have conventionally been made to glare at one another as non-speaking neighbours over the garden fence, whereas, in most of our lives, these two are engaged in a permanent symphony of gossip and mutual tit-for-tat. This epiphany, of the personal as political, introduced by feminism, still shines far more readily on women's than men's lives. People resist the filtering of legendary men such as Richard Titmuss through the prism of his unsavoury domestic moods, his distaste for women's agency, his inhabitation of The Family as a specious moral community. His daughter's academic study of gender, on the other hand, is easily blamed on her deficient adjustment to all this. Betty Friedan's *The feminine mystique* and Ferdinand Lundberg and Marynia Farnham's *Modern woman: The lost sex* were near-neighbours on the bookshelves of my father's study in the Blue Plaque House. There's practically no correspondence between these two texts, as the first documents the effects on women of the agenda that the second one complains women are most sadly in danger of losing. Did he read these books? If so, what did he make of them? Did my mother know and consider them and the possible application to her own life, and did she and my father discuss them?

We only remember a portion of what we experience. If we remembered it all we'd be unable to function in ordinary life, just like Solomon Shereshevsky, the Russian journalist whose struggle to deal with the burden of total memory was inscribed by Alexander

Luria in *The mind of a mnemonist*. The ability to forget is an essential element of the ability to remember.

We rely on other people to judge what we remember as true or false, to tell us about the origins of our memories, to offer alternative views of the past. We need our parents to tell us what happened in our childhoods, even if we disbelieve it. Last week I was in Moorfields Eye Hospital in London, where two doctors were quizzing me about a strange semi-paralysis I'd never really noticed on the left-hand side of my face. 'You must have had a palsy sometime,' they insisted. But no, I hadn't. And then a story of my mother's swam to the surface of the tossing sea in my brain, a story about how, in the polio epidemic that gripped Britain in 1949 when I was five, she brought me home from the park one day and I couldn't get out of my pushchair because the whole of the left side of my body was paralysed. My parents called one of their doctor friends, a formidable woman called Albertine Winner, the first woman Deputy Medical Officer of Health and an unshakeable defender of women doctors' careers. Albertine pronounced the diagnosis of polio. According to the story, I lay in bed in my semi-paralysed state with a high fever for two or three days and then I called out that I was hungry, after which I made a full recovery. Well, apparently not quite full. Sixty-four years on, the Moorfields doctors are in no doubt that the polio episode explains the paradox of my face.

Epidemiology knows so little about the really long-term consequences of disease; we know so little about our remote pasts, either because our memories don't reach that far, or because they've chucked out items from the storeroom in order to free up space for others, or because other constructed memories have intervened.

The problem is that we are what we remember. Memories are the building blocks of identity. Indeed, it's said (although some people query this) that you can't remember at all until you become a person with language – a time that has been set by psychologists with frightening precision as between 39 and 42 months. We also tend to remember things and people and places and episodes that support the identities we've constructed for ourselves, the ones that fit comfortably, so that we don't have to keep readjusting or fretting about them. Thus, fictional memories may also be inserted into these landscapes, for no better reason than that they match elements of what's already there. Identities do change over lifetimes, perhaps more so for women than men. When I interviewed women about housework and motherhood in the 1960s and '70s, I asked them how they felt about the identity label of 'housewife'. It was a question that made complete sense to them, as to me, at the time, but women now would stare hard at an interviewer who asked that question.

'Who am I?' is a question that bothers us more when we're young. It seems important to be able to pronounce on it, to locate oneself firmly on the map of the social world. As we age, the opinions of other people who aren't close friends or family generally start to matter less. Freed from the risk of others' opprobrium, we can re-engage with memory, whose psychodynamics permit a whole journey of fresh associations and integrations. Then the question becomes 'Who was I?'.

Asked to tell the story of their lives, most people will produce an already organised record, a linear staging of the gossip between public and private, a plausible arrangement of stored memories, all adding up to the project of a more-or-less successful life. The meaning of life is the metaphor of a clothes-horse. The clothes-horse is draped with the clothes of recognisably commendable achievements. The sociologist Peter Marris, an academic friend of Richard Titmuss, who proposed this idea of identity as a clothes-horse, also wrote: 'Whatever the new understandings someone may evolve in the course of a lifetime, he or she must start from the preconceptions of their upbringing – including the superstitions, cant, prejudice, ignorance and guilt they have been taught – in order to discover something else.'[26]

4

Family and kinship in London and other places

All houses have voices, said Virginia Woolf. The cadences of those voices shelter clues which speak directly of the lives that were lived there. Woolf herself was especially impressed by the battlefield of the Carlyles' home in Cheyne Row, Chelsea, where the composed dignity of middle-class life had to be wrought from a 'high old house' with no running water, electricity or gas. It was an effort for Thomas Carlyle and, even more, for his devoted wife, Jane. In contrast, consider the different habitus of the poet John Keats in Hampstead, where 'All the traffic of life is silenced. The voice of the house is the voice of leaves brushing in the wind.'[1]

Half a century after I stopped living in the Blue Plaque House, its voice echoes in my head. The voice is a strained, whispering spirit. In the early spring of 2012 when I sit with my notebooks trying to put memories into words, I while away a period of enforced idleness following a surgical operation (so-called 'sick leave') by sorting through some old family photographs. Faces from the past stare out at me curiously, uninformatively, mockingly: the faces of great-great-grandmothers in long dark dresses and bonnets, of stern upright gentlemanly ancestors with white whiskers and tight waistcoats, of small, disciplined children removed peremptorily from their play. There are posed family portraits in sepia with blurry edges, suggestive of the hazy distinctions that exist between life as it's recorded and as it's lived. What were those lives really like? What kind of family is this?

I notice some things about the photographs for the first time. My mother's mother, a thin sprightly dark-eyed woman called Katie Louise Caston, had a sister called Nora. It was in Nora's marital home in Yorkshire that my mother and I sheltered from the London bombing during the Second World War. I always thought it was just the two of them: Katie and Nora, but here is a little photograph stuck on card of Katie aged about four and her parents and a small boy held proudly in his mother's lap: 'her little brother who died' my mother has written on the back. What little brother? Is this little brother's untoward death the reason why Katie herself was said to prefer her own second-born child, a son, to her first, a daughter, my mother? This son of Katie's, Donald Miller, is an attractive boy in other photographs, bearing Katie's luminous dark eyes. One might think he would go on to lead a very interesting life. But I remember 'Uncle Donald' from my childhood as a rather dull and ineffectual person, whose occupation as an accountant and marriage to a red-cheeked, slightly stout woman called Muriel put him in a different league from those of us who lived in the Blue Plaque House. I had no sense of a relationship with him, or with Muriel, a sister-in-law whose company my mother eschewed, on grounds of personality or class – I was never sure which.

Donald and Muriel had one son, my cousin Andrew. So Katie Caston had two grandchildren only: a granddaughter from her daughter and a grandson from her son: Ann and Andrew, a euphonious duo. There are a few photographs of Ann and Andrew sitting on the lawn in the Acton house. Ann is scowling with a bow in her hair, and Andrew, a pleasant open-faced schoolboy, appears quite happy to be where he is. Donald and Muriel and Andrew came to tea once or twice a year. I don't remember ever going to their house in Shepperton, Middlesex. Those tea-times in the Blue Plaque House were always occasions of considerable huffing and puffing on my mother's part. And then, once a year, a few days before Christmas, she and I would also make the (what seemed to me then) immensely long journey from Acton to the steps of St Paul's Cathedral in Central London, where we would meet Uncle Donald, have tea in a Fuller's tea shop, and exchange carrier bags bursting with Christmas presents. I enjoyed those meetings, mainly I fear because of their proximity to Christmas and that riot of present-giving, but also for the excitement of walking through a festively lit London and seeing the dome of St Paul's carving such a wonderfully monumental space out of the navy blue December sky.

Biological affinity doesn't prescribe the emotional or social kind: if there's one lesson I picked up in my childhood, this was it. My father's collection of relatives was presented to me in what was possibly an even grimmer light than my mother's. In the legend of the childhood of the man who earned the blue plaque there are humble origins, material and social deprivation and multiple parental failings, from all of which corrosive obscurity he managed to climb, triumphant, entirely through his own efforts. It's a story repeated in virtually all the obituaries and commentaries on his work and enshrined as the orthodox version in a short biography published in the *Proceedings of the British Academy* by a woman called Margaret Gowing in 1975.[2] I remember Margaret, a beak-nosed woman with a commanding voice, and my childhood visits to her elegant home at the river's edge in West London. I was fascinated by the possibility of flooding, and by the tensions in the household created by an alcoholic musician husband and two boisterous sons. Margaret Gowing was a historian of merit, but her account of Richard Titmuss's life was weakened by its reliance on the singular perspective of his wife, my mother, who wanted people to understand how important she had been to his success and how unimportant, indeed damaging, had been the contribution of his own family. The story Kay Titmuss told Margaret Gowing and which Margaret Gowing told the British Academy caught on because it was such an attractive notion: this champion of equality and the welfare state transcending his own impoverished background through sheer hard work, a truly self-made man. It was a story 'assiduously fostered', not only by Kay Titmuss but by many who worked or associated with Richard.[3] The reproduction of this text in others is often accompanied by a typical media exaggeration of the poverty and deprivation of his origins (he left school even earlier than he did, his father died, drowned in debt, at an even more premature age). I bought wholesale this story that was fed to me in my childhood, seduced no doubt, like others, by its socialist romanticism, but also unwilling, as children are, to question tales their parents tell them.

As a child I learnt from my father that his own family of origin had nothing to recommend it: Morris Titmuss, my father's father, was a bad farmer in the country and a bad haulage contractor in the town where the family was forced to move in the early 1920s; he was a negligent father and a drinker who caused his own early death at 52. Maud Farr, my father's mother, was neurotic and equally incompetent: it's a wonder the children survived at all. Actually there was one who didn't, a little girl called Barbara; she died, said my father, of maternal neglect.

There are only two surviving photographs of Richard's childhood: each shows him with his older sister Gwendoline and his younger brother Harold. The children appear to be dressed in white. Richard is about seven or eight, with a serious look, neatly combed hair and long dark socks. Gwendoline, looking maternal, has her arm round baby Harold who wears a dress. They are all seated on an impressive piece of 18th-century furniture in a room with flowery lined curtains and a deep window sill. There's also a little photograph of Lane Farm, Stopsley, in Bedfordshire, now demolished, the house where all of them, and little Barbara who didn't make it, were born. Lane Farm was an ivy-clad Georgian building with a colonnaded porch and tall chimneys. There are no images of Richard or the other children with their parents, but there are a few pictures of Morris as a young man and a couple of his own father, Herbert. Herbert Titmuss was also a farmer. He was born in 1835 and evidently did rather better than his son, lasting until he was 83. His son Morris is a dashing fellow, with curly hair and a thick moustache: quite a ladies' man. He isn't smiling in his photographs, but no one is in these old images: I wonder when the tradition of saying 'cheese' came in?

In the enforced leisure of my sick leave, I do a little research on Richard's family. We know very little about this grandfather of mine, Morris Titmuss: he's been allowed to fade from history, remembered only in the imprint of his inadequacies in the legend of his son's advance to fame, and as the reason for Richard Titmuss's middle name – Richard *Morris* Titmuss. But was he really nothing more than this ruffian and unfit father?

The name Titmuss was originally Tychemarche or Titchmarsh, with variations as Tytchmarsh, Tychmerrs, Titchmas, Titchmersh, Titchmarch, Titmas, Titmous, Tittmus, etc. It is also the name of a parish in Northamptonshire, where there are de Titchmarshes recorded as living in 1199. The name means a fee or a tax ('tithe marsh'), a payment of cattle, property or land by a Lord on condition of homage or service. It probably has nothing to do with Titmice, for which association I was bullied at school, and which, more significantly, became the by-line under which my father and his colleagues conducted their work. By the early 15th century there are Titmusses recorded in Bedfordshire, and by 1630 they are farming the land a few miles from Richard Titmuss's birthplace, Stopsley, where his Aunt Lilian had a farm we visited very often when I was a child. Most of the Titmusses were farmers or corn dealers in Bedfordshire or in neighbouring Hertfordshire. There's nothing unusual about this geographical stability. English people stayed close to where they were born until the industrial revolution created a marketplace in manual skills. But those who worked the land clung to it long after that. There are still Titmusses living on farms in Bedfordshire and Hertfordshire. You can even buy 'Titmuss Rolled Barley' (£6.10 for 20 kg) from one of the rural Titmuss businesses. An online business directory turns up my father's namesake, a poultry dealer called R.M.Titmuss, living a mile from where he was born. My father undoubtedly had a lingering sense of belonging to the land; apart from those recurrent visits to Aunt Lilian's farm, one of his early books is a coffee-table sized *Report on Luton*, written jointly with Fred Grundy, the Medical Officer of Health there. Nostalgic photographs – 'Daffodil time at Putteridge', 'Sharpenhoe Clappers', 'Straw Plaiting, 1909' – are sandwiched between pages of tight demographic text.[4]

A combination of internet searching and visiting real places with the aid of real maps gives me a better sense of who my father's Titmusses really were, and the kind of material and cultural resources he inherited from them as tools of his own trade in the social science and policy world.

Morris Titmuss's paternal line goes back to a family of Tyttmusses who were the well-off inhabitants of a farm called Fairlands, now a public park in Stevenage. We know about their relative wealth because when William Tyttmuss died in 1685 three of his fellow farmers drew up an inventory of his possessions (which included nine beds, five dozen napkins, a cheese press, two 'carpitts', nine cows, ten horses, 240 sheep, two wagons, a lot of carts and many 'odd things Forgott').[5] The Titmuss men and women are long-lived (for the time) and fertile: Morris's father was one of ten children, and he himself had six siblings: three brothers and three sisters. Two of the boys, Frank and another Herbert, were farmers, and the third, Walter, was an actuary: thus Richard Titmuss had an uncle who knew about statistics. Frank ran the family farm in Almshoebury, and Herbert took over another at Tewinbury, near Welwyn. Of Richard Titmuss's three paternal aunts, Florence Emily never married but worked on the family farm, Ada became a nurse and lived with her brother Walter, the actuary, in Harpenden, a town not far away, and Mary married Charles Hill, another local farmer. All these Titmusses were reasonably well-off. Morris's father, Herbert, owned or leased several farms in Bedfordshire or Hertfordshire and was himself sufficiently wealthy to leave £7,818 (equivalent to £313,000 in 2011) when he died in 1918. Morris's mother, Mary Ann, left a bit less than half that to her daughter Florence and her son Frank when she died in 1920. What is notable is that Morris's parents left no money to him and his family. It looks as though there had been some rift in the family, that Morris had somehow become estranged from the other Titmusses.

In the 1901 Census, four years before he married Richard Titmuss's mother, Maud Farr, Morris is living on the family farm in

Almshoebury with his parents, three of his siblings and a 13-year-old housemaid. The farm today, when I travel there with the help of a map, is still inhabited by Titmusses. The farm buildings have deteriorated now; an events business has taken over some of the farm's redundant meadows; weeds and abandoned farm equipment litter the forecourt which is reached by a badly kept track, an effective deterrent to uninvited guests. There's a curious Marie Celeste air about the place – cars and vans parked outside, doors wide open, but no signs of human beings. One of the female Titmusses who lives there or nearby has contributed to Ancestry.co.uk a photograph which I didn't have of Maud and Morris's wedding, which took place in the summer of 1905. It's a posed arrangement of 11 elegantly dressed women and 13 suited and mostly serious men: the newly-weds at the centre look resigned rather than euphoric. An air of safe middle-class prosperity presides over them all. The wedding was reported in considerable detail in the local newspaper, the *Bedfordshire Advertiser and Luton Times*, complete with a misspelling of both the bride and the bridegroom's first names:

> The hamlets of Cockernhoe and Mangrove were 'en fete' yesterday for the marriage of Miss Maude Louise Farr, eldest daughter of Mr. and Mrs. Robert Farr, of Mangrove Hall, to Mr. Maurice Titmuss, third son of Mr. Herbert Titmuss, of Almshoe Bury, Stevenage. Bright sunshine favoured the happy event, which took place at Lilley church, where a large company of friends had assembled. Mr. A. Foll, of Lilley, was at the organ and played suitable music before the arrival of the bridal party. The bride, who was given away by her father, wore a handsome dress of pure white silk trimmed with panels of Parisian lace and flounces in true Lover's knots and caught up with orange blossom; she also wore a tulle veil with wreath of orange blossom, her wedding bouquet being of white roses. The bride's youngest sister, Miss Irene Farr, was a pretty train-bearer, attired in pale blue mousseline de soie, accordion pleated, with a wreath of cornflowers in her hair. The bridesmaids were Misses Edith and Ella Farr (sisters of the bride) and Misses Florrie and Ada Titmuss (sisters of the bridegroom), whose costumes were of pale

blue mousseline de soie trimmed with Valenciennnes lace, with picture hats of the same shade trimmed with cornflowers; their bouquets were of blue cornflowers and maidenhair fern. The bride's mother wore heliotrope silk with pleatings of the same, with toque to match in roses and chiffon. Mr. Walter Titmuss, the bridegroom's brother, acted as best man. The hymns that were sung were 'The voice that breathed o'er Eden' and 'O perfect Love', and the 67th psalm was chanted. The Rev. E.H. George, of Lilley, officiated.[6]

The Reverend Covey-Crump, Vicar of Stopsley, delivered a short address on the theme of how the Church had just received this woman from the hands of her natural guardians and given her to the care and custody of this man who promised to love and cherish her, and he hoped their union would always be inspired by the Divine Spirit. Maud and Morris passed under arches of evergreens and flowers erected by the villagers on their way back to her family home, Mangrove Hall, before leaving for a honeymoon on the Isle of Wight, Maud embellished in a pale grey travelling dress trimmed with French embroidery and a hat of tinted grey ostrich feathers and pink carnations. In the newspaper report, all 89 of the wedding guests were listed by name, along with 93 wedding gifts – a large quantity of silver items, gold bracelets and brooches, cheques, dinner services, vases, a barometer, Worcester tableware, household linen, and, most curiously, a whip.

The wedding photograph was taken in the garden of Mangrove Hall, about five miles distant from Morris Titmuss's home in Almshoebury. The house where Richard Titmuss's mother Maud was born and raised was spacious enough to house a family of ten children and several servants comfortably. When I go there, I instantly recognise the house today from the old photo I have of it: a self-possessed mansion, double-fronted with three floors and three pretty gabled attic windows in the roof, a farmhouse which for 400 years has been making a statement about the importance of the people who live in it. Today the farm buildings have been converted into other indisputably middle-class dwellings, and the whole site has become a desirable little niche of attractive homes with a view over open fields, yet only a few minutes' drive from the urban sprawl of Luton. Down the lane is Parsonage Farm in Cockernhoe, where Maud's brother Hugh farmed as an adult: I used to hear about Hugh and Cockernhoe as a child, but I never listened properly, as children don't, so the import of those remarks has sadly gone forever.

The alliance between Richard's parents, Maud and Morris, made agricultural and social sense: it brought together two people whose shared backgrounds should have bred common interests and at least moderate material success. Like the Titmusses, the Farrs had been in residence in the Bedfordshire/Hertfordshire borderlands for many centuries. The most prosperous- and cheerful-looking character in the wedding picture is Maud's father, 'Hoppy' Farr, as he was known. Hoppy farmed 587 acres, employing ten men and five boys. The Farrs made a good living, and were well respected locally. My mother, from a different background, seems to have taken a not wholly charitable view of farming as an occupation. She was convinced that Richard's statistical acumen, which enabled him to turn a rather mundane job in insurance into a career in social demography, came from another much more famous Farr, William, who joined the newly created General Register Office in 1839 and was responsible for all the early organisation and analysis of the country's vital statistics. Since William Farr was the son of a poor farm labourer in Shropshire, a direct link with the Bedfordshire and Hertfordshire Farrs seems unlikely. The fit between the rumour and the legend of the Blue Plaque Man is neat, but unconvincing. On the other hand, it's surprising that my mother never mentioned the actuary Uncle Walter, who must surely have conversed with the young Richard about their shared interest in the statistical calculation of risk.

Richard, and presumably his younger brother Harold (there's no record of what happened to their sister Gwendoline), were sent to St Gregory's, a small private school in Luton which described itself as a 'preparatory' school and which educated mainly farmers' sons. My mother kept a copy of the 1920 edition of *The Gregorian*, St Gregory's Annual Report. In that year 18 new boys were admitted, and ten left, all for well-known public schools, including Marlborough, Haileybury and Malvern. My father's memory of having learnt very little at St Gregory's apart from cricket and football is supported by the content of the Report, which is almost wholly devoted to sports – although in order to get boys into public schools some more academic instruction would also have been necessary. St Gregory's was, in other words, a bit more than the failed education of the Titmuss myth.

Why didn't Maud and Morris prosper? How do we conjure up people from the past, when the past is gone, and the living have no memories?

As I'm a researcher/detective at heart, I can't allow any stone to rest unturned in my search for an answer to Richard Titmuss's origins. I contact the Titmuss who put the wedding photograph on Ancestry, Ellie, the wife of John, whose grandfather Frank was one of Morris's brothers. Ellie brought up four Titmuss girls in the farmhouse where Morris Titmuss, my grandfather, lived as a child. Through her I find a whole host of relatives I didn't know I had. She and the pile of documents in the corner of her dining room are a treasure-house of information about the Almshoebury Titmusses and their kith and kin. For example, that rather dispirited-looking farmhouse is not what it seems: hidden in its core is an extraordinary 13th-century building raved about by architectural historians, erected on the foundations of a manor owned by William the Conqueror's brother, the Bishop of Bayeux. Ellie takes me round the house and shows me the huge timber beams that shout history above the clutter of 21st-century life. Morris's voice is wrapped in that clamour: here, in this magnificent medieval construction, he was born and grew up and reached his manhood as a farmer and progenitor of Richard. Ellie's mother-in-law, Ruth, remembers that there was some family row involving Maud and Morris, and she finds somewhere in her house a bundle of documents that confirm this memory of a family feud. When Morris Titmuss's sister Florence died in 1932, she left money to her family. Various nephews and nieces, including Richard Titmuss and his brother and sister, benefited, but it seems that some of them challenged the will. In the case of *Titmuss v Titmuss and others*, Richard and his siblings had writs served on them: the case was heard in the Royal Courts of Justice and Florence's will was upheld. All this testamentary detail ends up being more frustrating than revealing, since it's impossible to work out who sued whom for what, and neither the legal firm named in the papers nor the Probate Office have any records going back that far. So we can conclude nothing, beyond the fact that the Titmusses were materially and culturally resourceful enough to take each other to court.

The Bedfordshire and Luton Archives are housed in a modern building overlooking the Great Ouse which flows through the centre of Bedford. Fat ducks oblivious to human concerns about history swim on its rather immobile surface and on that of an artificial pond created in front of Borough Hall on the opposite bank. The photocopier in the Archives room has a particularly good view of all this. The Archives staff have apparently never been asked before for some of the files I want, which have to be fetched from another building. I am after the remaining records of Morris Titmuss's capacities as a farmer.[7] The story goes like this: Morris Titmuss leased Lane Farm, Stopsley, from a Mrs Frances Crawley of Stockwood, Luton, the widow of John Sambrook Crawley, in June 1903, two years before he married Richard Titmuss's mother, Maud Farr. He also leased from a 'Major Clutterbuck' a further 48 acres of adjacent land. Lane Farm was a fairish size: 329 acres of arable and 34 of pasture land. Morris kept ten cows, eight other cattle and six working horses. He made most of his income from selling milk, cultivating the fields to grow animal feed, and employing five men and one boy to do so. The farmhouse in which Richard and his three siblings were born was no mean establishment: it had a drawing-room, a dining-room, a kitchen, a scullery, a pantry, a 'lower kitchen', four bedrooms and a boxroom which Morris converted into a bathroom with a bath, W.C. and a geyser. There were roller blinds at the windows and a system of 'bell cranks and wires' in all the rooms. In the 1911 Census, Morris and Maud are living there with Gwendoline, Richard and Harold, all under five, and a 24-year-old nurse. My father once told me he was wet-nursed (a fate that hardly befell babies in really poor families), so perhaps the nurse was providing this service for baby Harold. Another clue that the family wasn't all that impoverished is that Richard's godmother was the wife of the Reverend Covey-Crump, who had officiated at Maud and Morris's wedding. Covey-Crump was a prominent figure in the local Freemasons. He and Morris were both active members of the Stopsley Parish Council. A trawl through local newspapers of the time revealed another of Morris's middle-class, and potentially income-draining, pursuits: horse-racing. In the 'Herts. Hunt Point-to-Point Steeplechase' at Sewell in 1908 Mr Morris Titmuss's chestnut gelding, Red Eagle, won the Farmer's Light Weight (race).[8]

Lane Farm was leased by Richard's father for 20 years, the period during which Richard was born and raised to be the slim, serious-looking boy of the photograph. It came with a rather tarnished pedigree, a previous occupant having been declared bankrupt. The fate of the farm took another knock after the First World War, when Morris was one of 134 farmers in Bedfordshire affected by government schemes to devote more land to cultivating human food and to provide smallholdings for ex-servicemen. Under the Cultivation of Lands Order 1917 (No 3), the Bedfordshire War Agricultural Executive Committee proposed to remove two fields totalling 32.65 acres from Morris Titmuss's control. One field was sown with white clover, but the other was pasture, and Morris objected that without this his cows would be unable to produce enough milk. Many farmers put forward these kinds of objections, and claimed compensation, as Morris did – a carefully itemised account amounting to £33 (£1,520 in 2011) – although he also sensibly agreed to give up ten acres.

This was the beginning of an uncomfortable relationship between Morris Titmuss and Bedfordshire County Council which lasted five years, in the course of which bigger claims for financial compensation by Morris were generated. The core issues involved the validity of the Council's claims on the land he leased, and the Council's view of his competencies as a farmer. Visiting the farm in July 1917, a Council Inspector deemed it in 'a very rough state', with 'very backward' swedes and 'foul' wheat. This confirmed the observations of the land agent for the Crawley Trustees, also produced in evidence by the Council, whose view was that things had been going from bad to worse for a number of years. Morris could surely only be scraping a 'bread-and-cheese' living from the farm; what had saved him was that Mrs Crawley liked him and didn't want to turn him out, and one reason for this was that he was good at looking after the game, planting crops with a particular eye to good game cover. Two years later, the Land Settlement (Facilities) Act of 1919 provided further grounds for the County Council's case against Morris Titmuss. This Act enabled farmland to be made available to ex-servicemen, and it led directly to the Council reaching an agreement with the Trustees of the Crawley Estate to purchase Lane Farm. The contract for the sale of the farm was signed in November 1919. Morris had all his implements taken away, was unable to use the farm buildings, and had to sell his animals 'at an unprofitable time'. He was given notice to quit the farmhouse by Michaelmas 1920.

It is a tribute to Morris Titmuss's staying power, if nothing else, that he managed to hang on there for a further two-and-a-half years. Over this period, relations between him and Bedfordshire County Council and the Crawley Trustees deteriorated further, with Morris's rising claims for compensation being counter-claimed on grounds of his agricultural mismanagement and non-payment of rent. A hearing took place in the Shire Hall, Bedford, in the summer of 1921. According to the verbatim transcript preserved in the Archives, at one point Morris is asked to confirm that he had been warned about his poor farming practice. In response, he points out that he had been told that once the Council had decided to buy something, they did. When the opposing lawyer suggests that Morris has been making only a hand-to-mouth existence for a number of years, his quick response is, if that is so, what have I been living on since the land was taken away from me? 'You are not here to ask me questions,' reprimands the lawyer. Asked how much profit Lane Farm made in 1919, Morris replies that he never kept any books. Did he have a bank account? Yes, but he was always paid weekly in cash for his milk, he didn't remember how much profit he made from it, and he couldn't recall how much he paid for feeding stuffs. He did write his accounts on a slate but then he would rub them out. 'You have got one of the most convenient memories I have struck for a long time,' remarks the lawyer. Morris's own lawyer claims vindictiveness against Morris and cites evidence that he wasn't such a bad farmer after all; an independent inspector from the Surveyors' Institute testifies that Morris was 'very open and very fair' and 'gave me every facility for inspecting the farm'.[9]

Tempers are heated and opinions are strongly held and voiced, but the momentum of the law marches on. By early 1922 the Ministry of Agriculture and Fisheries in London is writing to say that Morris Titmuss and his family must be ejected forthwith from the farmhouse on Lane Farm since access to the land is now inconveniently restricted for the smallholders who have taken over the land. The case goes to arbitration in Westminster, but then Morris and his lawyer contest the arbitration agreement on the grounds of misconduct on the part of the arbitrator – prejudice against Morris and in favour of Bedfordshire County Council. The final hearing in this sorry litany takes place in the High Courts of Justice in March 1922. Morris Titmuss's case against the arbitrator is upheld. But on a technicality – his acquiescence in the arbitration proceedings – it's decided that the arbitrator's decision can't be overturned. Morris gets £1,277 6s (about £57,200 in 2011) compensation instead of the £3,288 12s 9d (£147,400) he asked for, and is awarded costs. A few weeks later he purchases a small house in London, 1 Wroughton Terrace in Hendon, and the family move there on 3 July 1922.

Morris Titmuss emerges from the Archive records as an engaging, quick-tempered character: he is both obstinate and logical, both compliant and obstreperous. He clearly has an eye, not only for game-promoting crops, but for the main chance. I warm to him; he's a character with spirit. Local newspaper reports show that he's not without experience as a litigant, having earlier taken to court five youths for damaging one of his stiles, and a local greengrocer for failing to pay for goods supplied (he won in both cases).[10] But he does sound like a rather poorly organised farmer. A list of repairs needed to the buildings and the farmhouse is monumental: fences, rails, gates, posts, stables, barns, sheds, the cowhouse and the henhouse all need mending, painting and tarring; the south wall of the house is damp because the overflow from the bath is constantly pouring down it; the two main entrance doors are rotting, as are the windows; slates are missing from the roof, the eaves, gutters and rainwater pipes must be cleared out; the brickwork needs pointing; many of the rooms need two or three coats of new paint, the scullery must be re-plastered and the internal brickwork demands attention. But

Morris is a tenant, and his contract with Mrs Crawley is for limited repairs only. I can almost hear him pointing this out.

In 1917, when this saga starts, Richard is ten, his sister Gwendoline is eleven, his brother Harold is seven, and their little three-year-old sister Barbara catches whooping cough and dies. There's no mention in the Archives of Morris's family, of his responsibility to look after them, and there's no sign of the help of any relatives, despite their quantity and proximity. One wonders why Morris's mother, dying at the height of her son's disputes over land and farming efficiency, left all her money to another, prosperous, son, and not to Morris. Nonetheless, Morris does have sufficient resources – enough to survive the removal of Lane Farm without going into debt, enough to continue to send Richard and perhaps at least Harold to school, enough to buy a house in London. The Titmusses' modest end-of-terrace house in Hendon looks rather down-at-heel now, but it would have been sparklingly new then.

In the story of the self-made man, Richard leaves school early in order to help care for the family. Actually, he would have abandoned St Gregory's in that summer of 1922, when the family relocated to Hendon. The house at the end of Wroughton Terrace must have seemed cramped and mean after the sprawling, albeit slightly disintegrating, Lane Farm. There was certainly no room for a servant in it, only three bedrooms, and hardly any garden at all. The row of small two-storey, cement-rendered, houses, strung together in a line facing another identical one, was part of Hendon's emergence from a place of farms and country lanes to an industrial London suburb. The fastest population growth, urged on by the extension of the Underground and the building of new traffic-dense roads, was in the 1920s, when the Titmusses landed there. Richard was nearly 15, and his parents probably thought he ought to be equipped for an occupation other than farming. In that, they were right. They sent him to do a book-keeping course at Clark's College in Chancery Lane, an establishment founded to prepare young men – and later young women – to pass civil service examinations. In Hendon, Morris ran a struggling haulage business for a few years before dying, I was always told, of drink. I order Morris's death certificate: '*morbus cordis*' it gives as the primary cause of death. Apparently doctors go for a morbid heart when they aren't really sure what happened. But it could have been true. Morris's little daughter Barbara's certificate arrives, too: she was three when she died at Lane Farm, not of maternal neglect, as my father alleged, but of whooping cough, pneumonia and heart failure. No one would write 'maternal neglect' on a death certificate, of course. Yet whooping cough was killing around one child in every thousand under 15 in England and Wales around that time: the fall in deaths associated with better public health came too late for little Barbara.[11]

When Morris died of his morbid heart, the young Richard was 19 and working in the offices of Standard Telephones, an American-owned telephone and telecommunications company in nearby Southgate. Despite Richard's help with the family accounts, Morris's death did bring financial problems: debts and the absence of a family wage. The extent of the family's poverty has perhaps been a little exaggerated: Morris left the equivalent of £53,907 in today's money when he died. Maud lost no time in trying to increase the family income and place her son on a career path. Six weeks after her husband's death she wrote to someone she knew at the County Fire Office (perhaps through her brother-in-law Walter, the actuary) whose offices were in London's Regent Street. Less than three weeks later, despite the existence of a long waiting list for such positions, and after Maud had completed a medical report on her son, Richard was taken on as a Probationary Clerk. There he learnt not only the essentials of the insurance business but how to read and analyse the statistics of life, sickness and death. For the first 11 years of his 15-year stint in the County Fire Office, Richard went on living in Wroughton Terrace with his mother, brother and sister. The first to leave was Gwendoline, when she married in 1936; Richard was next when he married Kay in 1937; and Harold left on his marriage in 1938.

Deeply embedded in the pile of photographs I sort through is a newer one dated 1969. This is a faded colour snap of Gwendoline and Richard and their mother in the back garden of Gwendoline's house in Mill Hill, a short distance from Hendon. Some time after her children left home, Maud went to live with Gwendoline in Mill Hill. The two women had little to occupy their lives apart from Gwen's dog and the television. This they would watch every night past the National Anthem until the signal was switched off. My parents made regular visits to Mill Hill in my mother's cream Ford Anglia, registration number MBW 178, otherwise known as 'Maisie Bramble-Wilkins' – such is the power of some kinds of memory. These visits were much resented, at least by my mother, and they both came home in bad moods. Gwen had moved to the Mill Hill house on her unsatisfactory and childless marriage to a hospital radiographer. Her husband more or less abandoned her – there were unspelt-out rumours of his misbehaviour with other women. My mother kept a letter my father once penned to this neglectful husband, reporting his having taken Gwen, then aged 55, to see a Dr Evan Bedford about her heart. Dr Bedford, 'a master cardiologist' who had rescued Winston Churchill from congestive heart failure in Tunis in 1943,[12] pronounced that Gwen had to lead a restful life free of all exertion and worry. This didn't seem very likely. 'Aunt Gwen' had a rasping, mannish voice, and a curiously pitted face, which I was always told was due to chewing grass as a child – a most unlikely cautionary tale which nonetheless terrified me so much I never allowed a blade of grass near my own children's lips. Like her father, she did die prematurely, at the age of 65, and of that heart disease Dr Bedford had identified.

In that palely coloured 1969 snap Gwen is holding the dog, and Maud, a bulky woman with unbrushed bushy white hair, is supporting herself with two sticks: Richard stands awkwardly between them. The picture has a special poignancy, as within four years all of them were dead. On the back of the photo my mother has written 'the She-devil and her enmeshed son and daughter'. It's an unbroken 35-year-long line of hostility from two other photographs of Maud and Richard taken a couple of years after my parents met, on the back of which my mother wrote 'The Evil one', and 'Before he got away'. When I was a child I accepted my mother's version of Maud, that her hold on my father was impossibly malignant. I learnt to share her impatience with the long telephone calls that connected the house in Acton with the one in Mill Hill, my father hanging dutifully off the black Bakelite receiver. He always had reading material in front of him during these conversations. Yet now I wonder what Maud did to earn this reputation. Yes, she was a needy mother: after Morris's death, she clearly didn't know what to do with herself. Trying to hang onto the children may have seemed the only option. In the fashion of the time, Maud and her sisters, brought up in the middle-class comfort of Mangrove Hall, were expected to be idle ladies and get married; they were hardly educated to be resourceful women of the world.

In my childhood Maud and Gwen belonged in the category of Relatives to be Seen Occasionally and Not Heard Much. I had no meaningful relationships with any of these relatives, with one exception: my cousin Andrew, my mother's nephew, who was the 'kinkeeper' in the family, and who resiliently stayed in touch with both my mother and me. He remained the pleasant straightforward person of the schoolboy pictures. When Andrew married in 1960 I was a bridesmaid, and very proud of myself I was too, in a blue satin frock with matching shoes and a concoction of plastic flowers in my hair. I had never had a dress and shoes made of the same fabric before and never have since. My meetings with Andrew were always, I'm ashamed to say, initiated by him. We never talked about his work, which involved the Army and bomb disposal, and with his premature death from cancer in 1993 I lost my only sense of kin beyond the nuclear family.

I did have two other first cousins, the children of my father's brother Harold, little Harold of the photographs. They lived in Watford. Harold was an electrician who worked in the television and film industry. Once a year he and my father would meet somewhere on the train line between Acton and Watford and spend an evening drinking together, a fraternal ritual my mother barely tolerated, complaining that Richard came home late and smelling of beer. After Harold and his wife came to my father's memorial service in 1973, she wrote to my mother to complain that I wasn't wearing a hat. After my mother died in 1987, she wrote to me to complain about the length of time it was taking to sell my parents' house, an event of some significance to her as she was one of the inheritors named in my mother's will: her children, my long-lost cousins, were not, however, so remembered, she pointed out, with reasonable disgruntlement, especially as her son was my father's godson, a fact which I don't remember ever being mentioned during my growing up.

This son, David Titmuss, one of these two missing cousins, is dead too now, a fact I establish through yet more laborious relative-tracing. But his sister Margaret is alive and well and living in another Hertfordshire village (they aren't urbanites, these Titmusses). She meets me in the car park of the station with a puncture caused by a badly designed kerb; thus the conversation of these two elderly women, meeting after an interval of some 60 years, is at first all about how to mend the car. When that is taken care of, we sit in a leafy green space and consume two sandwiches and two sets of memories. My father and hers used to collect birds' eggs: she shows me a painstaking list in my father's teenage handwriting. He had an eye for statistical detail even then. Of our Aunt Gwen's scarred face she tells me a different story: that the scars were caused by Gwen's troublesome radiographer husband who over-treated some minor skin condition on her face. That sounds much more plausible than the chewing grass story.

Margaret gives me a most poignant little photo of Morris Titmuss at the back of Lane Farm with his two sons. They're moving what looks like a large bit of fence. Richard and Harold are at the edge of the photograph, Richard the taller of the two, Harold behind him. The boys are smiling slightly and you can see Richard's protruding front teeth (my mother got them fixed when she met him). Morris and his sons all wear starched white collars, ties and jackets and all look directly into the camera. Long grasses, bent in the wind, hide their feet. We all knew Maud, my father's mother, but none of us knew Morris, because he died before we were born. But there is one person alive who does remember him, a woman of nearly 100, Joan Harman, the daughter of Maud's sister Edith. Joan's memory of Morris is of a very nice man who fell on hard times. Her smile as she says this is reported to me by her daughters, in a final connection I make on this journey through the landscape of lapsed relationships. There seems to have been no sense of shared responsibility for one another in this kin network; it's the absence of such responsibility that allows family relationships to fade away.

This, then, is/was my family. This is what 'family' means to me: him and her and me in our tidy, self-contained house, with those other creatures out there, corralled a safe distance away, guilty of unidentified sins, yet yoked to us by invisible genetic codes. We were connected by a sense of obligation, and disconnected by what was probably a hefty dose of social snobbery. The blemished record isn't exactly that model of family and community and altruistic spirit my father preached in his public life. Yet it, and especially the disruptions of the Morris Titmuss–Lane Farm saga, may help to explain Richard Titmuss's own passion for the stable breadwinner-father formula of family life. No wonder I grew up wondering why people so glorify The Family that they are quite unable to see how actual families really behave. 'The chief means of fulfilment in life is to be a member of, and reproduce, a family,' wrote my father's colleague, Peter Townsend, in a volume called *Conviction* published in 1958 when I was 14. According to the blurb on the cover, *Conviction* was a compendium of essays by 'Thoughtful Young Men' who were trying to revitalise socialism (there was one token woman, the writer Iris Murdoch, who called for a new moral framework to replace the dull empiricism of modern sociological thought). What Peter Townsend contended in his essay was that the happiest and most secure family relationships are those involving the exchange of services, as when 'the old grandmother cooks meals and cares for the grandchildren, and her daughter does the shopping and cleaning and works part-time outside the home'.[13] Such unsociological nostalgia, a mostly male affliction, it has to be said, was the silently gendered altruism, the community spirit that my father upheld and lauded most of all in his last book *The gift relationship*, written and published in the years when the sad visits to Mill Hill dried up with the deaths of his enmeshed sister and the mother who enmeshed them both. I wonder if he pondered on the huge paradox of all this: the unsatisfactory family of the real world versus the vainglorious family of the cereal packets. And there was I, his only child, busy erecting a destruction of the whole sex/gender system, even as he took it for granted and lived in it and even, one might suggest, prospered from it.

Hilary Rose, who worked with my father in the late 1950s, wrote a paper called 'Rereading Titmuss: the sexual division of welfare'.[14] She had learnt about the injustices of the welfare system at first hand: when deprived of her husband in another polio epidemic in 1958, and left with a three-year-old son, a National Assistance Officer told her not to expect any help with her housing costs as she was pretty and would soon remarry.[15] Britain did have a welfare state, but it was one that embodied many such patrician views about women. The critical feminist scholarship, of which Hilary Rose's and my own work were both a part, exposed the field of social policy in ways that most of its male founders, including Richard Titmuss, might not have welcomed. My correspondence with Hilary Rose about her paper asked the question, which neither of us could answer, as to where Titmuss's moral fervour came from. What was the basis of that moral framework people so admired in his writings – not perhaps exactly the one that Iris Murdoch called for, but a moral passion nonetheless? I told Hilary her paper read 'like a history of parts of my childhood'; and thanked her for making me realise how selectively I had viewed those years.

In 1962 I went to Oxford to study for the uncomfortably triadic degree of Philosophy, Politics and Economics. Sociology was added in 1964, in which year I seized on it eagerly, in part because I sensed that the subject offered a way of understanding this contested space in which reality and myth so obstinately disagree with one another. Doing sociology, I read about The Family – how it is universal (or might not be, depending on how you define it), how it is functional (for whom, in what ways?), how it is extended or nuclear (explosive), how it is an engine for meeting (or not) and containing (or not) individual needs for sex, love and intimacy. There's nothing better since or before sliced bread. Actually, The Family *is* sliced bread: a formulaic arrangement of human beings in standardised plastic parcels which promise uniformity of taste and texture at the expense of creative difference. It was quite possibly my anger at the smirking self-satisfaction of the men who theorised about The Family or claimed to find their theories supported by observations of real families that first propelled me on the path to developing a less prejudiced kind of sociology. I wrote a long essay in 1964 on 'The Family and Industrialised Society' which competed with others in economics and moral philosophy for the annual Somerville College PPE prize. I was very surprised to win the prize, both because of what I had by then learnt to be Oxford's celebrated reluctance to embrace sociology, and because of my own innately poor self-confidence.

In seeking answers to the puzzle of family life which I dragged with me to Oxford from the Blue Plaque House, I was caught between two worlds of representation and understanding. On the one hand, there were the tendentious wordy theories of American sociological men – Talcott Parsons was the most celebrated offender – and, on the other, there was the accessible rosy romanticism of the British male empiricists. Peter Townsend worked then at the Institute of Community Studies in East London, which, under its energetic and extraordinary Director, Michael Young, was producing newsworthy reports about family life which foregrounded ordinary people's experiences. Michael Young and Peter Willmott's *Family and kinship in East London*, with its unpretentious language and insistence that the extended family is alive and well in Bethnal Green and is therefore likely to be so elsewhere in Britain, gave rise to generations of specious ramblings about kitchen matriarchs ('the Mother Goddess of Bethnal Green'[16]) by A-level sociology students (many of which I read and marked down when I myself became an A-level examiner a decade or so later). Young and Willmott 'put working-class mums on the middle-class map', doing for women more or less what the psychoanalysts and religion had already done, pointed out sociologist Ronnie Frankenberg.[17] They might just as well have called *Family and kinship* by their originally favoured title *Mother and daughter*.[18] Yet such idealistic models do nothing to encourage evidence-based understandings of real women. The word 'impression' occurs suspiciously often in Young and Willmott's book. My father's 'Foreword' to the original edition of *Family and kinship in East London* commended the authors for the qualitative richness of their text, but criticised them for lack of methodological rigour. This remark is probably the cause of the Foreword's omission from subsequent editions of the book.

I hadn't remembered my father's remark until a sociological friend drew my attention to it. Michael Young was a PhD student of my father's, although this affiliation doesn't do justice to Young's relative maturity and experience. Born eight years before Titmuss, he led a tremendously inventive life as a sociologist, political writer, and innovator. During the war he headed the policy think-tank Political and Economic Planning; then he went to direct the Labour Party's

Research Department, in which capacity he drafted the 1945 Labour election manifesto.[19] Young and Titmuss met around 1950 when Young had become disillusioned with the ability of policy-makers to understand people's everyday lives. Could academia do a better job? In 1952 my father agreed to supervise Young's PhD – 'A study of the extended family in East London' – though it seems, from the file of preserved correspondence, that Young originally wanted to study the social and economic position of women. There is the synopsis of a book called *Housewives and equality* – with headings 'The Mother's Day', 'Growing Burden of Work in the Home', 'Family and Community' and so forth. 'Is this a book? A campaign? A PhD?' my father has written. 'A middle-class ring about it.'[20] The idea was dropped at his instigation, though some of its themes appeared in his own piece about the position of women. Without Richard Titmuss's help, it's unlikely that Michael Young, skilled social innovator though he was, would have been able to marshal the resources needed to establish the Institute of Community Studies.

So far as I, with my personal/professional puzzlement about The Family, was concerned, there wasn't, in the end, a great deal to choose between the theoretical American and the empiricist British men, apart from the fact that the British men were a good deal easier to read. By the time I started to publish my own approach to the study of family relations I had become more adept at applying that methodological rigour my father recommended. *The sociology of housework*, my own PhD project, published in 1974, exposes a later version of the Young and Willmott thesis to straightforward quantitative scrutiny: there was nothing remotely symmetrical about *The symmetrical family* they celebrated in their 1973 book of that name: all you have to do is look at the coding of the *one* question on the division of labour in their 113-question interview schedule. Not only was there a certain amount of fantasy about The Family going on, but the entire notion of 'community' was, as the sociologist Margaret Stacey contended in an article published in the prestigious academic journal the *British Journal of Sociology* in 1969, an unevidenced and ill-defined invention.[21]

Michael Young's second wife, Sasha, a writer and radio producer, sent me in 1976, when I had started to publish other articles and books about the family and gender, a copy of a talk she had given some years earlier on the BBC Third Programme. The talk was called 'A view from the cage', and it was about the awfulness for a middle-class woman of being cooped up with small children (as she was at the time), living your life around their needs, experiencing a constant sense of failure at not getting anything right. 'Is it so odd to want work and a family,' she cried, meaning by 'work' paid work outside the home. 'This is the least that any man expects.'[22]

The first sociological treatise I was asked to read at Oxford was *Class and class conflict in industrial society* by Ralf Dahrendorf, a German sociologist who later became Director of LSE. Dahrendorf's book both excited and depressed me – excited, because it was about real social issues, which the rest of my teaching at Oxford was not, and depressed, because one could read the whole book without encountering a two-gender world at all. The sociologist in the opening sentence of the book was male. The theorists were male. The workers were male. The class system operated only through men. Conflict and capitalism were both male. Women were presumably stuck in their Bethnal Green kitchens.

Richard Titmuss was, of course, a splendid example of class mobility – from small farmer's son to grand university professor. Class puzzled me as a child – not in the self-conscious sense of class identity, which few children have, but because I was aware that the Blue Plaque family didn't really fit in. My family was my first lesson in social class. Perhaps this was one reason I later found myself drawn to sociology as a route to biographical understanding. I never had any trouble grasping those sociological texts about status and class and social mobility (or immobility) because I had imbibed it all in the Blue Plaque House. I couldn't have named it then – this curious distancing from kith and kin – but later I saw quite clearly that my parents felt, and wanted to be, socially superior to their culturally (but not materially) poor relations.

Tiny families of this kind pay a price for their isolation. I read about this, too, as a sociology student and instantly recognised it from my own experience. J.M. Mogey's *Family and neighbourhood*, a 1950s study of two contrasting districts of Oxford – a central city zone and a new peripheral housing estate – points out that in small families removed, for whatever reason, from their kin, the 'tensions of intimacy' have to be discharged by skills possessed within these tiny groups, but such skills are rare.[23] Taking Mogey's book off the shelf to re-read this observation is another act in which memory and history are fused: my memory, his history. Tucked inside the book is a letter to my father from Peter Townsend complaining about Mogey's research methods. Mogey liked percentages and Townsend didn't.[24] You can see why – I can see why and so probably could Richard Titmuss – when, as Townsend observed, 5% turns out to be actually just one family. I was born and grew up in the war between qualitative and quantitative methods.

Then there were the neighbours. The neighbourliness I knew as a child was quite unlike the *Family and kinship* paradigm proffered by the qualitative researchers like Peter Townsend and Michael Young. Our house shared a driveway with the next-door house, which meant that the two back doors faced one another. It was impossible not to know a certain amount about life in the house next door. The first family to live there consisted of a doctor, his half-Italian wife (who taught me the proper way to cook and eat spaghetti) and two children, a boy and a girl. The doctor used the front room of the house as a surgery, and patients came in the back door. After a few years, the doctor and his family sold up and left in a hurry; apparently he had been having an affair with one of his patients. That was about the most exciting thing that ever happened next door. The subsequent inhabitants were another family, also with a boy and a girl (this boy-and-girl business was another reason for my feeling a misfit), but this time the father was a well-off Indian who owned a car business, and his wife was a European Jew who had escaped the holocaust thanks to the Kinder transport. When Mr and Mrs Gasper bought the house next door, they were temporarily without their boy and girl, having left them in a nursery in Switzerland. They eventually fetched them and brought them late one night in a car to the shared driveway; proudly showing them to my mother and me. Mrs Gasper complained that her little girl's curly hair had suddenly straightened in the aeroplane; it never curled again.

Mrs Gasper and my mother were in and out of each other's kitchens in a manner superficially reminiscent of the scenes of working-class life sketched by Michael Young and his colleagues at the Institute of Community Studies. The kitchen in the Blue Plaque House was tiny, and the gas stove was opposite the back door. Every time my mother opened the back door to Mrs Gasper for what they both called 'a gossip', the gas blew out. This wasn't the only reason she was given to criticising Mrs Gasper. My mother made it plain to me that this was a relationship of convenience only: it was nothing to do with a real community of neighbours. Like our relatives, Mrs Gasper was from a different echelon of society and didn't share the Titmusses' important intellectual and political interests. She wasn't part of the story.

If we weren't working class, I didn't feel we were middle class, either. There was very little culture in the Blue Plaque House. We listened to comedy programmes on the radio – 'Much Binding in the Marsh' and 'Take it From Here,' with the mournfully engaged Ron Glum and his fiancée Eth – and we went to the cinema down the road in Acton occasionally. I don't remember ever going to the theatre or a concert or an art exhibition (when we went to Paris in my late teens I went to the Louvre on my own), and I don't remember my parents talking about going to any of these. I was taken to watch ballet though, at the Royal Opera House a whole world away in Covent Garden, precipitously high up in the cheap seats. I remember the diaphanous sets of Swan Lake and Les Sylphides as completely mesmerising. They were so unlike everything else in my life. Were we perched up there watching these alien life forms because my parents wanted to go or because I urged them to take me? I did do a ballet class for a short time as a child: there's a series of posed snaps of me with pointed satin feet and a starched tutu in the garden of the flats where we lived before the Blue Plaque House.

The other exception to the culture-free zone of my childhood was the momentous occasion when we were taken to the Broadway performance of 'My Fair Lady' by my father's university hosts in New York in 1957. I was quite overwhelmed by the splendour of this, and also by the discomfort of wearing stockings and a suspender belt (tights hadn't yet been invented) for the very first time. At home we had a piano on which my mother played light classical music quite well, spilling cigarette ash on the keys. Other than that, there was no music at all, and the record player they gave me on my 16th birthday was the only one in the house for many years. My mother kept a few books of poems – Rudyard Kipling, Walter de la Mare, Palgrave's *Golden treasury* – and a few novels, but I learnt about literature mainly through an imaginative English teacher at Chiswick Polytechnic when I was doing my A-levels, who enabled me to overcome the bad experience I'd had with Jane Austen at Haberdashers' Aske's.

I thought of our social class as rather like our street – uninteresting and quite undetermined. We were the inbetweens. We didn't seem to have much more money than my co-pupils at Haberdashers' Aske's, but they did tend to live in smaller houses further out of London (some, like my best friend's family, who took in lodgers, were clearly less well-off). My parents were always careful with money: in fact it's a bit of a puzzle what they spent their money on. My mother got this attitude from *her* mother, Katie Caston, who was given to such traditional utterances as 'Look after the pennies, and the pounds look after themselves', and 'Waste not, want not' (applied particularly to food, and responsible for my own habit of preserving leftovers and other out-of-date substances). Perhaps my father learnt his pecuniary caution from Morris's mistakes. His course in book-keeping at Clark's College came in useful when doing our family accounts, which were always scrupulously kept by him in little lined cash books, and for his annual pilgrimage with the demanding Inland Revenue income tax form to the study upstairs overlooking the non-privatised North Thames Gas Board Playing Fields. The door of the study was firmly closed at these times, and I was instructed to stay away.

The answer, of course, was that our class was based not on property, or on inherited identity, but on the labour of ideas, the politics of mind. Richard and Kay Titmuss collected around themselves a coterie of people who shared their commitment to improving public and personal welfare through the analytic and prescriptive power of thought. They thought about it and talked about it, and the politicians and the social engineers tried to manifest these ideas in action. Actually, *he* thought and discussed and *she* served the meals, keeping a little notebook in which she wrote down what was served – 'roast lamb and cherry pavlova', 'Greek fish dish and apple pie' – so the same people wouldn't eat the same meal twice, which would have been a *faux pas* of unforgettable proportions.

My mother preserved a lingering sense of the importance of personal friendship by maintaining intermittent contact with several friends. Two of these had emigrated to Canada and South Africa, so the contact was mainly by letter. She also had a friend who ran a hotel in Bognor Regis, a town with aesthetics that matched its title. We went to stay there several times, and it wasn't very regal. The last time we visited was when our son was a baby and not given to sleeping in strange hotel rooms or behaving well in hotel dining-rooms. I vowed, with the same decisiveness as I had given up camping for life after the first disastrously wet experience with a boyfriend on a French campsite in 1962, never to stay in a hotel with small children again. Helen Johnston, the fourth of my mother's friends, was a rich Scottish woman who had helped to fund my mother's work in clubs for unemployed men in the 1930s. She was a beautiful, poised, elderly woman who visited our house occasionally to participate in rather stilted conversations. When I got married she gave us a mohair rug, which shows the same propensity for longevity as its giver – it's still going strong after nearly 50 years. The fifth friend, Dorothy Blythe, was utterly different: she was large, very funny and effervescently talkative. She was an actress and sometimes she would have a small part in a television play or film – 'The Adventures of Robin Hood', 'The Love Match', 'The Avengers', 'Citizen James', 'The Tony Hancock Show' – and my mother and I would watch her (my father was never amused by such entertainments). Dorothy represented for my mother a life that she might have had but didn't: a life of economically precarious fun as a single woman.

Did my father have friends? What replaced for him the extended family that had been shoved out of the way so the nuclear one could have centre stage? Men don't have friends the way women do. They don't gossip, or, if they do, they call it something else. Men's conversations don't bear witness to the enduring domestic events (the original meaning of gossip is *godsibb*, a person with whom one has a spiritual affinity: *godsibbs* were witnesses at childbirth). In my father's diaries, bequeathed to me by my mother, it is impossible to distinguish any assignations there might have been with friends from the inventory of meetings, lectures, supervisions and more meetings. I think now he might have been lonely. They were both lonely, the way you can only be lonely in a publicly successful marriage. We were all lonely, all three of us in the Blue Plaque House. Isn't that sad? Mrs Titmuss left a record of her loneliness in her diaries, she left it as a permanent reminder of nothing, yet everything, in particular, for her only daughter.

5

Mrs Titmuss's diaries

In my memory my mother's persona is unchanging over time: iron-grey hair captured in a curious style – a comb to one side at the front and a bun at the back – perhaps the style was fashionable in the 1920s, and it just stuck with her; misty pale blue eyes; that smoker's cough; a brittle, restless energy, expended in darting movements around the domain of the Blue Plaque House. The rounded shoulders did grow more noticeable with age, and she dropped in height as the curse of osteoporosis kicked in; and the grey hair whitened and eventually, when its daily dressing became too much for her, she asked me to cut it. I can't remember at all what my mother looked like after I had cut her hair, but I do remember the act of cutting it: the terminal snap of the scissors, the heavy silk of the hair falling through my fingers onto the floor. Because she plaited it before rolling it into the bun, the hair had a snake-like waviness which made me feel slightly queasy. I was surprised she trusted me enough to ask me to cut it. She wasn't fond of hairdressers, and hadn't been to one for years. She had had her long hair cut once, as a young woman – perhaps as a fledgling sign of protest - and she arranged for the thick brown tresses to be woven together and thus preserved. As a child I used to play with them. Sometimes I pinned them to my own hair: the colours matched exactly. I was fascinated and horrified by their liminal status: both alive and dead, part of my mother's material body and yet not so any more. They reminded me of the dead fox fur that used to hang round my grandmother Katie Caston's neck, its little mouth and paws extended tight with horror.

Man and wife, the book I wrote about my parents' early years together, was an act of obeisance to the frustrated spirit inside my mother's edgy body. She never said to me that, had she not married Richard Titmuss, she might have had a satisfying career of her own, but the documentary remnants of her life bequeathed to me and the way she talked about the past, that past before I was born, did speak wistfully of an uncompleted journey. The letters she wrote to my father during the War, drawn on for *Man and wife*, are the only written record of their relationship and her life. She was an able woman with competencies that languished in the confines of that marriage and that house. Her sense of incompleteness and my failure as her only child to be the product she wanted (conformist, domestic) dominated, not only my childhood, but my whole life. This was the greatest conundrum of my childhood: *her* secondary citizenship versus *their* profession of equality.

In *Man and wife* I wrote of my mother's careful pruning of the documentary evidence concerning her own and my father's life and my childhood. She threw away much more than she kept, and what she kept was intended to tell a particular set of stories: of Richard's humble beginnings, of her own role as teacher and helpmate, of the great love they fell into, of the successful raising of a well-behaved little girl. It was a story of how native wit and ambition could triumph over material adversity: a true tale of capitalism and the protestant ethic, mixed with a noticeable dose of the fashionable-at-the-time eugenics. This was the narrative I picked up from my first examination of the evidence contained in the brown suitcase my mother left me. I noted then some of the gaps: nothing about her own schooling, for example; no indication of any non-domestic interests she might have had after she gave up social work to conceive and care for a child. This is a missing life. Women 'chose' then to dedicate themselves to husbands and children. The language of choice is often backhanded: choice among fixed alternatives can be no choice at all.

My mother left her diaries, though: well, some of them. I didn't read the diaries properly until yesterday, 25 years after I inherited them, although I had noted the puzzle of the unbroken series of 1970–87 diaries with only two earlier ones, for 1941 and 1951, preserved. Assuming she kept a diary for every year of her adult life, that's 41 diaries disposed of. People get rid of evidence *for* reasons, and those gaps and reasons are a biographer's nightmare. Yet people also *keep* evidence for reasons and that creates another predicament: one is called upon to decipher the code of what's left. Possibly the selection of documents my mother bequeathed to me in the brown suitcase was random and/or she had forgotten just what they contained – but I don't think so: too much effort had gone into organising that collection, and there's too much coherence in the jigsaw puzzle they create. But the problem then is, that if we tell only those stories about people's lives they want us to tell, we are no more than objects of manipulation. Well, perhaps a little more, since we can elaborate and enhance the story with a few fluttering asides here and there, a scattering of suggestions and suppositions. But the effort to be faithful to *their* story will cancel out any sustained investigation of other possible narratives.

Instead of her own work, my mother had health problems. As a child I was vaguely aware of these, but more as an atmosphere of tension between my parents than as a named disorder. Indeed, what she suffered from might well have been, at least partly, 'the problem with no name' identified by American feminist Betty Friedan in that 1960s tract *The feminine mystique*, a copy of which lingered so mysteriously on my father's bookshelf. The problem with no name is the problem of women's frustration and loneliness and depression when tied to the home, the 'view from the cage' that Sasha Young described. There are scattered references in my mother's tiny leather-bound diaries to her less than optimal mental health and the treatment she sought for it. 'Saw Macdonald' (a doctor). 'Events too much for me,' she wrote in 1941, and then 'Barton Hill after a private storm. Acute depression. V. tired.' My father's letters to his friends Maurice Newfield (of the Eugenics Society) and Jerry Morris, another doctor and epidemiologist, record the diagnosis: 'functional nervous syndrome', 'a breakdown' for which my mother was prescribed the drastic-sounding remedies of belladonna and bromide. That summer of 1941 was a summer of ill-health, not aided by the bombing of London and events abroad. At home my parents were bent on achieving parenthood. My mother was 39 and my father 35 and they thought they had better get on with it. Medical advice, to rest and take vitamins, or perhaps just the passage of time itself, eventually worked.

My mother's other problem was with her bones. By the date of the next preserved diary, 1951, she was taking 30 grams of calcium gluconate three times daily. She was 48 in 1951 so the osteoporosis must have been sufficiently obvious by then for her to be prescribed calcium. It wasn't common in the 1950s for people to self-medicate with vitamins. Why did she have osteoporosis so badly and so young? The epidemiologist in me recites the risk factors: an early menopause, only one child, no exercise, an addiction to cigarettes (at the front of the 1975 diary is a note 'Silk Cut 32 ½ for 20'). Her dislike of exercise was equally legion. She never went for walks or swims. MBW 178 was taken out for even the shortest shopping trips, a mere two blocks to the butchers' or the fishmongers' or the greengrocers' on the Uxbridge Road.

By 1970, aged 67 when the diary trail resumes, my mother has been put on something called 'santolan' and other vitamins. In March, her legs won't function and she's admitted to St George's Hospital in Hyde Park where she has X-rays and blood tests and is put on a hormone regime – stilboestrol 0.5 mg and methyltestosterone

5 mg on alternate days, according to the diary. Having collected this armoury of pills, my mother discharges herself from St George's Hospital by taxi in order to attend with my father a dinner for the Swedish Prime Minister at 10 Downing Street. This must have been the occasion I remember when she came home in her dressing-gown. She must have discharged herself against medical advice, anxious not to miss the party at Downing Street, and so her clothes hadn't been brought back in – in those days when people went into hospital their clothes went home. But where was her husband, and why didn't he fetch her from hospital himself?

Stilboestrol is a synthetic oestrogen that was licensed in the 1940s for conditions which included menopausal symptoms (but not thin bones). It later acquired fame under the name diethylstilboestrol (DES) as a cause of vaginal cancer in the daughters of women who were given it (ineffectively) as a prophylactic for miscarriage. The other hormone my mother started to take, methytestosterone, is an anabolic steroid mainly used today to treat testosterone deficiency in men, or taken by male exercisers to boost aggression and strength. In the 1970s it was combined with stilboestrol in an effort to allay menopausal discomfort. It seems odd that doctors prescribed these powerful synthetic hormones – hormones with a known adverse effect on mood – for a menopause that had occurred at least 20 years previously.

The diaries also tell me that in that summer of 1970 my mother was sent to see a psychiatrist. She was experiencing fluttering in her back and pain in her legs. Diazepam, 2 mg three times a day, was added to the drug regime. There are constant notes about tiredness, about the need for 'night pills', about the debilitating effect of seeing 'Ann and the children'. 'R at Mill Hill evening,' says one entry, referring to one of my father's visits to his mother and sister in North London, 'Row with him'. In 1972, eight months before her husband died, she 'tore' her back and was in more pain. After he died, everything got much worse. The appointments with the doctors at St George's multiplied, and a different anabolic steroid, durabolin, was used, this time via injection. In November she was prescribed further sessions with a psychiatrist, and ibuprofen and phenylbutazone, both non-steroidal anti-inflammatory drugs used for arthritic pain (today phenylbutazone is restricted to animal use). 'V. v. tired … irritation in back then pain felt sick. Panicked,' records the diary.

One evening, a few months after my father's death in April 1973, my mother rang me in a very distressed state. I was alone at home with my first two children, then aged five and six, who were asleep in bed. I woke them up and drove them in their pyjamas to the house in Acton. She was pacing restlessly around the front room weeping and shouting, and she appeared to have caused some injury to her hand, which was bleeding. She had wiped the blood over the white walls of the room. The children were very frightened. I telephoned her GP, who agreed to come. 'What do you want me to do?' he asked.

In the autumn of 1974 she was put on another course of steroids, and then she went into another hospital, Atkinson Morley in Wimbledon. An outpost of St George's, founded originally as a convalescent home and then converted into a neuroscience and psychiatry centre, Atkinson Morley in the 1970s was using new approaches to psychiatric treatment. These included the wearing by doctors and nurses of ordinary clothes so you couldn't tell them apart from the patients. This didn't suit my mother at all. She liked to know who was who. Most of all, she wanted the doctors to cure her, but they were all useless, or so she confided to her diary. One of these doctors observed to me on one of my visits that depression doesn't show up on X-rays. One of them, a consultant rheumatologist, wrote to her, in a letter I found only yesterday, frankly about her depression as the underlying cause of her poor health; she responded to his interest in her by sending him copies of her dead husband's books.[1] In the hospital she was invited to join a counselling group, an invitation she declined with some hostility. My mother wasn't a group person, and she disliked, in a quite uninformed but also rather reasonable way, everything psychiatric. Actually, it's a wonder she consented to see a psychiatrist at all.

A few weeks after coming out of Atkinson Morley, she was back in St George's for 12 days. It seems that one hospital was looking after her mind and the other one her body.

My mother had lots of X-rays and tests for this and that, and consumed many pills during 14-and-a-half long years of lonely widowhood. She went on living in the Blue Plaque House, in her later years sharing it with several Bible College students, young men with their own sets of difficulties. They were installed upstairs and she slept in the downstairs front room which had been my father's study. She slept here with his books and a spitting gas fire and a low table where she ate frugal meals of soup and toast and marmite, with one easy chair for visitors. The faithful Mr Pearce constructed an illegal bathroom for her at the end of the kitchen. The house went on receiving a frightening amount of attention during these declining years of hers: the walls were washed and redecorated several times, the curtains and carpets were cleaned regularly with the help of the Bible College students, and the window-cleaner continued to earn a steady income. All this was noted in the little diaries right up until the last weeks of her life.

With Richard's death, my mother lost contact with many people who turned out to be more interested in him than her. She became increasingly dependent on a small coterie of helpers, especially Graham, one of the Bible College students who was also a nurse, a tall dark-haired young man with a remarkable physical resemblance to Richard. Quite early on in this arrangement Graham and I understood that my mother complained to me about him and to him about me. Twenty-five years on Graham still sends me Christmas cards. I don't know his address so I can't reciprocate. Graham, if you read this, please get in touch.

My mother was good at complaining. Almost everyone she had contact with is deemed 'useless', 'no help' or 'unsatisfactory' in those diaries. Her contacts with me are especially flawed. I was away, or at work, or too tired to talk: sometimes our phone calls or meetings were 'disastrous', although more often they were just 'unsatisfactory'. The exact times were noted: 'Ann rang briefly 10.20 pm.' 'Oakleys 12.15–12.45.' In letters to friends she confessed her resentment of my work and the sacrifices it entailed: 'I made many for Richard's work, lacking his company when he was preoccupied with his writing, and the pattern continues now with Ann'.[2] Over the last years of her life I did a lot of work for the European Office of the World Health Organization in Copenhagen, which meant not only visits there but all over the place: Brazil, China, Germany, Italy, Kazakhstan, the Netherlands, the USA. Depressed by my cowardice, I would delay calling her until the departures lounge at the airport. I would stand there and she could hear the flights being announced with unavoidable finality. One 'disastrous' Sunday, at lunch in our house in Ealing not far from hers, she swept all the plates and cutlery and glasses off the table and screamed 'I wish you'd never been born'.

I wasn't short on intellectual understanding of her position: a woman born in a changing world, unallowed by circumstance and character to seize that world with open arms, and held in the vice-like grip of powerful ideologies about gender. After her husband died, and she was marooned in the wasteland of grief, she wrote to their politician friend Richard Crossman about how, when she first met Richard, she had 'recognised in him someone who could be of more use than I ever could'.[3] Self-sacrifice in supporting men's careers was a habit of the time. But it could have been otherwise. In the specialist world of LSE which she knew well, there were examples of academic partnerships. The sociologist and demographer David Glass married Ruth Lazarus, another sociologist, who continued with her own work while having two children: the Glasses were known as the 'Heloïse and Abelard' of sociological research.[4] Margaret Simey, the first British woman to take an honours degree in social science, and the wife of Richard Titmuss's Liverpool University colleague Tom Simey, wrote about her experiences as 'Mrs Prof' in her own autobiography published in 1996. Inside the copy Margaret sent me was a letter explaining the parallels:'Your mother's story and my own are identical. I faced the same choice as your mother, but I opted to hang onto my career'.[5] Margaret Simey's unbendingly radical work as a Labour councillor in Liverpool defending the unemployed, the miners, the protesters and the dispossessed, brought her name often into the media and onto politicians' lips. She enjoyed, she said, in her letter to me, the excitement of it all, even the task of combining public life with the care of home and family. She wrote to my mother, too, when they were both widowed about political work being a 'splendid way of diverting one's self-pity'. 'I do hope,' she ended, 'you have found an outlet for your own energies.'[6]

Reading the obituaries of Richard, Kay must have felt confirmed in the path her life had taken: 'like all great men he enjoyed her loving support in all he did'.[7] Without her, what might he have been? The asymmetrical commitment – her to him, him to his work – was part of the legend of the Christ-like figure (with his disciples) who rose to fame from nothing. But even in their lifetime there were those who queried this picture of a companionate and helpful marriage: 'I found her small-minded – someone who often made carping or destructive comments about others and who did not have interesting things to say about her own activities,' observed Peter Townsend. The point is the expansion of horizons and interests that comes as a package with involvement in the public world. 'She may have felt thwarted too many times in her early years in getting a career going, like many women then and now, and retreated into an extreme version of a safe traditional marriage. Perhaps this was the only version of marriage which she felt could work. If by doing this she thought she was responsible for his achievements she was certainly wrong. In truth he had done some fine things despite her. She may even have held him back from doing things better.'[8] As a child I began to suspect that the way my mother presented their marriage concealed her imperfect understanding of what her husband's work was all about. The acronyms that peopled the house – SBC, UGC, SSRC, MRC, PEP – were mantras rather than intelligent references in her conversation: she shared my childish ignorance of what they meant. As the years passed, her seclusion in the home increasingly cut her off from any real acquaintance with his world of demanding public issues. It would do that for anyone. I feel sad, even now, that my mother wasn't able, like Margaret Simey, to take a path that involved claiming some agency for herself.

The emotional wasteland of my and my mother's relationship has always left me floored. In my memory, she stands there, always slightly apart from me, as in the photograph at the head of this chapter. She invites my gaze and my speculation about the nature of (her) motherhood. When I was a child, my father was always the gentle, physically affectionate one. My mother's arms struggled to reach out to me, like the staccato movements of Dr Coppelius's doll in Delibes' ballet, which my parents took me to see. There was something quite hypnotic about that doll: its fabrication, its dancing to someone else's tune, and then its triumphant independent vitality. I saw myself there. It's a cliché, but I can't help it: it seemed to me that an element of dissembling was at work here too, that my mother's love for me was not for the person I really was. This was all the harder because the conditions of that love were mysterious. I wasn't a boy, I couldn't become another Richard.

In 1986, the Hebrew University of Jerusalem invited me to give the Richard Titmuss Memorial Lecture. I wrote a piece called 'Social welfare and the position of women' in which I took two of my father's classic texts – his 1955 Eleanor Rathbone Memorial Lecture 'The social division of welfare' and his 1952 Millicent Fawcett Lecture on 'The position of women' – as starting points for arguing what was by then the fairly uncontentious position that most social policy has been flawed by unarticulated assumptions of gender difference. The welfare state presumes the oppression and dependence of women's unpaid labour in the home. 'Received Ann's Israel lecture,' noted my mother's diary when I gave her a copy of it, 'Told her it would do.' That's more or less what my hosts in Israel felt. My political soliloquy on gender just about did because it was presented in a scholarly way and I took the trouble to dress and behave appropriately, but it could hardly be considered an achievement worthy of Richard Titmuss's intellectual legacy. Who wants to talk about the position of women when there are so many more interesting issues to be considered? I found Israel a shockingly uncomfortable place to be and wish I'd never accepted the invitation. I did accept it because I wanted to be a good daughter, and I foolishly thought my mother would be pleased.

The awful thing about all this delving into the past is finding things you'd completely forgotten, often for very good reason. Some time in the year of my father's death I must have given my mother the manuscript of my book *Housewife* to read. She commented only on the last chapter, which is called 'Breaking the circle' and is a daunting list of steps that need to be taken in order to abolish the oppression of women as housewives. Not only the role of housewife and gender roles must be abolished, say I, the not-to-be-daunted young author of this book with its declaratory red, blue and white OMO packet cover, we must also get rid of The Family. There are many references in the chapter to research and other literature drawn on to compose my argument. The first was a quote from Lenin: 'No nation can be free when half the population is enslaved in the kitchen.' 'People could assume you were a communist,' commented my mother, '& I think this is a bad quote anyway because he was wanting to get them enslaved in a lot of equally drab jobs. Also 90% of the population were slaves at the time he spoke – both men and women.' A few pages later I cite a journalist who wrote about the use of housework as a community service sentence for criminal offenders: this journalist sagely noted that many thousands of women in Britain were routinely interned week in and week out performing the ultimate deterrent of housework. My mother didn't like my including this quote: 'It is snyde [sic] and not worthy of your work.' But most of her criticism is kept for the section on The Family, in which I discuss the transmission of domesticity from mothers to daughters via what research on mothers and female babies demonstrates is a close identification that doesn't need culturally, as in the case of male children, to be broken. 'I suppose you expect me to disagree, & I do,' said my mother. 'Of course you are wrong – mothers cannot relate to a female baby as a separate person? Of course they can. This stems possibly I think from your own personal misconception that I wanted you to be like myself. Never, from the first moment you were born I regarded you as a person who as far as I had any influence should be free to develop independently & certainly not as another edition of myself. I can see that by adopting this attitude & sharing you so completely with my life partner (being ever conscious of the part he played in your existence) I may have contributed to your excessive attachment to him. Work that one out!!'

I can't really. What excessive attachment? Does this perhaps reek of something as basic as jealousy? Perhaps it *was* hard for her, perhaps there was a real sense of competing with me for my father's attention. But what did she mean, sharing me so completely with him? He was hardly there, except as an ideational presence, the reason for it all: her devotion as a wife, my exemplary girlhood, our happy family life. As a young woman striding (or teetering) out into the unkind world of academia and the volcanic territory of motherhood, I desperately wanted my parents' approval, a parental pat on the back: well done, Ann. After all, by the age of 30 I had given them two grandchildren, three books and the beginnings of an international reputation as an expert in the sociology of gender and women's health. They accepted all of this as their due, although with the unspoken reservation that they would have preferred my work to have been less controversial. They wanted a conformist daughter, but I misread the signs and thought they wanted me to be me.

The psychological effect of reading my mother's melancholy diaries in sequence, all in one sitting, wasn't as bad as you might think, because I already knew the outlines of her story. I knew she thought I had failed her; I just wish she could have explained to me how and why. I was unprepared for the diaries' attention to detail: the exact specification of minutes spent with me, the noting down of the times she called and couldn't get my attention. I could find no explanation in those diaries for why they had never told me of my remaining grandmother's death the year before my father's, or why she didn't share with me his own diagnosis of terminal cancer: if she was punishing me for something, what was my crime? Just as I reflected, looking at the old family photos, on the fact that my grandmothers never actively involved themselves in my care (Maud was unlikely ever to have been given the chance), so I am now aware of how little active grandmothering my mother did for her own grandchildren. The 1970–73 diaries record how she and my father took Adam and Emily to the park for an hour sometimes on Sundays, but little else. The years of her widowhood were crowded and momentous years for me: three further pregnancies, two brushes with death, the birth of a third child, cancer, the dissolution of my marriage, and five changes of job. Through all this, my mother was obsessed with my absence from her life, with my negligence and failure. As the scientist R.C. Lewontin once noted, in an exchange on the subject of 'Sex, lies and social science': 'Even when diaries are only a form of talking to oneself, one may engage in an elaborate composition of a self-justificatory autobiography, much of it unconscious.'[9] Perhaps she was conscious – perhaps we both were – that her widowed loneliness was the cause of her wretched longing for my love and attention. Perhaps we both knew I didn't do enough, partly because I had my own children to look after and I had to earn a living, but partly also because of the legacy of whatever had disrupted our bond many years before.

I'm not bitter about any of this: my mother was who she was, my father also, and they made a reasonable job of me. I'm just puzzled. I don't understand the nature or cause of the problem, although I do understand more as a consequence of writing this book. 'To write is to get on top of it', to fight alienation, establish identity and effect reconciliation.[10] I think that reconciliation is an over-used word. The past is nothing to be afraid of. It is as it is; it was all as it was. We work through layers of feelings, passing several ice ages on the way; we learn to value what was good and not to forget the bad, but to tuck it away safely somewhere.

A fond memory of my mother returns us to a beach in an English summer, probably one in Cornwall or Devon with or without the grandmothers. It could have been Treyarnon Bay, on the North Cornwall coast, and I like to think it was, since this was a house belonging to social reformer Eva Hubback who had lent it to Eleanor Rathbone for the writing of Rathbone's renowned plea for the financial endowment of motherhood, *The disinherited family*. The symbolism of the location pleases me, but it isn't necessarily accurate. Anyway, there I am in the choppy Cornish sea. It's a typically chilly summer's day: the sun isn't shining. I emerge from the sea, a shivering mess of goose-pimples, and my mother is there on the sand with a large towel into whose scratchy warmth she enfolds me. I am saved, I am safe. She rubs me down to pinken my skin, slips off my wet bathing suit and dresses me quickly. She gives me something warm to drink and something sweet to eat. If there are other people there – the grandmothers, my father – I'm not aware of them: it's just the two of us and the towel and the shared damp sand between our toes.

My mother died in 1987 at the age of 84 when I was 43 and away for a month at the Rockefeller Foundation Centre in Bellagio, Italy. There I was above the splendid calm of Lake Como writing a novel about mothers and daughters, and I'd just finished a scene about a mother dying when the telephone call came from a doctor friend of my mother to say she had fallen out of bed and he had given her a pain-relieving injection. He said this 'might depress respiration'.

I've thought about this conversation many times since. I didn't understand then, and the doctor friend certainly didn't spell it out, that depressing respiration with morphine is a humane way of hastening death. It would have been more humane for all of us had he made this clear, and had he held back the injection until I had time to come home. Since he didn't do this, and I didn't understand that my mother's death was imminent, I decided to wait until the following morning to catch a flight.

My mother died that night. I managed to speak to her on the telephone before she died, and she was able satisfactorily to complain to me about the loss of her false teeth. I was glad to be able to commiserate: yes, surely someone had stolen them. We found them later safely tucked away in her handbag. At the end of the conversation I told her I loved her. I think this is what she wanted to hear. Graham told me later that she turned her face to the wall beside her bed after speaking to me, and a little after that she died.

6

Love and solitude

The dawn chorus is a mighty paradox for a country-loving insomniac. It's four o'clock or five o'clock or some other unearthly hour, and you awaken in panic: it's those bloody birds again. 'The chickens woke me up,' objected Zoe, my eldest grandchild, when she first slept here as a small child. The birds clatter with size eleven feet on the roof above my bed and whoosh with cymbal-like wings across the palely dawning sky.

I came to this part of England 25 years ago and put down unexpected roots. I am a town child, born near Paddington Station, raised in a block of flats a few miles west of there, and then in the Blue Plaque House. I'd always lived in a town: the noise and the pace and the crowds are built into my identity. But I did have, from early on, that other experience of the countryside: nothing especially wild, just the placid green undulations of Bedfordshire, where my father's parents and their ancestors lived their now-unknowable and probably quite unremarkable lives. There's nothing remarkable about the countryside – it's just here, this land, with its effervescent birds; it isn't at all pretentious. This, where I am now, isn't pretty-pretty tourist England, just ordinary trees and fields and hedges and lanes and medieval churches with comfortably leaning gravestones. It makes me think of Kathleen Raine's poem 'Vegetation' which opens 'O never harm the dreaming world, / the world of green, the world of leaves'.[1]

Love & solitude is the title of a set of poems composed by the Swedish-speaking Finnish writer Edith Södergran. She wrote her poetry first in German, French and Russian, before turning to her native Swedish and becoming the first Scandinavian modernist poet. For this she was ridiculed in her lifetime, a reputation since reversed. Södergran contracted tuberculosis from her father when she was 16 and died of it 15 years later in 1923. Her poetry was written against a backdrop of illness, poverty, failed love affairs and war – the 1917 Russian Revolution cut off her family's financial support, and the Finnish civil war brought fighting and near starvation. The poems are uncompromising, lyrical and biting at the same time. There is a keen sense of resilience in a landscape of harsh inequality: 'You looked for a flower/and found a fruit. / You looked for a well/and found a sea. / You looked for a woman/and found a soul-/I disappoint you.'[2]

Edith Södergran lived in an isolated village in eastern Finland on the Karelia peninsula where everything that lived was important – the trees, the flowers, the birds, the shimmering sea. The countryside fed her joy in life, her poems, her self-confidence, which came from 'the fact that I have discovered my dimensions'. 'It does not behove me,' she wrote defiantly, 'to make myself smaller than I am.'[3]

When I first started to spend time in my rural retreat, I was afraid to be alone, particularly at night. Solitude and silence both impose disciplines quite alien to the main drift of modern culture. They drive one into the manias of one's own head, demanding the cultivation of a special sort of vigilance. Yet the countryside at night is an appallingly noisy place, full of the spooky sounds of owls and foxes and sheep and unknown animals, even before the birds start their own concert. The dark is darker than the town, the scents of planet earth far more pungent. At first I barricaded myself in the house with bolts and keys, kept the windows closed, sat up startled with my heart in my mouth whenever the old pipes in the house creaked. At first I didn't grasp the difference between loneliness and solitude: they are negative and positive names for the same state, being on one's own. One is about pain, the other about the intense pleasure of being free from the constraints of others. I was younger then, when I worked this out. Those ancestral memories of which I write in this book were yet to be recovered. Now I am more at home here than anywhere else. In the daytime I look out at a garden full of gifts, from a gardening daughter, from my late friend Vera Seal, from a sociology colleague: brilliant blue hebes, bell-like white clematis, Japanese wineberries shooting out in all directions, a pink rose, just blooming for the first time ever. If you sit under my magic apple tree in the autumn you will, like as not, be hit on the head by a large green globe, but it only happens every other year: old trees, like old people, need periods of rest. *My* position in the garden is in the corner outside the kitchen looking at the apple tree from an angle where any sun there is will be keenly focused on my wintery English skin.

Writers need solitude, and most of us need silence, which is hard to find in our modern noisy lives. Silence is a condition of solitude. Sylvia Plath wrote those astonishing last poems alone in the early hours of the morning before her little children woke up. One is always, anyway, alone in the presence of small children, a fact whose impact on mothers' mental health has been hugely overlooked; perhaps the combination of solitude and uninvited noisiness is the most lethal of all. The writer Sara Maitland's search for solitary silence revealed a depth and range of sensory impressions that normally escape us: the porridge was intensely porridge-y; the wind was composed of different noises, like an orchestra; being hot or cold or tired or amused produced 'monumental waves of feeling'.[4]

My own rural solitude is about freedom. Only when I'm not 'on duty' in the sense of having to respond to other people's needs am I free to scurry around in my own head, and find out what's there. Being tied down by responsibility is, of course, what has held creative women back throughout the ages. I know there's some boundaried and shadowy mental space which is busy with all sorts of excitements, premonitions, analyses, understandings, metaphors, images – immaterial nonsense which can only be turned into sense when I am alone with it. I sleep (or not) when I want to, get up at dawn or in the middle of the day, eat vegetables for breakfast, scatter nuts on the stairs in my haste to carry snacks up to the attic where I write. I hope no one calls at the door because my jeans have mud on them and the moths have dined on the old jerseys I keep in the cupboard.

This afternoon, a triumphal moment in late spring, I took myself for a walk across the fields and down the lanes. It was late afternoon, and the sun was shining after a day of rain. The saturated ground released a nosegay of perfume. Apparently the older one gets the more it is smells that set memories off, although the sense of smell itself actually declines. After a while, when the rhythm of walking had calmed my mind, I came to a bend in the road. As I turned, the whole green world opened itself out to me: the narrow silver road between bright green hedges heaving with creamy blossom, with the lazy umbrellas of meadowsweet and the honeycombs of hawthorn, with the pale lime green of elderflowers just starting to whiten on their journey to becoming those bitter blood-black fruits. There are times when one's body and mind are peculiarly open to sensations – sights, scents, the sun's warmth, the rustle of life in the hedgerows, the cuckoo's off-the-cuff remarks, even the incipient taste of the apple and elderberry concoctions expecting to be brewed in country kitchens at summer's end. I know nothing more intoxicating than this. No draught or potion or psychotropic medicine could be nearly as mind-altering. I have the strongest feeling of having walked like this in this kind of place for centuries, but also of walking here for the very first time. Everything that's old is also new, and every new experience contains the old.

My father will probably be coming round the next bend in the road in a moment. I remember him walking with me as a child in sunlit country lanes, where he would have been steeped in his own boyhood memories of roaming the fields round Lane Farm, Stopsley. Here he'll be now, in a transubstantial moment, tall and stooped with his neatly combed black hair and his yellow tie, there he'll be with his smile and his lean hands and his penknife to show me how you peel acorns from the trees. There's so much I want to talk to him about. I missed my chance when he was alive. He wasn't a man to welcome such talk. What kind of disappointment is that?

7

The story of the Titmice: an alternative version

Brian Abel-Smith's biographer, Sally Sheard, says the welfare state we have in Britain today is essentially the dream of three men: Richard Titmuss, Peter Townsend and Brian Abel-Smith, otherwise known as 'the Titmice'.[1] Through a variety of routes – academic analysis, policy research, political networking – they adapted and promoted the implementation of the 'cradle-to-grave' philosophy of William Beveridge's original vision. The Titmice's *modus operandi* established an unbeatably effective model for the research–policy relationship. Their department at LSE was the only place in Britain in the 1950s and '60s where serious social policy research was done; its work informed the Labour Party's social policy programme for a decade, and was the inspiration behind the policies of the Labour government in 1964–70.[2] It's probably the most influential 20th-century example of an academic group capturing governmental thinking, and the key to its success was the intellectual and moral leadership provided by Richard Titmuss.[3] In an alternative, pseudo–religious representation, the Titmice were known as God the Father, God the Son and God the Holy Spirit. This formula chimed with the depictions that crowd the obituaries of Richard Titmuss as a 'high priest', 'a saint', 'a prophet' and 'an ascetic divine' who, with his lean face and compelling eyes, might well have been painted by El Greco.

So long as I was a child, I was firmly annexed to the repository of perfect family happiness represented by the Blue Plaque House. But once I began to emerge from childhood, matters were bound to get more untidy. Even children like me, good home-loving daughters, ultimately grow up. In my first account of my childhood, *Taking it like a woman*, I saw my emancipation largely in terms of entry into the world of male friendships. It was boyfriends who broke the spell. Deprived of brothers, and with only two distant boy cousins and no male schoolmates, the erotic pull of masculinity provided the spur needed for me to question the Blue Plaque House's occupation of my life and identity. But, yet, hang on a minute, who were those masculine mischief-makers? I met no boys through my own restricted social circles, although I did have an avid correspondence on thin rice paper with a young man in Nagoya, Japan, whose exact address I can still recite. We exchanged photographs, of me with my cat and him with his dog, and stories about life in Nagoya and Acton; at one stage he declared himself in love with me, but the point of the correspondence was that we never actually met and we knew we never would.

No, my early adolescent stirrings about sex and men all latched themselves – or were purposively latched by others – onto the men who encircled my father: his research assistants, his protégées, his disciples, his collaborators. I was the pubescent jewel in the entourage, the icing on the cake. François and Eileen Lafitte were friends of my parents: François, a social researcher and journalist and later a professor of social policy and administration at Birmingham University, was the son of a French feminist called Françoise, who, during her son's childhood, had been financed by the American birth control campaigner Margaret Sanger to become Havelock Ellis's wife-like companion, and cure him of his lifelong impotence.[4] François's exposure to Havelock Ellis's line on sexual freedom made him prone to gossip about sex, a characteristic which didn't accommodate itself well to the Titmusses' own prurience about such matters. His wife Eileen was a beautiful blue-eyed woman, an untrained social worker like my mother. They all met through the activities of the Eugenics Society, a much-written-about organisation that dominated right-wing and (some) left-wing thought during the 1930s and '40s. Both Richard Titmuss and François Lafitte were aspiring young intellectuals who found the Eugenics connection socially useful. It *was* a fertile place for the meeting of different kinds of minds which shared a fondness for the role of biological inheritance in a variety of reformist agendas.[5]

François and Eileen had a son called Nicholas, a year or so older than me. There are photos of me and Nick as toddlers on the grass in West London in our double-breasted woollen toddler coats. I imagine our parents speculating happily about a later liaison between their two precocious only children. Fast-forward a dozen or so years and there we are, Nick and I together in Nick's bedroom, somewhere in South London. Our parents are downstairs. Nick talks, he talks all the time, about everything. He is trying to impress me, I think. He talks especially, like his father and his adoptive grandfather, about sex, and then about what he would like to do to, or possibly with, me. It's my first conscious experience of men's unwanted physical attentions. On the way home, I tell my parents about it. They exchange meaningful looks, but (so far as I know) say and do nothing.

Nicholas Lafitte was later diagnosed with schizophrenia, and when he was 27 he killed himself, leaving behind a body of terrifying Plath-like poetry. I did realise, some years later, that I was lucky to have escaped the same fate. Actually, suicide was a motif among the children of my parents' friends: there were at least two other political and medical families who lost a son that way.

With two of my father's research assistants I had relationships that included sexual contact. It was a process at once logical and insane. A psychoanalytic interpretation would be all too easy, but it would be facile.

Some time after the Nick Lafitte episode, when I was about 15, I met a young man whom I will call Simon. When he wasn't assisting my father with research, Simon was a musician: he played the piano and conducted choirs. Music was the great anchor of my adolescence. My father had contracted tuberculosis in 1958 when I was 14, and I was bought a flute as a consolation for a cancelled summer holiday. With lessons from the kind of charismatic teacher who simply didn't exist at Haberdashers' Aske's, I quickly became a competent flautist, and I began to plan for a career in music. In order to take the higher grade flute examinations, I needed to pass a theory examination, and Simon agreed to teach me for it. We did the teaching mainly by post, but we also had some practical sessions. During one of these, Simon broke off what he was saying about some aspect of music theory, and said 'this is for you'. The piece he played, gazing soulfully into my eyes, was Liszt's Consolation Number Three. It was a filmic moment: the adolescent Acton version of Casablanca.

Simon and I used to go to concerts, usually at the Royal Festival Hall on the South Bank of the Thames, but also in the summer promenade concert season at the Royal Albert Hall in Kensington. After each concert, he would steer me to a bench beside the darkly flowing Thames or under the trees of Kensington Gardens and there he would kiss me twice. It was always twice, interspersed with conversation. The rhythm, like that of one of choruses he conducted, was determined entirely by him.

I have a batch of letters Simon wrote me, in nicely legible blue ink on pale blue writing paper. I was like Brahms' Third Symphony – unpredictable but exciting. He thanked me for joining him and his choir to play the flute at a concert, and was relieved to hear that I had got home safely and that therefore he wasn't going to lose his job. I had obviously written to him to commend him for his sense of duty in making sure I got the right train at the right time, which sentiment prompted him to make the remark I wanted him to make, that his concern for me wasn't motivated just by duty, because I was 'the Professor's daughter'.

I met Simon through Tony Lynes, who worked as Richard Titmuss's researcher. Tony was a grammar school boy, the son of a scrap metal and rag dealer, who trained as a chartered accountant and thus shared my father's love of actuarial calculations. After a colourful life in Malta, with regular trips to Tripoli and Benghazi auditing large commercial companies, Tony did the social science certificate course at LSE and then worked as Richard Titmuss's research assistant, later becoming an assistant lecturer at LSE. The Titmuss projects to which Tony contributed most were my father's book on *Income distribution and social change* (the one that was informally known as 'Alice in the Board of Inland Revenue'), and the inquiry into social services in Mauritius, which was commissioned by the colonial government to address the problem of a high birth rate combined with poverty and restricted natural resources. His duties for the Mauritius Report positioned Tony in a terrifying encounter with what was probably the worst cyclone in Mauritian history. He hid in the basement of his hotel listening to corrugated iron roofs being torn off buildings. Not much was left of the sugar crop, and work on the Titmuss Report was shelved, as Tony offered his clean-up and food-getting services to the local old people's home and orphanage. LSE complained about the wastage of Tony's salary while he was engaged in this essential relief work; Richard Titmuss complained back and instructed them to forget it.[6]

Tony was, and still is, an extraordinarily self-effacing and kind man, with a role in the Titmice's work which has never received proper credit or attention. Unlike the other men in the Titmuss entourage, he kept his physical distance from me. One of my clearest memories is of his explaining to me (we were walking somewhere along a pavement) that in the past gentlemen had always walked on the outside to protect ladies from the unsavoury effluents chucked out of upstairs windows. Tony was a flautist, too. He and I played flute duets together. He encouraged me to join the LSE orchestra. Thus I came to do that journey my father did every day, on the Piccadilly line from Ealing Common to Holborn, and walking up to LSE by Lincoln's Inn Fields. Everybody else in the orchestra was older, a student or member of staff at LSE, except for a clarinettist, the daughter of LSE's Registrar, who was my age. Susan and I were entranced by our premature membership of a university community.

By the time of the second physical relationship with a man who worked in my father's Department, I was a couple of years older and more interested in what might come after the kisses. This man – I will call him Harry – had done the same degree in PPE as I was embarking on at Oxford. He lent me books and we discussed Wittgenstein. He took me to a May Ball in his old college and we danced together – an event which was a considerable achievement on his part, since I never danced at parties, or at balls, although that ball proved to be the only one to which I have ever been. One day Harry bore me off to his parents' home, somewhere suburban like Beckenham. His parents were away. We went to bed but he refused to have sex with me. I recall feeling far more disappointed than I had ever been after a couple of Simon's kisses.

It took only the sight of these men's writing on the correspondence retrieved from my attic, the feel of the notepaper in my hand, even, I imagined, the abiding scent of their bodies and our encounters, to remind me of how I felt in those days, of how they made me feel. The recaptured excitement is primarily emotional and psychological, a flood of anticipation, the promise of another land which will be different, but also reassuringly the same. As a child and a teenager, and despite my small rebellions, I was full of horror and fear about the prospect of life outside my home. What these men offered was an external world with a permanent connection to the world I knew. These men knew me better than I knew myself because they came to me through my father.

Simon and Harry were bit-players in one of the major performances of my father's life after he joined LSE: the story of the Titmice.

Brian Abel-Smith was the first other Titmouse to appear on the stage. He was an economist who used his economics expertise to advocate and implement health and welfare and legal reforms, both in Britain and internationally, for some 40 years from the early 1950s to his death at the age of 69 in 1996. His analysis of Britain's NHS, written jointly with my father as *The cost of the National Health Service* in 1956, was the first to show just how well the NHS performed, given the limited resources devoted to it. Twenty-eighth or thirty-seventh or thirty-eighth in line of succession to the throne – the estimates varied – Brian was tall, blue-eyed, intensely charming, a fast and easy talker, a *bon viveur* and entertainer of the great and good in his Vincent Square flat and later in a house near Victoria Station, convenient for the travel to which he devoted a good portion of his life.

In 1955, Brian joined the Titmuss Department at LSE as an assistant lecturer. The following year, when I was 12, he drove me and my parents through France, Germany, Austria and Italy in his glamorous white car, which was called 'Jones'. Cars did have names in those days. I always thought of Jones as a sports car, but I realise now it couldn't have been, or it wouldn't have been large enough for all of us and our luggage. It was the first time I had been outside England. The excitement caused me to throw up twice all over Jones's side before we even reached the English coast. There we drove the car onto an aeroplane, as you did in those days, and I was sick again. When we got to Calais, Brian stopped at a garage and had Jones thoroughly washed down.

We drove first to Bonn, where my diary records that 'Daddy and Brian wanted to see a man, so they dropped us at the Houses of Parliament situated on the Rhine'. Later, we crossed the Rhine on a ferry and made for Munich, where the men were to attend a conference. There we met up with my father's young and attractive secretary, Judith: my mother always said, rather proudly, that Judith was in love with him. Also in Munich was a woman called Geraldine Aves, whom I found very forbidding, and Anneliese Walker, a social worker with a false leg. Dame Geraldine Aves led a distinguished career as a civil servant and social reformer. I didn't know it then, but Anneliese Walker had originally been a dancer with the Ballet Jooss, a politically inspired German dance company which sought refuge from the Nazis in Dartington Hall in Devon in 1934. In that insanely satisfying logic whereby everything is connected to everything else, Dartington Hall is the legendary utopian community where Michael Young of Institute of Community Studies fame, Richard Titmuss's ex-PhD student, was educated and grew up. The women in my father's entourage were generally single and middle-aged, not seen as prepossessing role models by an adolescent girl. The exception was Judith, who left her post soon after our European trip, being replaced by a very controlling middle-aged widow who arrived with her husband's Greek surname and then abruptly disposed of it. The sign on her office door was changed overnight, an event my father considered worth reporting to my mother and me at the end of that particular day.

My childish diary of that first European trip, littered with sellotaped-in restaurant bills and museum tickets, records diversions such as a visit to Schloss Neuschwanstein and a lake called Chiemsee, where Brian gave me a diving lesson. Once or twice I contrived to be alone with him in Jones. Many years later, when Brian and I had a conversation about all this, he admitted that he knew I had what is known as a 'crush' on him in those heady teenagery years, and he knew I didn't know he was gay. Brian followed with amused interest my path through the education system and a rather difficult adolescence. When I walked out of Haberdashers' Aske's finally, in disgust at its narrow attitude to education, and then decided I wanted to go to Oxford from the unlikely habitus of a polytechnic, he supervised my taking of the Oxford entrance examination from my father's room at LSE (the polytechnic being unable to provide a room for this purpose). The examination papers were posted to Brian who gave them to me, and then posted my answers back to Oxford. We both thought this very funny. Three years later it was Brian's address that was recorded on our marriage certificate: in order to claim status as a London resident, so we could be married at Caxton Hall by the man who married one of the Beatles, Robin left a suitcase in Brian's house. And it was Brian who arranged the wedding supper in Rules Restaurant, London's oldest, where they cook game birds raised in the High Pennines. Our table consisted of Brian, my parents, Robin and me, and Robin's mother, a merry widow from Kent who fell visibly under Brian's spell. Like almost everybody else in those days (homosexuality was illegal in Britain until 1967), she failed to notice that his romantic and sexual interests had nothing to do with women of any age. Brian knew how to flatter older women – he had a lot of practice with his own mother. My mother took longer than I did to fathom his homosexuality, partly because the Blue Plaque House was riddled with quite conventional values. My parents disapproved of gay couples, fancy cooking, fashionable clothes, reliance on credit, large unplanned families, law-breaking (even for radical political motives), single mothers and also to some extent mothers who laboured outside the home. This illiberality was interred beneath a veneer of modernity,

In my childhood perceptions of men, sexuality and family life, the third Titmouse, Peter Townsend, played a very different role. He had a different sort of attractiveness, with thick dark hair, a masculine face, a direct way of speaking, and a very beautiful wife called Ruth. The Townsends lived in two converted cottages in Hampstead and had three small boys (a fourth was added later) who slept under brightly coloured crocheted blankets. At a conference in Italy another year, I helped to look after the youngest Townsend, a toddler with a halo of blonde curls. The Townsends camped, whereas the rest of us stayed in the conference hotel. We went to their campsite once, which was on a beach, and Ruth emerged from their family-sized tent quite unashamedly wearing only a silk petticoat. I thought I would like to be a mother and a wife like her. This was the family that Peter had idolised in that book *Conviction* which formed part of the gender-blind landscape of the 1950s social policy world. This was the kind of family I would have liked to have belonged to as well as the kind I aspired to create. By the time I discovered that all was not what it seemed — although perhaps it was then? — and Peter's devotion to The Family was more of a devotion to Families, as he married twice more, I had myself acquired a more realistic knowledge of family life. Peter Townsend and I had an extraordinary accidental reunion many years later when our eyes met in the changing-room of a little ballet school in North London, where his daughter Lucy, from his second marriage, and my daughter, Laura, from my only one, were both struggling into their pink tights and baby-blue leotards.

Peter Townsend came to the social policy world from a working-class background and a moral sciences and social anthropology degree at Cambridge. He joined LSE in 1957 at Richard Titmuss's instigation, taking with him a Nuffield Foundation grant to study residential accommodation for older people. This ultimately became a fat, far from dispassionate, and enormously influential book, *The last refuge*. When the end of Peter's Nuffield grant was in sight, Richard negotiated for Peter an Assistant Lectureship in Social Science in his Department — and 'negotiate' is the right word, for in the correspondence Richard baldly states that he is getting Peter a job at LSE, although there are unfortunately a few committee hurdles to overcome first.[7] Universities worked like that in those days (they still do, although the mechanisms are generally better concealed).

John Vaizey wasn't one of the Titmice, but his incisive intelligence haunted the edges of the Titmice circle, and he was responsible, indirectly, for creating it, since it was he who introduced Brian to Richard, and Brian in turn introduced Peter Townsend. John was an incredibly clever man with a pale aquiline face and a taste for laughter and scurrilous rumours about other people. His air of impatience, which led him to hurl himself through life at a fantastic pace, stemmed from a dreadful boyhood experience of two years' institutionalisation with osteomyelitis of the spine. At one stage John and Brian lived together in a flat in Vincent Square. They had met at Cambridge. I always assumed they shared the same sort of privileged background, but John's origins, as the son of a wharfinger from South-East London, were much more humble. His trajectory to Cambridge was achieved through the grammar school system and a scholarship. John met my father in 1952 when they corresponded about my father's social history of the War, *Problems of social policy*, a book John much admired. The economics John had studied at Cambridge was entirely devoid of any reference to social policy, and he was anxious to remedy this. The meeting with Richard Titmuss was important in driving his work in this direction, and one result was his founding of a new sub-discipline, that of the economics of education, which he practised for a while at the Institute of Education in London, where I now work.

John described my father at this first meeting as 'very professorial with dark hair & tired, wise, kind eyes'.[8] He and my father never worked directly together, but John was enthusiastically welcomed into both the LSE office and our house, and he became a family friend. The letters he wrote to my father in the late 1950s are warm and affectionate and funny, telling of events in Oxford, where he lectured in economics; in Paris, where he worked for the OECD (Organisation for Economic Cooperation and Development) and wrote a novel; in Pakistan, where he was a visiting lecturer; and in Siena and Colorado, where he was simply holidaying. My father reads, and urges John to publish, his riveting autobiography of illness,

Scenes from institutional life, which makes many Titmussian points about the failings of institutions: John reads my father's lecture on 'The hospital and its patients', later published in his *Essays on 'the welfare state',* and is equally admiring. Many of his letters begin 'Dear RKA' (Richard, Kay and Ann). In a portrait of my father published shortly before his own premature death in 1984, John talked about getting to know the Titmuss family, 'a small daughter, later an attractive girl, to whom Richard was devoted; Mrs Titmuss, at first rather stern'.[9] He remembered being included in family Christmases, mainly as a chauffeur for the distinguished social historian R.H. Tawney, who was brought to Acton from his house in Mecklenburgh Square, Bloomsbury, for Christmas lunch. John bought me expensive presents – clothes and jewellery – and he used to take me to concerts, too. What would these men have done without the excuse of classical music?

One Christmas is prominent in my memory. I am wearing a new royal-blue silk dress with a low neck, a tight waist and a full skirt. I must have been about 14, since the dress accentuates budding breasts which grew late on me. I am standing by the baby grand piano my mother bought when her mother died, the lid is open and I'm about to sit down and play. The air in the Blue Plaque House is seasonally wintry but the fire in the sitting-room is lit with the aid of carefully arranged smokeless fuel and a gas-pipe of which my mother is exceptionally proud. The turkey (it was always a turkey) is in the oven. I won't eat it, of course, I will stick to my cube of cheese, but I will enjoy the Brussels sprouts. My father in his customary suit is arranging the sherry glasses on the tray by the 'hatch' into the dining room. Our Christmas tree is nothing like the magnificent specimens at those Christmas parties at LSE to which I was taken as a child: it's small and artificial and sits ungenerously on a corner of the mantelpiece. The whole atmosphere is anticipatory: we are waiting for the guests to arrive, And then John Vaizey pulls up with the retrieved pipe-smoking Tawney. John gives me his present: a single pearl in a gold mount on a thin gold chain. I have never had, or seen, anything quite so lovely. He fastens it round my neck, murmuring something with the word 'beautiful' in it. I am momentarily released from my signature role as the daughter of the Blue Plaque House, and have become instead a cherished woman.

I was flattered by John's attention but I never knew quite what to say to him. He was frighteningly clever – he confided in me once, walking through the back streets of Oxford when I was a student there and he was a fellow at Worcester College, that being cleverer than anyone else was such a handicap. When he decided to marry an American art critic, Marina Stanksy, he came to the house in Acton to tell me that I was losing one of my admirers. For a while he continued to visit us, with Marina and then two small children in tow. The Vaizeys' third child, the Conservative politician Ed Vaizey, was born just after I gave birth to my own second child. The Vaizeys lived in Chiswick near us, and Marina, hugely pregnant with Ed, came to admire baby Emily and bring me a pot plant.

My knowledge of the Titmice and their entourage as a teenager in the Blue Plaque House was of a very particular kind. I knew little about the logic and power and impact of Titmussian ideas: what I did know about was the enormously focused energy that flowed between these men as they sat and talked: the penetrating eye contact, the quick repartee, the excited circumlocutions of hands in the air. There was something intensely intimate about these encounters. Women, in their roles as hostesses, wives and daughters, were marginal to them. I suspect now that my adult understanding of how patriarchy works was developed partly through my witnessing of these masonic interactions.

At the core of the intellectual liaisons that developed around my father lay for me, as an adolescent trying to come to grips with these things, a definite confusion of sexuality. I eventually worked out Brian Abel-Smith's homosexuality, and John Vaizey clearly entertained the idea of a close relationship with Brian before he settled into marriage. He used to have photos of both Brian and my father by his bed, and he once suggested that he and Brian live together at Madingley Hall, an adult education centre near Cambridge, where John taught part time, an offer Brian refused, although they did later share a flat together in London.[10] There is something ineffably safe for such men about a girl on the verge of womanhood. She is only on the verge, so they are saved from the compunction of declaring their sexual orientation one way or the other. Such a girl, a girl such as I was in the Blue Plaque House, personifies unsullied femaleness. This is how I was, I think, to my father. Brian Abel-Smith told me years later that my father appeared to be so madly in love with me when I was in my early teens: it struck him forcibly whenever he visited the Blue Plaque House.

I don't suppose I would have used the phrase 'madly in love' of the relationship between Brian and my father, but it was a manifestly solid and passionate thing. Brian's biographer has observed that Richard Titmuss is central to understanding Brian's life,[11] and the same applies the other way round. Brian was 'the power behind the throne'.[12] For nearly 20 years these two men met or phoned one another almost daily. They shared ideas, projects, ambitions, humour, an abrasive insider analysis of the British political scene. I don't have to struggle to remember them: there they are, standing up or sitting together talking, looking into each other's shining eyes, faces and hands animated, in one of the Blue Plaque House's bland rooms, or in the grey environs of Houghton Street, or at some international conference with a backdrop of snowy mountains and shadowy female social workers. In the photograph at the head of this chapter Richard and Brian are in my father's study – the place where he kept, but didn't write, his books.

Other men with important public reputations, like Richard Titmuss, have relied on untarnished images as upright family men to camouflage more complex identifications. There's little evidence to contradict the public image to which my parents both signed up: of Richard Titmuss, the happy heterosexual family man. Brian himself was of the opinion that my father's physical interests *were* purely heterosexual. He cited two grounds for this: my father's attitude to me as a teenager, and the love letters my father wrote to my mother during the War.[13]

Their marriage was unusual in various ways: the age difference (he was six years younger than her), the totality of my mother's ambition to make Richard Titmuss famous, their apparently united front against the attributed awfulness of almost all their kin, especially Richard's mother. Perhaps, beyond the problem women typically were for men of his class and generation, women were a problem for him. Brian summed up my father's attitude to women's minds as 'Men could be intellectually interesting. Women hardly ever', in a letter to me after reading the manuscript of my book *Man and wife*.[14] Men were the essential fascination; Richard Titmuss's mind was drawn only to very exceptional professional or academic women, mainly Americans, such as Ida Merriam and Eveline Burns. Ida, a quietly spoken woman with a cartographer husband, headed the Social Security Administration's research and statistics division in the USA. For many years she was that country's leading civil servant and academic in the social administration and policy field. The more forceful Eve Burns was an England-born and LSE-trained economist, a Columbia professor and a social welfare expert. She and her economist husband, Arthur, took us to their New England retreat on my first visit to the USA when I was 13 in 1957. The small, square, faded Kodak photos show my parents, me and the Burns sitting round the residue of an all-American barbecue. I formed a particular attachment to their Siamese cat, who was called Ficelle because of her fondness for string. The pungently dusty and woody smell of the house and the sensation of creatures smaller than Ficelle operating in the woodwork accompanied my nightly insomnia. Neither the Merriams nor the Burns had children in their households, although I believe that the Merriams did have a badly disabled daughter with Down syndrome who lived in an institution. Thus these women were free to share Richard Titmuss's masculine public life.

One function of the contacts I had with Titmuss men was to hold at bay safely for a while the threat of my transition to womanhood and exit from the regime of my childhood. The complex dynamics of our relationships and the attentions of the Titmuss men anchored me there. The fusion of the erotic, the aesthetic, the intellectual and the political was a potent glue. It ensured that I remained my father's daughter long past the normal sell-by date. When I started to have real boyfriends of my own age things did change – although not immediately: my first 'real' boyfriend was the son of the woman who ran what was then euphemistically called the National Council for the Unmarried Woman and her Child, and it was through her professional relationship with my father that I met this young man. Only yesterday, trawling through my father's papers, did I come across letters from John Vaizey which underline how stitched up even this liaison was. My father wrote to John to ask him to intervene in the business of the young man's application to Queen's College, Cambridge: and Vaizey did: the young man was in.[15] Why did I not know this before? There was also a short dalliance somewhere in this chronology with the son of one of the few married women in my father's LSE Department, a young man with an earthy smell and pale leather boots who was about to embark on a farming career. I wasn't into the rural life then; he and I clearly weren't made for one another.

My father was awkward in the presence of real boyfriends and didn't want to listen to me talking about them. When I was 17, my parents and I went to Paris for a short holiday (this was the occasion of my solitary visits to the Louvre). We sat separately on the plane, because there was no spare set of three seats together. Next to me a dark and delicately charming young man engaged me in conversation. He was an Armenian dress designer called Sébou, some years older than me. By the time we landed, he had invited me out. I had to confess to him that my parents were tucked away at the back of the plane. On the way to the hotel I told them about Sébou. My father was silent and non-committal; my mother said Sébou had to come and be introduced to them, and that I must be back at the hotel by 10.30 pm at the latest. I didn't go out with Sébou the first night, because we met John Vaizey, who was working in Paris, for dinner (I wonder now if he was composing one of his novels), but the second night, which was the celebratory French July 14th, Sébou took me to the funfair at Les Invalides, where we boarded very dangerous flying machines and had a memorable view of illuminated Paris sprinkled under the bright navy sky.

The paternal silence about my engagements with the opposite sex was maintained, but my mother campaigned violently against my second real boyfriend, a working-class Irish Catholic who worked in a pub and wrote poetry. I met him at the polytechnic where I did my A-levels, and where I enjoyed a much wider social circle than I would have done had I remained locked up at Haberdashers' Aske's. My mother's antagonism helped to prolong the relationship beyond its natural end. She also played a curious role as a kind of intermediary for my father in such matters. She would tell me that he thought so-and-so about my behaviour, or wanted me to do or not do something: he was apparently unable to tell me himself. When I got married at the age of 20 rather suddenly – the suddenness being caused partly by my decision finally to emancipate myself from my parents – she told me that my father had asked her to ask me to wear a dress with a waist for the wedding, so that his colleagues wouldn't think I had 'had' to get married. Why did other people's opinions matter to him more than I did? Of course now it all seems horribly symbolic – of my awkward place in the carefully constructed life of the high priest of the welfare state, of the ambivalences and ambiguities attached to women in a world they neither made nor own.

What I now understand as the colonisation of my adolescence by Daddy's men didn't strike me as unusual when it happened. Nor did it occur to me in this form in the earlier accounts I transcribed of my years in the Blue Plaque House. Memory isn't a fixed thing: it changes over time, with the alteration of contexts and interests. The intellectual labelling is imposed on it: true 'afterthought'.

In between the Catholic boyfriend and the marriage in a straight-waisted dress, my father sent me to see another of his men, a famous child analyst. Donald Winnicott was only loosely a Titmuss affiliate. He was married to a social worker in the Titmuss Department at LSE, a gentle-voiced woman called Clare Britton who had been embroiled in a Machiavellian story about the fate of women social workers, a story told in a later chapter of this book.

Living one's life as a good middle-class daughter is troublesome in different ways from the experience of poverty and deprivation. I did find it troublesome. I felt both confined as my parents' child and an abiding sense of exclusion – from their lives, and from the world beyond. I saw Donald Winnicott professionally only once in his elegant white-painted house in Chester Square, in a thickly carpeted room discretely equipped with children's toys. Donald wrote my parents a letter afterwards, and at the end he said he was happy for me to see it. I found it only 25 years later, when they were both dead. The letter rambles on for several pages in florid blue-ink writing, as though Donald can't quite come to terms with what he needs to say, which is that it's difficult being the daughter of a Blue

Plaque Man, and that I should enter an analysis with a colleague of his, for which my father will unfortunately have to pay.

Who was Donald Winnicott? A gentle man, like his wife, with a high-pitched feminine voice, and a head that seemed too large for his body so he resembled a garden gnome. His extraordinary sensitivity to the needs of very young children and the inner worlds of their mothers earned him a permanent place in the iconography of child psychiatry. Like the Titmusses, the Winnicotts were a perfect couple, and at the time it was this that was impressed on me. But it took only a little digging around in the British Library to find a less perfect history. Before Clare, Donald Winnicott had been married for 25 years to an artistic first wife called Alice who was said by him to have mental health problems. These were probably not alleviated by his habit of taking home various disturbed children for her to look after.[16] He didn't have children with either wife, and is thought by his biographers to have been totally impotent.[17] Alice was eventually divorced and consigned to a farm in Wales, where Donald's nephew, a professor of botany, was paid by Donald to take care of her.[18] Donald himself was analysed for ten years, six days a week, by James Strachey, brother of the slightly more famous Lytton, and he applied to the famous Melanie Klein for a second analysis. Klein said no, as she wanted Donald to analyse her son Erich.[19] Alice herself was sent for analysis to the Canadian psychoanalyst Clifford Scott for whom, at the time, Clare Britton worked as a personal assistant. Clare herself was psychoanalysed by the same man whom Donald suggested, after our one brief meeting, my father should pay for me to see.

The social world of psychoanalysis is as mysterious as that of eugenics to ordinary mortals who believe in (social) science. I knew all these people from my days as a child and a young woman before the world outside the Blue Plaque House opened itself up to me. Now, as an old(er) woman, I read extra meanings into my knowledge of them. It's the shadowy spaces behind and between the official texts that hold my interest, the rich pickings of an insatiable curiosity about the way private and public interact in making people, and particularly women, who they are.

8

Meeting Win

In Remembrance of
SARAH ANN TITMUSS,
OF STEVENAGE,
WHO DIED THE 12th OF OCTOBER, 1863,
AGED 73 YEARS.
"The memory of the just is blessed."

We enter through a dark garage. The side door to the house is open, framing the solid and unexpectedly bronzed figure of her carer, who tells us Win has just had a fall and is very shaken: we may come in, but only to say hallo. The house is cool after the heat outside – the kind of heat wave the British, who can't avoid being obsessed with the weather, are going on and on about. Our feet sink into comfortable cream carpets in a well-ordered sitting room with French windows opening onto a tidy garden. Win lives, in her 98th year, on a modern crescent in a Domesday book village called Wheathampstead. The village is near the town of St Albans in Hertfordshire; Win has always lived here, at first with her parents and grandparents, then with her husband and her son. Wheathampstead is deep in Titmuss country. There are Titmusses everywhere – Titmuss fields, Titmuss farmers, Titmuss millers, Titmuss poultry dealers, Titmuss pet food suppliers, Titmuss catering businesses. I am introduced as 'Ann Titmuss': I have come home.

Win, short for Winifred, is my third cousin. Well, she's one of them: there are many more, all of whom, like her until now, I haven't ever met. Win and I have the same great-great-grandparents: Samuel Titmuss, born in 1776, who married Sarah Ann Aldham, or Oldham, born in 1791. Samuel and Sarah Ann had 11 children, beginning with James, the eldest, Win's great-grandfather, and ending with Herbert, the youngest, who was mine. This was a 'long' family: 20 years between the first and last child.[1] I tracked Win down through the wife of another unmet third cousin, the amateur historian and constructor of family trees, Ellie Titmuss. It's Ellie who takes me to meet Win.

Win is turned towards us in her wheelchair as we come into the room. She dominates the wheelchair, not it her; she hasn't sunk into it, given into its denotation of dependence. She's smartly dressed in a black-and-cream frock. Her legs are bare because of the heat and her psoriasis, which she points out to us, although it isn't too bad today. I remember recoiling from this kind of old lady's skin, thin like tissue paper and spangled with purple-blue sores and erosions, when I saw my mother's, but that was a long time ago. Now my own skin is edging in that direction it doesn't feel quite so alien any more. Win is still in command of her life: 'I'm lucky to be in my own home,' she says, despite waving a dismissive hand at the tidy garden outside the sparkling French windows, which isn't the size we Titmusses are used to. She has her back to the garden: it's paradise lost to her, although for anybody else the green and golden landscape of rolling hills and summer fields beyond the garden would be paradise gained.

Win starts talking about her/our family. The concerned carer hovers, then exits. Win's face lights up as she takes herself and us back through the years and across the fields, remembering stories, of Titmusses who died suddenly while out shooting, Walter in the pub that's now called the Rusty Gun, Titmusses who took over mills as reluctant teenagers – that was her father, James. She talks a lot about this James Titmuss, who once invited George Bernard Shaw to attend a village meeting, and so Shaw came from his own Hertfordshire village not far away, swinging his hurricane lamp. The stories are well organised, which is a feature of ageing: the clothes-horse of identity becomes very tidily draped and very stable as we age, so there's absolutely no chance of it falling over. The stories are almost word-for-word the same when repeated, which the primary ones are. When I ask Win questions, she doesn't know the answers; my questions are an unwelcome interruption in the flow of time remembered. I am a Titmuss interloper, a person she can't quite place, despite our explanation that I am the granddaughter of that couple whose splendid wedding photo hangs in Ellie's dining-room. Telling her this is no substitute for a lifetime of familiar association, which is what Win and I don't have. Our DNA connects us, but I am a stranger. 'How can "blood relations" not be related?'[2] Memory doesn't work with DNA, only with the social and emotional fabric of lives as they are actually lived.

I puzzle about this a lot these days. 'Relatives are always a surprise' is the subtitle of a book about kinship by the social anthropologist Marilyn Strathern. Kinship appears when one can imagine, or at least form an abstract idea of, people who are relations. In modern Euro-American culture there are two ways of getting at 'relational knowledge': 'uncovering what is in nature and making new knowledge through culture'.[3] Kinship is 'an amalgam of genetic position and cultural construct'[4]: in a knowledge-based society it has a technical lexicon which impresses us, but what does it mean? Win in her wheelchair talking about the mill in Wheathampstead when she was a girl in the 1920s, and me with my questions about whatever it was that divided Morris and Maud Titmuss, my father's parents, from the rest of their kin – there *was* something, I'm sure of it, but nobody will tell me. What Win and I have in common is only this hot day, this meeting, which she will probably forget and I will remember, the only thing we really share is our interest in the history of the many Titmuss lives played out in the hollows and rises of this arcadian landscape. Whatever lurks in our cells may be material but it's immaterial to us.

And yet as I watch her remembering – the moving contours of her face, her dark animated eyes, the angle of her nose, the slightly swarthy skin – I imagine I can see my father there. This is the yearning for simple stories that the cultural icon of genetics plays into. I know about the power of the imagination, so I make myself look again: yes, it *is* real. Win does look like her Uncle Richard. She doesn't remember ever meeting him, or his parents, although they lived only nine miles away. In the 71-page booklet Win put together 12 years ago – 'The Life and Times of the Titmuss Families from the Thirteenth to the Twentieth Century in Northamptonshire, Bedfordshire, Hertfordshire', Richard Titmuss doesn't appear at all. Win's big concern in this history was the difficulty of arbitrating between four William Titmusses (Tytmuss, Titmouse, Titmus) who were all born within a few years of one another in the 1660s and 1670s in the same small area of Hertfordshire, and any of whom might have been our direct ancestor. My own searches have got stuck at exactly the same point, on the enigma of the four Williams. I promise Win that one day I will crack the problem. We may live in a knowledge-based society now, but it wasn't one then, and solving the mystery is likely to involve multiple and time-consuming sleuthing through parish records.

Ellie and I are there for an hour perhaps, conscious of the hovering carer, and not wanting to outstay our welcome, although on the way out the carer remarks that our visit was appreciated because it has taken Win's mind off her fall. Ellie gives her a pink orchid. I hold her surprisingly solid hand in mine and tell her how good it is to meet her. The cool canopy of the room hangs over us, white and cream, china ornaments, small polished tables, a gigantic Panasonic in the corner imposing the knowledge-based society and much else besides that isn't the world Win remembers from her girlhood in the mill in Wheathampstead.

On the way back to Ellie's house, we stop at G.J.W. Titmuss's, Win's brother's Pet Supplies, Food, Products and Accessories business, a highly modern cavern of animal foods, clothes, objects and general trinkets, to buy some sacks of chicken feed. I wander around, only half-seeing the doggy beds and the rabbit cages, the coloured bridles and the bags of organic cattle and goat pencils (pencils?): I am involuntarily hung up on the 'haunting powers'[5] of what we call 'blood relationships', much as, I suddenly realise, my father must have been, not in relation to his own relations, but when he analysed and understood the gift of blood in that final book of his: blood, he wrote, unites us all, it proves 'that the family of man is a reality'.[6]

9

Harem in Houghton Street

In 1950 the first hydrogen bomb was developed and the first credit card was issued; in Britain, the wartime rationing of soap and petrol came to an end, and the Labour Party, under Clement Attlee, secured a second term of government after its post-war triumph, but with only a tiny majority. In 1950 Richard Titmuss, a man whose only formal educational qualification was in commercial book-keeping, took over the headship of a university department that had once housed the newly victorious Prime Minister. Richard Titmuss became Professor of Social Administration at the London School of Economics and Political Science, in charge of a department devoted mainly to social work training and staffed mainly by women. Over the course of the next decade or so, he transformed it into a centre of social policy expertise populated mainly by men – 'the leading centre of its kind in the world'.[1] He achieved this despite knowing little about social work (aside from the untrained social work activities of his own wife), having no experience of management or administration and having never worked in a university before.

This is a story about social mobility and about personal effort, about networking and the opportunities that unfold when useful friends are made. It's a story about a decade that was bad for women and good for social policy. But it's a great deal more than that. The social world came later than the natural world to the attention of the probing human mind, perhaps because it's harder to feel we really know what we're part of. In this appreciation of the social – the way our relationships and communities and structures and rituals and traditions work – knowing and doing have had an especially intimate connection. The connection is reflected in the terminology – *social* science, *socio*logy, *social* work, *social* policy, *social* reform, *social* action.

Most of the people, both before and after Marx, who have wanted to understand society, have also wanted to change it. Sociology and social work are both children of the impulse to social reform. 'Social work' and 'social worker' were terms that only began to be used in the late 19th century in Britain. They described the practical activities of people, chiefly women, who had a sense of community and enough time and money to provide aid for those who weren't in such advantaged positions. There was no welfare state. The state provided welfare through its citizens.[2] Social policy, known when Richard Titmuss went to LSE as 'social administration', came later, with a more mixed pedigree. These terminological relationships are key to the story of Richard Titmuss's life and also to that of my own. The early social workers saw a seamless relationship between activities aimed at promoting public welfare on the one hand, and both evidence and theory, on the other. Reform wouldn't work unless it was based on facts, and facts needed to be embedded in analysis of how communities and social action function. Much of this pioneering work, both in Britain and the USA, was carried out in 'Settlements' – neighbourhood social welfare agencies based on the idea that 'settling' in an area was the best way both to help and to understand the poor – thus giving rise to the term 'Settlement Sociology'.

The most famous Settlement, Hull-House, in a rundown district on Chicago's West Side, was set up by 'Saint' Jane Addams and her friend

Ellen Starr in 1889. Addams was a saint of a peculiarly American kind: benevolent, self-sacrificing and committed to the welfare of the poor, yet also practical, and possessed of a sharp business sense. In fact her reputation as a saint concealed what she was actually supremely good at – organisation, administration, drawing together people with similar interests. What also singled Jane Addams out from other American saints was her sociology.[3] Hull-House was a centre for social research and a 'Working People's Social Science Club', as well as a community centre, a nursery, a school, an art gallery, a bath house, a coffee house, a supplier of cheap meals for working parents, a co-operative coal association for the neighbourhood, a boarding house for working girls and a general hive of community activity. Addams saw it as an experimental effort to find solutions for modern social and industrial problems; such settlements, she said, demanded from their residents 'a scientific patience in the accumulation of facts'.[4] For example, when she and her co-residents came across the problem of child labour among the many immigrant families who lived round Hull-House – a four-year-old pulling out basting threads hour after hour, a 13-year-old exhausted from heavy laundry work committing suicide – they proposed to the Illinois State Bureau of Labor that systematic data on children's work should be collected. An investigation was duly carried out by Hull-House residents, a report prepared, and legislation then introduced regulating the age and conditions of child labour. Other studies looked at garbage disposal, housing, the typhoid epidemic and sanitation, tuberculosis, cocaine, midwifery, truancy, fatigue among factory girls, and children's reading. But Hull-House's most famous research initiative, *Hull-House maps and papers*, published in 1894, developed the technique of 'mapping' demographic information onto the geography of urban populations. This marked the birth of Chicago sociology, the first major school of sociology in the USA, and a central plank in the whole professionalisation and institutionalisation of sociology in the 20th century.[5]

Women 'social workers' everywhere played a key role in the institutionalisation of social science. They believed in its science, its sociology. Every sociology had a strong cast towards social action: in the early years of the 20th century, women predominated in the

Schools of Sociology, Social Science and Social Study that sprung up everywhere, although male sociologists, especially in the USA, were good at sidelining the women into Schools of Civics and Philanthropy or even household administration/home economics departments.[6]

Reading about the pioneering activities of women such as Jane Addams in Chicago and Elizabeth Macadam in London, I suddenly remember a buried episode from my own past. In a gap between the end of A-levels and the beginning of university, it was suggested (by whom I don't remember) that I might spend some time as a volunteer at the Blackfriars Settlement in South London. This was originally the Women's University Settlement, founded by women at Cambridge, Oxford and London Universities in 1887. I remember little of the detail of *my* Settlement Sociology now, except for the strangeness of bus journeys in a part of London that felt to me like a foreign country, exposure to the terrible grey poverty of council flats, and revulsion at the invasions of people's privacy I was called upon to commit in the interests of discovering whether they might be entitled to some benefit or other. What I had forgotten is revealed by another brief scurry into the attic and my own archives: I had actually helped to set up a holiday play scheme for children in Greenwich. For 2s 6d a week, the children were invited to play in an old London County Council Open Air School, with (warmer) afternoon trips to museums or the cinema. I have no idea whether my efforts were worthwhile, but the result was that I knew I never wanted to be a social worker.

By the time Richard Titmuss entered the university world, social work and sociology had become securely gendered and much more hermetically sealed communities in Britain. LSE was the centre of it all – the first place to offer formal social work training, the first to collect together a critical mass of (male) sociological theorists and political scientists – Ernest Gellner, Morris Ginsberg, L. T. Hobhouse, T.H. Marshall, Karl Mannheim – whose occupation of the School complemented the *gravitas* of its many (and also male) economist heavyweights. The Department of Social Science and Administration to which Richard Titmuss was appointed had a curious history. Its establishment in 1912 represented a carefully negotiated 'marriage of mutual financial and administrative convenience'[7] between LSE and the Charity Organization Society (COS). Those incorrigible pioneers Sidney and Beatrice Webb oversaw the creation of the new Department, as they had that of LSE itself. A condition of the arrangement stipulated by the COS was that Edward Johns Urwick, the social philosopher who ran the COS's own School of Sociology, should head the new Department. There's a direct line of descent from Urwick's writings to Richard Titmuss's own social philosophy. Altruism, the spirit of community, was a central value for both men; both protested in print about the divorce of social work from social action, and both saw the importance of social reformers acting only on the basis of sound evidence. It's for this reason that historian José Harris calls Richard Titmuss 'Urwick's apostolic successor'.[8] Interestingly, this connection seems to have escaped other narrators of the Titmuss story, and it isn't acknowledged at all in Richard Titmuss's own writing.

The most curious aspect of the Department's origins isn't the 'grandfatherly wisdom' of the twinkly-eyed Urwick,[9] but its bizarre financing by an Indian millionaire who lived most of his life as a reclusive semi-invalid in Twickenham. Ratanji (known as Ratan) Tata came from a family that made its fortune out of the cotton mills, the iron and steel foundries, and the hydroelectricity and construction industries of India. The family pioneered industrial welfare there, and Ratan and his brother tried unsuccessfully to endow a social and economic research foundation in India. The story goes that the Webbs happened to be on their travels in India at the time, they met Ratan Tata, and they suggested he transfer the endowment to LSE.[10] For its first five years (1912–17) the Ratan Tata Foundation was only housed at, not owned by, LSE. It was called 'the Ratan Tata Department' and was run by a Trust under the direction of Urwick – hence its alternative patriarchal name, 'Urwick's harem'.[11] With the help of L.T. Hobhouse, Britain's first proper academic sociologist, Urwick recruited the socialist historian R.H. Tawney to join them in 1913. The man who was Prime Minister when Richard Titmuss arrived at LSE in 1950, Clement Attlee, came to LSE in 1912. In 1920, Attlee published a book called *The social worker*. It's a manual for social workers, 'a general introduction to the subject of social service', a thoughtful history of how the modern conception of social work developed out of older charitable endeavours, drawing on both

Urwick's moral philosophy and the history of 'Settlement Sociology'. (Attlee had worked at Toynbee Hall, the first British Settlement, in the East End of London before he went to LSE.) His chapter on 'varieties of social workers' is particularly engaging on the topic of how the interrelationships between social work, social reform and social investigation were seen at the time. The social worker's job, says Attlee, is to be a pioneer in 'discovering new social groupings and new methods of advance'. Each group of social workers, each Settlement, is therefore 'a laboratory of social science'.[12] Social investigation is a form of social work in which social workers have the opportunity to offer back to the community a store of systematic data and observation. The example quoted by Attlee is William Beveridge's study of unemployment, carried out when *he* was at Toynbee Hall, a project which led directly to the system of nationwide Labour Exchanges. I don't know whether Clement Attlee and Jane Addams knew one another, but their ideas about social work and sociology do have a lot in common.

A good deal of exciting social research was done in the Ratan Tata Department – into poverty, educational welfare, low-paid work, taxation and living standards – alongside the task of preparing women for social work. Little of this is known today. There is, for example, a precocious 1917 study by one 'V. de Vesselitsky' of the economic effects of war on East End families. *Expenditure and waste* carefully documents those systems of financial management practised in working-class households that were later discovered by sociologists.[13] 'Miss' de Vesselitsky, a shadowy figure so described by R.H. Tawney in an introduction to another of her forgotten studies, also wrote a pungent short play about poverty and the sometimes misdirected practices of charity workers.[14] What brought the cheerful liaison between social work training and social research in the Ratan Tata Department to an end was the collapse of the Tata fortunes in the recession of the 1920s. Urwick departed to Canada to give his sons a better life and develop social work education there. The interregnum after his departure wasn't especially memorable. From 1922 to 1944, C. Mostyn Lloyd took over, combining the post with his work on the weekly political magazine *The New Statesman*, but the running of the Department was effectively left to its Deputy Head, Edith

Eckhard, an energetic woman who wore red stockings twisted round her legs like a spiral staircase,[15] and who often sported a cap, a legacy from the days when the Department was housed in a hut with flaky cement ceilings.[16] Eckhard features in Ralf Dahrendorf's history of LSE as 'the heart and soul of the Social Science Department' for over three decades, and one of 'the great and long-remembered teachers of the School'.[17] 'What a help Edith was in Richard's first days at LSE,' reads a note in my mother's handwriting: 'The memory is with me of the little mousy woman with the ever bright eyes & smile & sympathetic voice.' Richard Titmuss's dependence on Edith Eckhard was limited by her illness: she died of liver cancer in 1952, only two years into his sojourn at LSE.

Richard Titmuss's journey to this repository of unlikely stories is really quite an ingenious one. Self-made man (well, not quite self-made), aided by encouraging wife, carves out on unpromising ground an institutional base for an international career as a welfare and policy expert. How did he manage this? It's surprising that none of those sociologically-minded men and women who have written about this stage of my father's career have ever asked this question. At least part of the answer involves what was unstudied then, and is far from a mainstream subject today, the business of gender politics, intermingled, as always, with the potent dynamics of class.

First of all, how did Richard Titmuss get to LSE? He had relinquished his occupation as an insurance inspector – the job he had taken up when his mother Maud arranged it for him in the financially tight aftermath of her husband's early death – and had become instead a government social historian. This move was made on the basis of his spare-time writings on demography and health, and his networking in the Eugenics Society. It isn't really possible to ascend the professorial ladder from Lane Farm, Stopsley, and St Gregory's School for farmers' sons without a little help. Richard Titmuss joined the Eugenics Society in 1937 and remained a member until a few days before his death in 1973. It was his active networking within the Eugenics Society that brought him new influential friends and entrées into both the publishing and academic worlds. In return, his innovative social demography helped to dig the British eugenics movement out of the nasty hole of its association with German national socialism. One of the members of the Eugenics Society was Eva Hubback, the social reformer and Principal of the adult education centre Morley College in South London. Hubback knew the quixotic Australian historian Keith Hancock, who had come up with the unusual scheme of writing the social history of the Second World War while it was still happening; Hubback recommended Titmuss to Hancock as the historian for one of the volumes.[18] (This business of who knows whom is absolutely pivotal in stories of social mobility (and in maintaining patriarchy).) Hancock, who was fascinated by Titmuss's status as 'the academic equivalent of an *enfant sauvage*', would later say that the one thing that had to be mentioned in his own obituary was that he had been responsible for discovering Richard Titmuss.[19] The volume of war history Richard Titmuss produced as a government social historian established his academic credentials in that expanding institutional space – the study of social policy. His *Problems of social policy* was greeted especially rapturously by Tawney, and later by sociologist T.H. Marshall as 'a flawless masterpiece'.[20] It did have flaws, of course, as everything does, but the only people who at the time noticed any of these were the civil servants who tried to stop its publication on the grounds that the story it told was unflattering to the government.

In 1950 Richard Titmuss was 43 years old, with a wife and six-year-old daughter to support. His Cabinet Office salary had come to an end. His post in a Medical Research Council-funded research unit – to which he had migrated when the war history post finished – was insecure. He needed a financially stable, sustainable career. The Director of LSE, Alexander Carr-Saunders (whose daughter Flora never gave me the fairy off the top of the Christmas tree) was another usefully prominent member of the Eugenics Society. Titmuss and Carr-Saunders had been in contact about Eugenics Society matters for at least a decade, with meetings at the latter's gentleman's club in London, The Athenaeum. It also helped that Richard Titmuss's old boss, Hancock, and his new one, Carr-Saunders, were close friends. The sociologist T.H. Marshall, who had taken over, and was struggling with, the burden of running the Department of Social Administration, proposed the creation of a new job which would free him to concentrate on sociology proper.[21] Marshall thought

Richard Titmuss was the man for the job. But he probably didn't quite anticipate the degree to which the new man would lead social administration so decisively away from sociology.[22]

LSE *was* an obvious destination for Richard Titmuss, with its socialist origins and its empiricist social science. The Chair in Social Administration was actually his second attempt to gain entry to this unique place – his first, in 1945, had been an unsuccessful application for a Readership in demography. The successful candidate, sociologist David Glass, would later be one of Richard Titmuss's professorial colleagues, although the two men never got on well. LSE's history gave the Department of Social Science and Administration roots in both the tradition of women's voluntary social work, and in the endeavour to construct a science of social relations. A tiny memento of the former lingers in the remnants of the brown suitcase of family papers my mother left me. Clipped to an obituary of a woman called Charlotte Marsh is a note in my mother's handwriting explaining how the two women met when Marsh worked for the National Assistance Board in Fulham, and my mother had dealings with that office through her work running clubs for unemployed men:

> I have memories of lunching with her in a friendly little restaurant where we pored over the regulations under which she laboured searching for loopholes which would enable authorisation of special help with perhaps bedding, cooking utensils, shoes for children etc. From this friendly & understanding cooperation with her began my interest in what became 'Code A' & the value of 'discretionary payments': long before I met Richard or the Supplementary Benefits Commission had been envisaged.

Charlotte Marsh led a much more high-profile life than Kay Titmuss, a life that included three periods of imprisonment for suffragette activities, being force-fed 139 times, and acting as Lloyd George's personal chauffeur during the First World War (apparently he told her it would help the cause of women's enfranchisement).[23]

And so Richard Titmuss arrived in Houghton Street. The functional grey building in which he was housed in a 'pokey and inelegant office'[24] didn't look much like a university at all. 'The man and the building seemed made for each other.'[25] His office was located high up via a serpentine maze of stairs. Although not large, it did sport two windows, a sizeable desk, many bookshelves, and the status symbol of a secretary whose annex next door needed to be braved by anyone who wished to see The Professor. I remember my father's office as thick with cigarette smoke and political negotiations. A main substance of these in his early years at LSE concerned the domestic relationship between social work and social policy. His new, mainly female, Department was seen as marginal to LSE's main interests. Its staff had historically been paid on a different, lower, scale from their colleagues because they were considered non-academic practitioners. Richard Titmuss enjoyed repeating to others the enquiry he once had from an academic colleague about how his 'good-looking midwives' were getting on (women's caring roles always being conflated in the minds of the patriarchs), and the common assumption that his students' main function was to provide girlfriends for the School's more important male students.[26] The union between social work and social administration was itself definitely 'a marriage of convenience rather than love at first sight'.[27]

Their names peopled the accounts my father brought home to me and my mother in the Blue Plaque House: Clare Britton, Christine Cockburn, Pearl Jephcott, Janet Kydd, Kay McDougall, Pleasance Partridge, Kit Russell, Nancy Seear, Kitty Slack, Eileen Younghusband. That extraordinary name 'Pleasance Partridge', together with those of 'Younghusband' and 'Kydd', evoked for me a totally misplaced rural imagery for the stable of LSE women. There they are in the official photograph, arranged on the roof of LSE, the women smiling, their male head looking perhaps a little overwhelmed. I was fascinated by the upper-classness of the golden-haired Kit Russell who was Kit Stewart until, at the age of 48 in 1957, she married Britain's first male almoner, Sheridan Russell. Sheridan's other main accomplishment was music-making: he had been a virtuoso cellist until a hearing defect diagnosed by Debussy persuaded him to give up music as a career.[28] I tagged along with my parents to exclusive soirées in the Russells' home on the Chelsea embankment. Janet Kydd was Scottish, known for her 'good tweed suits and knitted stockings',[29] so it was hard for me to tell whether or not she was upper class. Clare Britton, 'a pretty, feminine, stylish woman',[30] and an authority on the care of separated and troubled children, married the child analyst Donald Winnicott in 1951 when she was 45. Kay McDougall, a psychiatric social worker, and Christine Cockburn, an expert on superannuation systems, also departed from the prevalent social worker norm in having husbands. After the arrival of Richard Titmuss to head their Department, all these women with their various liaisons and specialisms were involved in a series of most dreadful ructions about the future of social work education. This was 'the LSE Affair', 'part of the folklore of social work',[31] a testing ordeal, described in the next chapter, that brought tears to the participants' eyes even decades later.

Apart from my father's end-of-the-day stories, and the imagery of their names, my memory of these women is of them smiling benignly at me, rather in the manner of childless great-aunts (they *were* all childless, except for Christine Cockburn, who had a son) whose attitude of kindliness towards the young is founded on absolutely no practical experience of them. I see them always on their own, whether or not each was half of a couple, because it was their autonomy which impressed me. They came to the house, to my mother's economical dinner parties, although not as often as the autonomous men, who brought their wives. One of the LSE women, Janet Kydd, took upon herself a particular role in helping with my annual birthday celebrations. These were big events for me, since I was allowed to invite some 20 or so girls from Haberdashers' Aske's, thus earning myself much-needed kudos. My mother's speciality was a kind of bun called coffee kisses. Each was made of two light coffee-flavoured biscuits clamped together with a squodge of coffee butter icing. Delicious: I can taste them still. Janet Kydd brought her own cake offerings, and also the woman she lived with in Canonbury, North London, a woman called Pat Smith. With a name like that I haven't been able to trace her; I think she was a teacher, or perhaps even a social worker. I even had trouble finding Janet Kydd, until I discovered that she was adopted and was originally called 'Jessie Agnes'.

Then there was Pearl, an absolute pearl among all the LSE women for her trailblazing social research into the lives of girls and women. Pearl Jephcott entered my childhood version of Urwick's harem in 1954, when she was recruited to the Social Administration Department as a research assistant to work on a study of married women's employment in Bermondsey. That's how the official history puts it: but now I wonder whose idea the study really was. When she went to LSE, Pearl was 54 with a solid career as an organiser in the Girls' Clubs Movement and three books about the lives of girls and young women behind her. The books used participant observation, interviews and autobiographical narratives to build a picture of women's lives, and included practical recommendations for improvements: Pearl Jephcott was exactly that combination of social investigator, social reformer and social worker Attlee and Addams advocated. She was, as I remember, a large-boned woman, rather clumsy and surprisingly shy, with rosy cheeks and a face that shone, like her eyes, with a kindliness towards others and a great passion for her work. Why, I wonder, do I remember all these women as smiling and holding out their hands to greet me? Were they aware, either directly or intuitively, of my awkward position as the Professor's daughter; or am I perhaps contaminating those early memories with a later interest in the doings of women social scientists and reformers?

Pearl Jephcott's passion was for exposing the accounts of girls and women caught in a cultural moment of heightened ambivalence: women in a man's world being allowed new freedoms in it, at the same time as being censored for trying these out. *Married women working*, the title of the book she wrote about the experiences of women employed in a South London biscuit factory, is ideologically very much a child of its time. Peek Frean's, the biscuit factory in question, had practised the habit of refusing to hire married women at all, disposing of any who did get married. But this was a new demography – of women having fewer children, of more jobs than workers – and so change was happening. Was the country ready for the mass migration of women back out of the home, and all the attendant problems of 'latchkey' children, delinquency and disgruntled husbands? 'At last some FACTS about Those Working Mothers' proclaimed the *Daily Herald*[32] in its review of the book. The *Daily Mail* quoted childcare expert Dr Spock on the subject ('It doesn't make sense to let mothers go to work'), extrapolating from

Married women working the conclusion that women want the status, social contacts and independence of a job as well as the money. The stigma of selfishness implied in this was dissolved by the purposes to which the money was put: holidays, treats for the children, consumer goods for the home.[33] Having gone to considerable lengths to check out the dominant suspicion that working mothers bred delinquent and/or otherwise unhealthy children, Jephcott and her team were impressed by the 'unexpectedly satisfactory nature' of their findings.[34] My father wrote a short uncontentious Foreword to *Married women working*, making no reference to what was elsewhere described as its 'troubled passage':[35] he had apparently been rather 'an elusive supervisor',[36] and had tried to persuade Jephcott to change the book's title to *Wage earning wives*, which she protested made it sound like a tract in favour of housekeeping allowances.[37]

Pearl Jephcott was regularly invited to the Titmusses' house, and my mother and I were taken by my father to hers, a Dickensian wood-panelled affair in an old warehouse in Bermondsey, in Rotherhithe Street, hanging over the muddy Thames. Jephcott went to live in Bermondsey because of the Peek Frean study, and she also worked for three months as a cleaner in a Bermondsey hospital and tried out all the various shifts at Peek Frean's itself. I remember a smell of fish and dank water in that Bermondsey warehouse, a sharp contrast with Pearl's exuberant and homely joviality. I always felt like a contrast myself in these social encounters with my father's LSE women: a child among adults, an appendage, even an orphan, but, most of all, an observer of performances and interactions. His embroilment in their professional lives, as it reached me in laboriously recited end-of-the-day stories, never quite rang true: well, it was truly *his* narrative, but it caused me to wonder what alternative narratives there might be. It was my first lesson in the pitfalls of qualitative data.

Whether or not she was consciously influenced by the Settlement idea, Pearl Jephcott believed that social researchers should always live in the area and with the people they were studying, and so she practised what she believed. She was only the 'research assistant' for *Married women working*; the man described on the title page as directing the study didn't move from The Blue Plaque House in order to familiarise himself with the area and its problems. She left

LSE reluctantly.[38] The Director, Alexander Carr-Saunders, wanted to give her a permanent post, but it seems that Richard Titmuss wasn't enthusiastic.[39] Actually, Pearl Jephcott's career illustrates another critical feature of academic social science: its dependence on the labours of contract research workers who don't really – compared to teaching staff – have 'careers' at all. They lurch from one short-term contract to another, outside the main frame of reference of university life; their social investigations, despite adding enormously to knowledge, all happen at the margins, where they can safely be either forgotten or claimed by those in positions of greater security and power.

Like many such researchers, Pearl Jephcott wasn't deterred. She moved to the University of Glasgow, where she researched and wrote more about the lives of young people, and then began another pioneering investigation into the horrors of family life in high-rise council flats. She lived in one of these herself while doing the research. Her *Homes in high flats* moved beyond simple notions of satisfaction/dissatisfaction to give a real picture based on residents' own experiences of this architectural and policy insanity. What she generated in her study was a new form of housing social science, combining traditional methods of representative sample selection (5% of the Glaswegian high-rise population, 1,056 interviews) with international data and imaginative ethnographic studies. Using a camera and a researcher perched on a ladder, for example, Jephcott demonstrated how the splendid views afforded by the windows of the upper flats were simply not available to residents when they were sitting in front of these windows. Her 'place-saturated science' offered a meticulous and sensitive portrait of high-rise living which housing policy couldn't subsequently afford to ignore.[40] Carr-Saunders and Titmuss clearly had very little idea of Pearl Jephcott's importance when they decided not to hold on to her at LSE. She, like some of the other women in this story, was a missed opportunity for the male academic establishment, but, then, missing such opportunities is part-and-parcel of how it constitutes itself.

Imagining myself a child again (with all the interpolations of other inbetween efforts to remember), I am sitting at the dark wood table in what was called The Breakfast Room (why? We ate all our meals in it) in the Blue Plaque House. The table is laid for supper. I can smell lamb chops and anticipate the insidiously fatty curve they will settle into on the pale brown plates. The yellow front door opens and shuts. I can hear my father taking a hanger from the wooden cupboard in the hallway to put his overcoat on. It's winter, my mother has turned on the storage heaters to take the chill off the house. It's the winter of 1956 perhaps, or 1957, when the ructions of the LSE Affair reached their peak. I know, with a childishly sinking heart, that my mother and I are about to hear yet another laboured story about his encounters with the women in the Department of Social Administration, whose difficult behaviour he didn't know he was going to have to confront when he first walked into Houghton Street as a Professor.

10

Difficult women

The first and most crucial point is that the Department Richard Titmuss took over in 1950 really belonged to Eileen Younghusband. By far the most prominent of the LSE social work staff, she already had a very considerable reputation outside LSE. She was the daughter of a well-known explorer and colonial services officer, Sir Francis Younghusband, who had won Tibet for the British Empire, and his aristocratic wife, Helen Magniac, and was said to look like a cross between Virginia Woolf and Captain Hook.[1] Her colourfully elitist family once had a parlour maid called Gladys Aylward, who left their employ in 1932 to go on a mission to China, thus unintentionally giving rise to the film 'The Inn of the Sixth Happiness', starring Ingrid Bergman. Aylward led an extraordinary life in North China for more than 20 years, becoming a Chinese citizen and leading campaigns against female foot-binding and trafficking.[2] Eileen herself had suffered from the usual disadvantages attendant on being an upper-class daughter at the time. A debutante who had been 'presented' at Buckingham Palace with ostrich feathers in her hair, she had no formal school education, only the expectation of a life devoted to home and family. Like other women in her situation, Eileen had to labour hard to overcome these obstacles. Immersing herself in voluntary work in London Settlements, she then became a student at LSE, taking the Certificate Course in Social Studies, followed by the Diploma in Sociology. In 1929 she discussed with Beatrice Webb what to do with her life; Beatrice was of the opinion that she should become a 'woman relieving officer' and help to change the old poor law from the inside.[3] Instead of taking her advice, Eileen joined the LSE staff as a tutor in social studies, where she occupied Clement Attlee's old room, occasionally taking advantage of the House of Commons stationery he'd left behind.[4] In 1947, she carried out an important survey of social work training for the Carnegie UK Trust. This stressed the need for expansion, greater consistency, and improvements in standards of training. Her report recommended the provision to would-be social workers of generic courses which would precede any professional specialisation by equipping them with a basic set of skills. It went on to suggest a major experiment in social work education, a School of Social Work attached to a university, which would house training courses, but also do research and link social work theory effectively with its practice.

In 1955, after Richard Titmuss had assumed the headship of the LSE Department, Eileen Younghusband built on her already substantial reputation in chairing a Ministry of Health Working Party on the role of social workers in the local authority health and welfare services. What came to be known as 'the Younghusband Report' changed the face of social work education in Britain. Above all, Eileen Younghusband was anxious to enhance the status of social work, to ensure its future as a profession and to increase its intellectual input.

Her work went a long way to achieving these aims. Her influence on the national perception of social work is regarded as 'second to none'.[5] Frederick Seebohm, who chaired the Committee on Local Authority and Allied Personal Social Services in 1968 which established the modern pattern of social service organisation in Britain, once told her that this reorganisation would never have been possible without her labours.[6] These were serially recognised in the British honours system, with the award of an MBE in 1946, a CBE in 1955 and a DBE in 1964. Richard Titmuss wrote to congratulate her on the CBE; he had to wait another 11 years for his.

Eileen Younghusband's reports on the state of social work evidenced a close relationship between her and the Carnegie UK Trust, a large charitable foundation set up by the Scottish industrialist Andrew Carnegie in 1913. This relationship would prove to be an especially sharp thorn in Richard Titmuss's side as he came to grips with his new Department. There was a particularly strong alliance between Eileen Younghusband and one of the Carnegie Trustees, (Baroness) Kay Elliott: the two women had met some years before through their joint work for the National Association of Girls' Clubs. With Kay Elliott's support, the Carnegie link eventually gave birth to the famous 'Carnegie Experiment' – a new course in generic social work training, along the lines Eileen Younghusband had suggested in her original 1947 report. Following some years of delicate negotiation, this new generic course was finally established in the Department of Social Administration at LSE in 1954. It was the material realisation of Eileen Younghusband's vision, and it did eventually transform social work training in the UK. Unfortunately, it was also the fuse for a prolonged argument about the running of social work courses, the place of social work in social policy, the status of social work and its practitioners, and the locus of power and authority in Richard Titmuss's Department.

In 1950, when he arrived, the Department housed three separate professional courses, in Personnel Management, in Child Care and in Mental Health. These had arisen organically in response to the development of the personal social services – the demand for social workers to fill particular institutional roles. The women staff in the Department had been running these courses happily alongside one another for years. Staff meetings were informal and the ethos was collaborative. As Eileen Younghusband remembered, Edith Eckhard as the *de facto* head of department didn't ostensibly manage them at all: 'She kept us together as a team ... we all liked each other very much. We never got in each other's hair.'[7] It was probably not clear to them what their new male head would be doing, especially since he knew so little about social work training. Titmuss's predecessor as department head, the sociologist, T.H. Marshall, was fond of describing the Department's mission as 'pouring oil on troubled daughters' – a reference to social work's function of soothing the social consciences of young upper-middle-class women.[8] Marshall had pretty much left the staff of the Department of Social Administration alone, having no interest or expertise himself in the field of social work training.

Marshall's Chair was actually in the Department of Sociology and the two Departments of Sociology and Social Administration were run as one. Marshall encouraged Titmuss to apply for the new, separate Chair in Social Administration, inciting him with the promise that the job would allow plenty of time for research, since the Department virtually ran itself.[9] This was more than a little disingenuous of Marshall, since he couldn't get on with his own work because of too much administration.[10] The notes Richard Titmuss made before his interview for the Chair show that he was already aware of this problem: 'How much administration? How much lecturing?' he reminds himself to ask. 'Why was the Chair created and what for? What are the responsibilities?' Tucked in the file is a note he made after talking to Edith Eckhard, who alerted him to a 'staff status problem' – the lack of publications and of research that were normal expectations of any university department.[11] By the late 1940s, the research base established by Urwick, Hobhouse and Tawney in the Ratan Tata Department had lapsed, and the Department was held together mainly by a shared moral commitment to enhancing personal and collective welfare through the expansion of statutory social services. Richard Titmuss must surely have been persuasive in his interview about his intention and ability to revert the Department to some new version of its former glory. Interestingly, the version of the *curriculum vitae* attached to his job application describes his occupation as 'Social Economist'.[12]

Some of the story, the story I didn't realise as a child in the troubled atmosphere of the Blue Plaque House's Breakfast Room, can be worked out from my father's archives. The struggle for ascendancy between Younghusband and Titmuss began early. When he first arrived in Houghton Street, Richard Titmuss asked Eileen Younghusband to let him have a note about the nature of her work at LSE. Her letter, which has undertones of irritation, begins with a historical digression. In 1944 she had taken over the organisation of students' practical work and 'public relations' – committee work and external contacts – from Edith Eckhard. Younghusband notes, not really in parenthesis, that this is far too much for one person to do. She also represents LSE on a lot of important committees, sits as a magistrate in the juvenile courts and does some teaching.[13] Eileen Younghusband's restlessness is evident from other letters. She is offered a United Nations job in Geneva (as Chief of the Social Welfare Section), which she decides to turn down, in favour of concentrating her energies on developing social work education at LSE (but Richard Titmuss isn't very willing to let her go anyway); she is invited to New Zealand, and this time he is decisively against the invitation because he needs to lean on her in the work to be done at LSE. Her letters are formal at first – 'Dear Professor Titmuss' – and then they warm – 'Dear Richard'. He keeps careful notes of their conversations on the back of some old Medical Research Council gastric ulcer study forms. He writes to assure her that her work is valued by the Department, that he is proud to have her on his staff; he asks if she realises how much other universities envy him for this.[14]

It's a cold day in February when I climb the small hill to the Modern Records Centre at the University of Warwick where Eileen Younghusband's papers have ended up. The archivist inside the glass doors of the Centre isn't keen on eye contact; he gives me forms to sign and directs me to a locker, wherein I must deposit all my personal belongings. The papers, which he hands me in small piles, are organised in neat brown card folders. I start with the little leather-bound diaries, cousins of the ones Richard Titmuss and his wife kept, and it takes me all of five minutes to find the first mention of Richard Titmuss: on 19 December 1950, three months after he started at LSE, Eileen is invited, not to the Blue Plaque House, because we aren't in it yet, but to the flat in Chiswick: 'Turnham Green–Chiswick Empire,' Eileen notes as helpful landmarks. Almost a year later, on 7 November 1951, her invitation is to the Blue Plaque House. After that, and despite at least another seven years' cohabitation as colleagues, there's no sign of her being invited there again.[15]

It's from these papers that I learn how Richard Titmuss spotted the opportunities that might follow if he annexed himself to Younghusband's plans. Before he began the LSE post, Eileen Younghusband was working on an update of her Carnegie Trust report on social work training, developing the ideas she put forward in 1947 for a university-based school of social work, 'a Carnegie School of Social Work'.[16] Titmuss went to see her in her house in West London, and asked if he could read the draft of the updated report. When he gave it back to her, he said, 'I think this is something we ought to do at LSE'.[17] At his request, she worked further on the details of the proposal, together with notes of the resources that would be needed to establish an institute for social work training, and the negotiations which would have to be done. Such an institute would have three main objectives: research into social welfare issues; short training courses for people in central and local government and voluntary organisations; and providing future teachers and leaders in social work with an 'all-purpose' social work training which would absorb all the present specialised courses.[18] This idea of 'generic' training was particularly important at a time of hugely increased demand for social workers. After he had formally taken up the LSE post, Titmuss presented the Carnegie idea to the Director of LSE. He was less than honest about its origin, telling Carr-Saunders that the Institute was his idea, that he had had a meeting with the Carnegie Trustees, and that he had been invited to put in a proposal. His letter made no mention of Eileen Younghusband. At the subsequent meetings with the Carnegie Trust, Eileen's role was to take the minutes.[19]

Getting external funding was important to Richard Titmuss's profile as the new Department Head, especially in the run-up to the next internal allocation of LSE resources which was due in 1956. Thus, associating himself with Eileen Younghusband's efforts to gain Carnegie funding, he put forward a proposal for a ten-year grant amounting to £75,000 (equivalent to about £1.83 million in 2013) to set up an Institute of Applied Social Studies. This was, in essence, the outline of the School of Social Work Eileen Younghusband's 1947 report had suggested. The Carnegie Trustees turned it down, but made it known that they would consider something more modest. In June 1952, Richard Titmuss and Eileen Younghusband travelled to Edinburgh to meet three Trustees and discuss a proposal for a demonstration course which the Trust would fund initially, but which would then be taken over by LSE. The following March a four-year course with funding of £20,000 (£472,816 in 2013), 'the Carnegie Experiment', was agreed – not the full-blown School of Social Work Eileen Younghusband wanted, but at least a beginning. The Director of LSE, Carr-Saunders, asked Richard Titmuss who should head the project. Eileen Younghusband's close friend Helen Roberts, another social worker, found it incredible that he should need to ask this question: the answer was obvious. The Carnegie Experiment was Eileen Younghusband's baby.[20]

In 1953 Eileen Younghusband went to the USA to study social work education in preparation for setting up the Carnegie Course in Applied Social Studies. This was another trip that Richard Titmuss wasn't happy about. He probably didn't realise that such Anglo-American connections were a well-established tradition in the social work community, especially among practitioners with a psychiatric bent. Many crossed the Atlantic courtesy of the Commonwealth Fund, a leading American charitable foundation, in order to learn about American social work ideas and practices. This is how the original Mental Health Course at LSE came about. In 1928, Edith Eckhard, of twisted red stockings fame, was invited to the USA by the Commonwealth Fund to see what was going on there; when she came back she persuaded William Beveridge, then Director of LSE, that a special course on mental hygiene, modelled on the American example, was needed.[21]

Twenty-five years later, it was in the USA that Eileen Younghusband met her own American counterpart, an established figure in social work education called Charlotte Towle. Towle had written a book about her views on social work, *Common human needs*, and Eileen had read it. The two women began a long-term friendship. Towle, a small vivacious woman 'with intensive eyes',[22] who taught Eileen Younghusband not only about American social work education, but how to enjoy American cocktails, taught at the University of Chicago, where she had pioneered a new client-centred casework curriculum.[23] She had also published widely on social work and the social services, and had acted as consultant to several government agencies. Towle believed that all social workers need an understanding of human behaviour, and that psychology shouldn't be taught only in mental health training courses. Effective social work depends on an appreciation of both the individual and the environment. The individual's needs – a home, job security, a sense of purpose, friends – are, she contested, much the same in all cultures. Her book *Common human needs* was originally a manual written in 1945 for the Bureau of Public Assistance of what was then the US Social Security Board. It was one of very few social work training textbooks available at the time, and it argued a position with which Richard Titmuss would surely have agreed: that society has an obligation to assist with the needs of individuals, that people hold rights to such assistance, and that effective assistance means empirical enquiry into needs and into people's own perception of these. Indeed, the concept of 'basic needs' elaborated in Richard Titmuss's inaugural lecture at LSE is very reminiscent of the cast of Towle's book.[24] The book achieved notoriety when, in 1951, the President of the American Medical Association noticed that Towle used the term 'socialized state' approvingly. The Government Printing Office was ordered to destroy all remaining copies on the grounds that the book was 'malevolently and viciously un-American'.[25] Charlotte Towle had already fallen foul of McCarthyist suspicion when she had helped to sponsor the Scientific and Cultural Conference for World Peace which was held in New York in 1949. Her name appears in a long list of others suspected of 'communism', a list that includes many leading social scientists and democratic organisations of the time, as well as some innocuously sounding obscure ones such as 'The League of Women Shoppers'.[26] Towle's application to the Fulbright Program for funding to spend a year advising the proposed LSE Course was blocked because of her suspected indulgence in un-American activities, and her passport withdrawn; Younghusband and Titmuss, who were both on the Fulbright Selection Committee, resigned in a campaign to get the decision reversed. It was.[27]

Richard Titmuss clearly appreciated Charlotte Towle's work at this stage. Younghusband had written to Titmuss about Charlotte Towle with great enthusiasm: 'She is like something out of a story of nineteenth century New England but with all the modern knowledge added to a first rate subtle, penetrating mind and a very rich, warm personality. I have no doubt that she would be right for us beyond our dreams. If we could get her help to what she calls "structure" the course … we could really get somewhere.'[28] During Eileen Younghusband's year in the USA, she and Charlotte Towle worked together on the plan for the Course, and Towle then acted as Course consultant in London for its first year. The Carnegie Course in Applied Social Studies was advertised as a 'One Year Course in Social Casework' and it got off to a flying start in the autumn of 1954. Students were to spend two days a week at LSE and three days a week in fieldwork, an integration of classroom teaching with field supervision that followed the American model, but was a new development for Britain. Despite Carr-Saunders' initial uncertainty, Younghusband was given a new contract at LSE to run the Course. She used the opportunity to inquire about the possibility of promotion to a Readership: she had, after all, been working at LSE for a long time (25 years), she had an international reputation as a social work expert, and had carried out and written those important Carnegie Trust survey reports. The Director, approached with this request and a c.v. not inferior to Richard Titmuss's own a few years earlier when he got his Chair, told Titmuss he thought the case 'rather thin'. Titmuss scribbled on the bottom of the Director's letter, 'Answered. Not now'.[29]

Charlotte Towle's presence at LSE exacerbated growing tensions. The Carnegie Course posed obvious threats to two of the other social work courses, in Child Care and Mental Health, since it took a different approach – that of a general rather than a specialist education. These issues did not affect the third course in Personnel Management, which was headed by another formidable woman, Nancy Seear, later Baroness Seear, a prominent Liberal politician and sponsor of sex discrimination legislation. Seear, who kept her

LSE post until her retirement in 1978, was judged by many to have experienced personally the glass ceiling effect on women's careers,[30] but at least she was saved the damage of being directly involved in the arguments about status and hierarchy that followed the introduction of the Carnegie Course. The Child Care Course was led by the gentle, conflict-avoiding Clare Britton, later Clare Winnicott, who quite early on in what became known as the LSE Affair contracted meningitis and withdrew from the battle. The Mental Health Course was run by Kay McDougall, a psychiatric social worker. McDougall stood out among the Department's staff both for her class background – her father was a brass finisher and her mother a dress-maker – and for her marriage at a conventional age to a printer six years younger than her (an age gap similar to that between Richard Titmuss and his wife). Both Britton and McDougall had high reputations outside LSE, as did the courses they headed.

The themes of the LSE Affair were a microcosm of wider debates raging at the time about the nature and role of social work, some of which endure today. Is social work an art or a science? Is it properly about a personal relationship between client and professional or about the provision of administrative expertise in the running of the social services (the kind of eye for detail Kay Titmuss and Charlotte Marsh fostered over their friendly lunches)? It's impossible to get very far trying to fathom the LSE Affair without confronting the mysterious term 'casework'. Casework was a process that took place within the individual professional relationships between social workers and their clients; it involved the social worker studying the client's background, circumstances and attitudes. The technique of casework gave social work an expert gloss, raising it above a purely administrative activity, and enabling 20th-century social workers to shed the 19th-century tradition of friendly visiting, with its connotations of patronising sentimentality and feminine intuition. It was thus an important plank in social workers' drive for professionalisation. The casework approach was born in the USA, and brought to British social work education largely via the Towle–Younghusband link. Sibyl Clement Brown, who taught on the Mental Health Course at LSE from 1932 to 1946, remembered visiting the New York School of Social Work in the 1920s and noting the 'extreme contrast' between social work training there and in Britain. In New York it seemed that postgraduate social work education focused entirely on 'what you could do wisely about individuals and families, whereas in England we'd had practically no teaching on this subject at all but did feel that we'd exercised our minds about broad social problems and the kind of vicissitudes into which social conditions led people and families'.[31]

Central to the curriculum of the Carnegie Experiment was the attempt to universalise the casework approach across social work settings. Richard Titmuss took issue with the dangers inherent in an individualised approach – that the aim would too easily be to adjust the client to reality rather than doing something about the defects of reality itself. But it was Titmuss's colleague at Bedford College, Barbara Wootton, who undertook the most damning review of the casework approach, most famously saying that it seemed the best way for the social worker to understand her client was to marry him.[32] Wootton's *Social science and social pathology*, published in 1959, took a critical look at the scientific understanding of what causes and prevents anti-social behaviour. The book was particularly negative about most research in this area, and about the perspectives of social workers. My copy was inherited from my father, who stuffed inside it a bundle of complaints about Mrs Wootton's text from the social workers in his Department. He himself wrote a judicious review, concluding that Wootton's attack on casework was wrongly based on the 'choicest fragments of the American casework literature'.[33] This is what the social workers in his Department told him, although when Wootton asked them for a reading list of the right literature there was nothing on it she hadn't already read.[34]

There were divided views in the LSE Department about the value of casework. The notion that people can be helped only by other people probing and pronouncing on their psychology drew its strength from Freud and the psychoanalysis movement, and was abhorrent to those, such as Richard Titmuss, who focussed on the material determinants of need. His own views of social work hardened as he began work at LSE. An academic colleague of his, Tom Simey, Professor of Social Science at Liverpool (a position inherited from Carr-Saunders), passed him a paper on the political assumptions behind casework theory – that the social worker's goal was to adjust the client to reality. Titmuss nodded approvingly. Social work, he considered, was increasingly inward-looking and ignorant of real social problems. The paper Simey and Titmuss read was written by the political theorist Alan Keith-Lucas, who argued powerfully that the casework approach was 'inimical to liberty' since it breached people's rights to their own understandings of their situation.[35] In the USA, the Keith-Lucas paper had already drawn Charlotte Towle's ire. She sent a strongly worded protest to the editor of the journal that had published it, objecting that 'Social workers in both public and private agencies have long shared the author's concern that there not be an infringement of the individual's rights'. An exchange of letters between Towle and Keith-Lucas got nowhere in resolving this basic disagreement.[36]

The importation of Freudian ideas into social work and its consequent move away from social science drove a wedge between social work and sociology. This 'psychologising' of social work was led by some female social workers and opposed within academia by social administrators, most, but not all of them, male. One of the first such opponents was actually Titmuss's predecessor at LSE, Urwick, who campaigned as early as the pre-First World War days against the corruption of social work by the encroaching American enthusiasm for casework. He thought that it turned social work from a means of achieving social change into the provision of aid for individuals defined as maladjusted.[37]

In the domestic setting of LSE, divergences of opinion about casework were underscored by real material resource issues. The Carnegie Trust had only agreed to provide funding for four years for the new Course: after that, the expectation was that LSE would take over. But Richard Titmuss's bargaining position in securing LSE financial support was weaker because there were now three parallel courses – Child Care, Mental Health *and* the new Applied Social Studies Course. His plan therefore was to amalgamate the old with the new. He asked the three women concerned – Britton, McDougall and Younghusband – to come up with suggestions about how to achieve this. Although both Britton and McDougall accepted the logic of integration, they wanted it to happen slowly and partially. There were endless time-consuming meetings, conversations, arguments, protests, proposals and threatened resignations. From Eileen Younghusband's point of view, her position as the person responsible for getting the prestigious Carnegie grant and running this pioneering Course was constantly challenged. In the summer of 1956, for example, she complained to 'Professor Titmuss' (the 'Dear Richard' time had passed) about the appointment without consultation of a clerical post to serve all the social work courses: she pointed out that the Carnegie Course needed, and could fund, one of its own. That same year, she was invited by the Home Office to become a member of the Central Training Council in Child Care. Richard Titmuss told her not to do it. Her response, in a letter to Charlotte Towle, was 'NUTS!!'[38] She disregarded his instructions and accepted, playing a key role in the Council until it was disbanded in 1971. When she was asked to chair the working party on the future of social work that would lead to the famous Younghusband Report, Richard Titmuss again told her she shouldn't accept it, citing the loss of attention to the work of the Department, and threatening to inform the Carnegie Trustees. But again she accepted the invitation, knowing that the Trustees wouldn't object (and surely he could have understood, she said crossly, that she would have thought hard about the implications for both Carnegie and LSE?). His response was frosty. 'Your statement that the Director and I saw no objection to your accepting this invitation needs some qualifications.'[39]

When plans for integrating the three social work courses were clearly getting nowhere, Richard Titmuss asked a new young member of staff, David Donnison, to sort it all out. 'When I arrived your father said to me I've been trying to make some sense of the social work courses, I'm absolutely at my wits' end … please will you see what you can make of it and come and tell me what you think.'[40] Donnison had been at Toronto University in Canada, and before that at the University of Manchester. He had written two books on the social services, and would later develop an interest in urban studies and housing policy. Accepting Richard Titmuss's challenge, Donnison set about attending some of the social work courses in his new institutional home, talking to the students, and so forth. 'Who is this little boy?' asked Charlotte Towle suspiciously in a letter to Eileen Younghusband. 'How old is he?'[41] Eileen Younghusband called him 'a stripling'.[42] (He was actually 30, to Eileen's 54 and Charlotte's 60.) They saw him as a Titmuss puppet. 'Little David has great propensity to tip the apple cart each time so that the apples roll papa's way,' remarked Charlotte Towle ferociously.[43] Roy Parker, who took the Carnegie Course in its second year in 1955, recalls 'a certain tension in the air', and that students knew David Donnison had been 'wheeled in' to sort it out.[44] Now it was a cold war between the 'Three Musketeers' and the 'Quagmire Quartet'.[45] The Three Musketeers were Charlotte Towle, Eileen Younghusband and a woman called Kate Lewis, a trained psychiatric social worker, from a wealthy and well-known Northamptonshire family, whom Eileen Younghusband had met at the Tata Foundation in India and had recruited to help her, conscious of her own lack of any formal social work training. The Quagmire Quartet consisted of Richard Titmuss, Kay McDougall, Clare Britton and Janet Kydd, who was Deputy Head of the Department when she wasn't helping my mother with my birthday parties. The Quagmire Quartet benefitted from an alliance with the Director of LSE, Carr-Saunders, that the Three Musketeers lacked. When Carr-Saunders left and was replaced by Sydney Caine in 1957, the Three Musketeers and their allies felt that Richard Titmuss 'got at' Caine and was less than honest about the origins of the Carnegie Course, claiming a much bigger role in it than was in fact the case. Caine quickly decided that it was all very tiresome anyway – why couldn't these women stop squabbling with one another?[46]

The argument had now acquired the air of a gothic drama. Donnison was unable to see an easy way out. Finally Richard Titmuss decided to unify the three courses in stages, with one person in an overall coordinating/administrative role. Donnison's advice, to make that person Kay McDougall,[47] again fitted with Titmuss's own disposition. She would have the title 'Lecturer in Charge of Professional Education for Social Work'. The plan was announced in a staff memorandum in January 1957. It didn't go down at all well. Even Kay McDougall, who appeared to be the victor, complained to Titmuss that the wording of the document made her sound like 'a kind of dogsbody carrying out instructions'; it wasn't really his intention that she should be in charge of anything, was it?[48] Eileen

Younghusband and Kate Lewis resigned in protest at McDougall's elevation and at that offensive title 'Lecturer in Charge'. Eileen Younghusband was ten years older than McDougall and much more experienced: like Florence Nightingale, she was creating the profession to which they all belonged. 'I daren't really let myself think what the hurts have been & are to you over the child of your creation, & over LSE in general,' wrote an impassioned Kit Russell to Eileen Younghusband.[49] Another female member of staff, less directly involved in the ructions, commented on Eileen's wisdom in going and letting Richard Titmuss have his way. She found working under him sufficiently difficult to consider resignation herself.[50] Charlotte Towle wrote to Eileen Younghusband about the prospect of her last days at LSE: 'The tug of your heartstrings ... I know how much the course meant to you.' There was, she said, nothing wrong with Eileen Younghusband's ego. 'In contrast, R.T.'s is a lacy one – full of holes.'[51]

Once news of the resignation was out, Richard Titmuss had to tell the Carnegie Trustees, who were less than happy: 'the effect of these developments on Miss Younghusband and Miss Lewis is greatly to be regretted,' replied their spokesperson.[52] The correspondence is stern on the Carnegie Trustees' support for Younghusband. In their letters to Richard Titmuss, they all but accuse him of incompetence. Richard Titmuss's neglect of the close historical alliance between the Carnegie Trust and Eileen Younghusband had come home to roost. It's possible, of course – and really quite likely – that Younghusband and Lewis actively mobilised the Carnegie Trustees to admonish Richard Titmuss for his behaviour.[53] But one very important thing he hadn't considered was the need for close cooperation between LSE and all the professional organisations responsible for providing student fieldwork placements. These working relationships would be severely jeopardised were Eileen Younghusband and Kate Lewis to leave. There are many letters of protest in both the Younghusband and the Titmuss Archives from important people at the London Probation Service, the Family Welfare Association, the Middlesex Hospital, the Central Training Council in Child Care, and so on and so forth – letters of indignation and sadness that such an outcome has been allowed to happen. Sibyl Clement Brown, now in a responsible position at the Home Office, called the resignations 'a great source of alarm and despondency' and warned that the Home Office might no longer be able to sponsor students for the Course.[54] Twelve members of the Carnegie Course Supervisors' Group signed a letter to Richard Titmuss expressing their concern that his decisions about the future of social work training at the LSE were being taken without any consultation with any of the professional training bodies: 'Two people of this calibre would not have resigned without very good cause'.[55] Dr Gordon Stewart Prince, a psychiatrist who taught on the Course, recorded on his Harley Street notepaper how 'appalled' he personally was by the resignations and that his teaching days on the Course were consequently over.[56] 'I wonder if he is jealous of Miss Younghusband?', one of the protesters wrote to another one about Richard Titmuss's motives. 'Does he come from a different social background?' It was suggested that Kay McDougall's background had much more in common with Richard Titmuss's, and that this threw much light on the situation.[57] Everybody wrote to everybody, and many people threatened to resign. It was even rumoured at one stage that Richard Titmuss would himself be forced to do that in order to avoid a personal breakdown. He recorded getting a total of 31 complaints, accusations and allegations of non-cooperation, plus five threats of resignation.[58] The Chairman of the Carnegie Trustees writes to the Director of LSE to say that they have 'lost confidence in the direction in which Professor Titmuss is pushing the Carnegie Course', and they intend to withhold their payment for the final year of the Course unless they can be satisfied that the success of the Course won't be prejudiced. They make it clear that, as far as they are concerned, Eileen Younghusband and Kate Lewis are the pioneers and owners of the Course, and LSE is merely the administering authority.[59] Richard Titmuss, aided by the Director, has to work hard at bridge-building to make sure that the Trust does pay up. Charlotte Towle writes to the Director, too, and she writes to the Carnegie Trustees, who find her comments 'helpful'.[60]

In the aftermath of the decisions about Kay McDougall taking over and Eileen Younghusband resigning being made public, Richard Titmuss had some of his own regrets, admitting in a letter to Eileen that perhaps 'Lecturer in Charge' hadn't been the most diplomatic choice – he always intended that Eileen and Kate should continue running the Carnegie Applied Social Studies Course until the experimental period finished, and for as long as it continued thereafter. He accepted that some of his actions 'may have been mistaken in the sense that they have led to misunderstandings'.[61] When Eileen Younghusband suggested that he might change Kay McDougall's title, he refused, although he was later persuaded by two other women in the Department to make this offer, in the hope that Younghusband would reconsider her resignation.[62] Writing to Charlotte Towle, he called the resignations 'tragic'. 'He really is consciously & deliberately dishonest or suffers pathological amnesia,' responded Charlotte to Eileen. 'He knew full well you would resign, thus <u>wronging poor Richard</u>, to whom it was a tragic surprise!!'.[63] Towle wrote to Titmuss herself making this point:

> It must be a relief to you to have placed the generic education venture in hands responsive to your reservations about it. I recall that whenever the future of the professional courses was skirted in your conferences with me, you brought up Miss McDougall as the likely Head. Reservations implied in my criticisms were never explored by you. I left London with the conviction that you had never entertained any other idea than to turn the generic education project over to the regime responsible for the kind of education the Carnegie Course (as a pattern setting venture) was designed to correct.

How could he possibly be surprised, she went on to ask, at the resignations, when it was clear to all concerned that McDougall's appointment as Lecturer in Charge would have this outcome? Towle was particularly critical of McDougall's deficiencies as an academic leader and the unstable feelings of rivalry and ostracism she had manifested when asked to discuss the amalgamation of the three courses. Eileen Younghusband and Kate Lewis would perhaps not have resigned had they been able to respect and trust Kay McDougall as 'a properly behaved professional person'.[64] Towle's long and very articulate letter survives, not in Richard Titmuss's papers (which were carefully pruned by his wife) but in Eileen Younghusband's, because

Charlotte Towle sent her a copy – with a spiteful note attached: 'I'll venture a guess as to what he'll use this bit of tissue for??'.[65]

She may have felt the same about the letter she wrote to Sydney Caine about Richard Titmuss's decision to hand the Carnegie Course over to Kay McDougall. Towle informed Caine in no uncertain terms that McDougall wasn't qualified for this position; she lacked commitment to the Course, had been a reluctant and infrequent participant in meetings about it, was given to stereotype rather than individualise social work clients, and was unable to regulate her feelings in the interests of professional behaviour. Moreover, it was bizarre to use one person (Younghusband) to develop a course and then hand it over to someone else. This indicated a failure of management on Titmuss's part. Anxious to please everyone, Caine refused to sort out resistances and relationships, thereby confirming his own reservations about the project.[66]

Clare Britton, who was on sick leave throughout most of this unpleasantness, learnt about the amalgamation of her Course and the planned change in her role, at second hand. She was angry and upset, particularly since she and Kay McDougall had already worked out a strategy for amalgamating the Child Care and Mental Health Courses, but she knew Richard Titmuss didn't want to listen to their ideas. She had also worked with Eileen Younghusband on planning the Carnegie Course, and had been disappointed not to have been more closely involved with it. LSE was no longer a comfortable place for her. Although married to Donald Winnicott since 1951, she had continued to be known under her unmarried name: from 1958, she changed this to 'Mrs Clare Winnicott' and decided to begin training as a psychoanalyst herself.[67]

In 1957, at the height of the awfulness of the LSE Affair, Richard Titmuss went to the USA for the first time to give some lectures. Before he left, he wrote to both Younghusband and Lewis asking them to reconsider their resignations. Younghusband's reply referred to 'lack of consultation and of adequate machinery for consultation' as a fundamental reason why they both had to leave.[68]

My father had his family with him on that USA trip. We travelled on the Queen Elizabeth (this was before the era of commercial transatlantic flights). I slept in a windowless cabin on the top bunk above a complete stranger called Mrs Burgess. But I still think that drifting into New York harbour on a boat after a week of that was worth it for the view: it was March, and wet and misty, and the small square black-and-white photos that survive show the towers of Manhattan and the Statue of Liberty as some kind of ethereal alien city, out of this world, and certainly beyond the imagination of a sheltered 13-year-old girl.

Richard Titmuss's preoccupations with the LSE Affair were not obvious to me during that trip, which took in the New York School of Social Work and the Universities of Yale, Harvard and Michigan. I found staying on the 18th floor of the Hotel Paris in New York extremely exciting, but puzzled over the tremendous domestication of American university wives, who seemed to spend all their time giving dinner parties, driving children around and ironing underwear. We did a lot of sightseeing, of course: the skeletons of dinosaurs, turtles and gorillas in the Peabody Museum of Natural History, the amazing Empire State Building, Radio City, the Statue of Liberty, the FBI, Harlem, the United Nations building. Everywhere we went, the excesses of American culture impressed me: I counted the number of lamps and cupboards in the hotel rooms, once achieving 17 and 24 respectively: in one there was even a pencil sharpener attached to the bathroom wall. Towards the end of our tour we went for a few days to Toronto, passing on a train the weather-clouded Niagara Falls. In Toronto my mother had a friend who shared her first name, and my father had someone who was introduced to me as his ex-girlfriend. I don't remember feeling at all curious about this odd configuration of networks, especially since I had a small social agenda of my own in the shape of a girl I had known slightly at Haberdashers' Aske's who had now emigrated with her family to Canada. There we are in the photograph, smiling in our green school raincoats – although why either of us was wearing them there is a mystery.

David Donnison clearly had a very difficult time with the difficult women at LSE during the two months Richard Titmuss was in the USA. It was to Toronto that Donnison sent my father 'a progress report' on events at LSE. It was a long letter, on that thin crackly blue airmail paper that always expressed an air of excitement (and illegibility). I can imagine sitting there in some hotel dining-room while my father read it over breakfast, but actually I don't have any memory of that: it was 56 years before I knew of its existence in the LSE Archives. The substance of the letter was that Younghusband had still not withdrawn her resignation, and Donnison had threatened to close the Applied Studies Course completely. The Director of LSE had (perhaps unsurprisingly) arrived at the view that social work training probably shouldn't happen in universities anyway, since it all seemed such an emotional business.[69] On his way back from a tough meeting with the Carnegie Trustees, Donnison was working off his hostility by running downstairs when he fell and twisted his ankle badly – which was a good thing because he could stay at home for a week and get some reading done. Apprised of this by Eileen Younghusband, Charlotte Towle noted, unkindly, 'Poor little boy!'[70]

Towle also wrote to Eileen Younghusband about our visit to her country. 'Saw R.T. he looked so thin & sick & ailing from all he'd been through.' She and her colleagues found what he had to say about teaching social policy and the social sciences very disappointing. Charlotte wrote at length of a report back from a colleague of hers:

> Of R.T. Marion said – how well did you know that man Titmuss – did you have anything to do with him? Before I could answer she launched into an account of how thin his context was and how she took him to town – when he was presenting a report on the Research he'd done on Health matters in the course of which he told how he wore a white coat & sat in on interviews with doctors & patients & that he didn't get to know what the patients thought because the doctors did all the talking. Marion said – of course – what did you expect – with you present, in the interview – didn't your presence color the response? He said no – it should not have because he had on a white coat & was passing as a doctor. She said, well you didn't fool the doctors & probably not the patients. She had to spell out for him the defensiveness of the doctors under these circumstances & how anxiety would push them to take over. Also the implications of a three-cornered interview – the interference with the doctor–patient relationship etc. She said ... you could see he did not know one thing about human nature. She talked on, & I can

tell you she had him taped. <u>Diag.</u> neurotic delinquent. He could
be pushed into saying anything for approval or contrariwise
– provocatively got himself into traps. She picked up that he
was essentially feminine with a terrific rivalry with competent
females & yes-yes to the males, in fact ingratiatory. I did not
get time to tell her much about my experience with him. But
I did say he behaves like a schizophrenic at times. [She said] ...
whether he was a schizophrenic or not, he had a very sick little
girl who was suspiciously schizophrenic in her behaviour on
the occasions when she saw her. She then told a sad story of the
dinner party [?] gave for R.T. Both Kay his wife and Anne (?)
was there. The young people, four – invited by Anne – sat at a
separate table. After dinner when they went to watch TV, play
games or whatever, Anne crawled onto her mother's lap, refused
to go, lolled all over her mother? Finally [?] said I think you
need to go lie down ... Mrs T immediately arose – said she must
take Anne home & insisted that the Professor accompany them.
Guests offered to drive her & Anne but both insisted R.T. go
with them. So he left at 9 o'clock & the guests gathered in his
honor lingered until 11 o'clock. Kay Titmuss, on insisting R.T.
go, said – he is so tired from his week at Yale. Marion said she sat
next to Mrs T. & she talked only of R.T ... what a wonderful
man etc – but with much concern for his health & frailty. She
told how he had gone only to the 8th grade because of T.B.,
how she had never hardly known she had a baby when Anne
was born, because Richard had insisted on being the one to care
for her – gave her her bottles at night, changed her, bathed her,
dressed her etc. Also endlessly about how hard he works when
he should not, all his committees, responsibilities etc.[71]

So this is another story about my father but also about me. The
account of my parental care as an infant isn't one I recognise from
what my mother told me about my father's presence in our lives at that
stage. I don't remember the evening Charlotte Towle's letter described,
although I do remember being dragged around to people's houses,
much as I was unwillingly exposed to musical soirées in Chelsea. I

was 13, a young 13. In the 1950s, in Britain then, a 13-year-old was a child still. Not so in the USA.

Other diagnoses these women offered of my father's personality were that his lack of conscience and contact with reality suggested a psychopath, 'an altogether infantile character'.[72] We must remember, in digesting these labels, that the labellers were psychiatrically trained social workers and thus prone to that habit of quick psychologising rightly complained of by many outside the profession, including Richard Titmuss himself.

I do, nonetheless, find a perceptiveness in Charlotte Towle's comments on what she called 'the battle of the Thames'. Richard Titmuss wanted to own the Carnegie Course and he wanted his rival, Eileen Younghusband, deposed. This was a professional disagreement, a dispute about the ownership of ideas (and funding), the kind of internal fight for which academia is famed. That's why, when Donnison came to write it up some years later, he took it as an example of the way university departments work (or not).[73] Unfortunately such fights also tend to generate huge personal animosities. When Kate Lewis wrote to Charlotte Towle early in 1956 about all the arguments in the Department, she mentioned that Richard Titmuss had been ill: 'well he deserved to be,' commented Charlotte unpleasantly. 'And as far as I am concerned I would not weep. He could kick the bucket sky high for all I care.'[74] Her diary for the year in London is full of remarks about Richard Titmuss's insincerity, negative attitude and general 'enmity' towards the Carnegie project. When she's invited to dinner at T.H. Marshall's house, Charlotte notes that it's too bad Marshall no longer runs the Department instead of Titmuss: he's 'a much more simple, straightforward man'.[75] Later, when the outcome for her friend Eileen was even more negative, 'He is the kind of bird that fowls [sic] his own nest & bites the hand that feeds him … I cannot see why or how anyone of integrity can now face working with him'. He was 'a redcoat for whom shooting is too good. I'd sink him in Boston harbour in a bag of garbage – not tea – we could send him to the bottom in style & we would clap gaily.'[76] The diagnosis offered by Kay Elliot, one of the Carnegie Trustees, was critical too. 'I feel very cross about the whole thing,' she wrote to Eileen Younghusband, expressing her concern that Caine had not been told the truth by Richard Titmuss about the origins of the Carnegie Course, so that he didn't understand how crucial Eileen Younghusband was to it. 'Machiavelli seems quite a normal character compared to R.T.'[77]

As the 'tragic' early months of 1957 drag on, and we come back from our testing trip to the USA, Eileen Younghusband begins to negotiate with the Director of LSE the circumstances in which she might be willing to return in some part-time capacity to finish her work on the Carnegie Course. Her conditions are that she and Kate Lewis should be regarded as responsible for the Course, that a third person should be appointed, and that the 'in Charge' bit of Kay McDougall's title is dropped.[78] Caine is conciliatory. Donnison persuades the Carnegie Trustees to wait before withholding the rest of the grant. But Eileen Younghusband wants Richard Titmuss to apologise. Donnison gives up: 'my own determination to find a way through has evaporated,' he confesses to Eileen Younghusband and Kate Lewis. 'Should we meet some time? I don't want to lose my friends as well!'[79] He had been an unwilling negotiator in the LSE Affair from the beginning. It distracted him from his own research and policy interests, which effectively made him one of the Titmice after Peter Townsend left in the early 1960s for the University of Essex and a more overt engagement in political activity.

Historical research changes perceptions of history and the fabric of memory. That year, 1957, was the year of another American connection whose link with the LSE Affair was unknown to me until I came across it in the correspondence. Karl de Schweinitz, an American Professor of Social Welfare, visited London for a year in 1957 on a Fulbright Fellowship. These transatlantic funding bodies have a lot to answer for; their support was key to the entire 20th-century network of Anglo-American links between social reform, research and policy.[80] De Schweinitz was already the author of a respected history, *England's road to social security*, and was working on what he intended as a definitive two-volume account of the development of social welfare on both sides of the Atlantic. He brought his wife, Beth, with him to London, as male academics tended to do; she was also an academic, and had co-authored with him a manual about interviewing which was widely used by social service staff in both Britain and the USA. They were a hugely animated and enthusiastic couple, who embraced both the Titmuss family and the staff of the Social Administration Department in what were trying times for both. Beth and Karl, but especially Beth, involved themselves directly in the awfulnesses of the LSE Affair. She would visit Eileen Younghusband and Kate Lewis every day: they would tell her what was happening; she would listen. As Younghusband later remembered, 'she never took sides in one sense but we knew very well indeed where her friendship and her sympathies lay'.[81] It must have been a difficult line to tread, supporting the Three Musketeers while not falling out with the Quagmire Quartet. But what I remember the de Schweinitzes for is not this impressive mediating role (which was either kept from me or I chose to ignore). Karl de Schweinitz shared with the adolescent Ann Titmuss a consuming interest in music, and especially in playing wind instruments. He was learning the recorder and I was playing the flute. We played together, and also with the Simon who taught me Grade Five theory and respected my position as the boss's daughter.

In the end, the Carnegie Trust agreed to continue their funding provided the professional organisations were satisfied with the arrangements that were set up. Eileen Younghusband and Kate Lewis's resignations were revoked, with Lewis becoming the Lecturer in Charge of the Applied Social Studies Course, and Younghusband taking on the role of part-time 'advisor on general policy'. In 1958 the Child Care and Applied Social Studies Courses were merged, and a new member of staff, a refugee from the Polish resistance, Zofia Butrym, was hired as a 'Lecturer in Social Casework'. Butrym remembers coming in at the end of the conflict, being aware of the residual strained atmosphere, and trying not to get involved.[82] Lewis and Younghusband left to join the new National Institute for Social Work Training, and Clare Winnicott became Director of Child Care Studies in the Home Office. The Mental Health Course was finally amalgamated with the Applied Social Studies Course in 1970. But in what seemed to some a terminal insulting twist, another man with no social work experience was appointed to a professorial post in the Department in 1978: Robert Pinker's brief was to 'get something done about the research profile of the social workers'.

Their resilient habit of protest now resurfaced to fix on his title, 'Professor of Social Work'. As 'a peace offering' this was changed to 'Social Work Studies'.[83] But they co-operated with Pinker's efforts to raise the research profile of the Department; indeed, they had argued for such a professorial-level appointment. Pinker was notably successful in his brief.

In his history of the LSE Affair, ex-Director Ralf Dahrendorf notes merely of its conclusion that Eileen Younghusband left, 'though her ideas became the new orthodoxy of social work education', while Richard Titmuss 'was on his way to becoming much more famous than his colleague'.[84] Actually Richard Titmuss was exhausted from a struggle that no one had warned him about. His response was to ask the Nuffield Foundation to endow a new Chair in Social Research at LSE with himself as the first incumbent. He acknowledged that this was an outrageous suggestion. In its support he quoted the absence of any serious academic study of the development of the social services. 'In my present position,' he went on to say, 'over-burdened as I am with an immense load of administrative responsibilities, I now despair of ever having time to stimulate some of these needed developments let alone take part in them.'[85] The LSE Affair hadn't given him a breakdown, but he was ill now, with tuberculosis, and about to embark on a long course of streptomycin which produced various unpleasant side-effects. Most of all, he needed to resign his headship of the Department in order to do what professors in universities are supposed to do – research and scholarship. The tone of his appeal reminds me of Barbara Wootton's decision a few years earlier to resign her professorship at Bedford College on similar despairing grounds. Wootton and Titmuss were colleagues and friends, but *her* application to the Nuffield Foundation for financial support had been successful as a way out, whereas his (perhaps inspired by hers?) was not. Perhaps the difference was that he just asked them to pay his salary while she put together a well-thought out research proposal. It's one of those splendid ironies that Barbara Wootton used her Nuffield funding to research and write her meticulously passionate critique of social science research and of the casework approach in social work, *Social science and social pathology*, which earned her the wrath of social workers everywhere. This book would never have materialised had Wootton succeeded in another of her earlier ambitions, to work at LSE. In 1944 she had applied unsuccessfully for the Chair T.H. Marshall got, and had reluctantly accepted the second prize of a Readership at Bedford College. Her fights with colleagues at Bedford College to establish a research unit preceded her own exhaustion and resignation. I wonder whether, when things got difficult for Richard Titmuss at LSE, Barbara Wootton talked to him about how it had been for her at Bedford College? It's impossible not to wonder what might have happened to social work education, to social science, to LSE, to Eileen Younghusband and to Richard Titmuss had Barbara Wootton taken over the Department of Social Administration at LSE instead of him.

Most obviously, the story of the LSE Affair is about conflict, about unwise management decisions. But gender and class shadow each other through the story. Its participants may have surmised the presence of these themes, but the power of the analysis is something we – I – impose looking back. Strands of 'appraisal, discernment and memory' all play a part in my construction of it.[86] The Three Musketeers came from backgrounds of social and material privilege that were not matched by those of the Quagmire Quartet. But the Quagmire Quartet, through their leader, Titmuss, had access to other forms of power, those that controlled academic resources and decision-making. The behaviour of men can't be understood without an understanding of men's power. This is perhaps a story in how the injustices of gender override those of class. In its painful remembering towards the end of her life, Eileen Younghusband especially regretted how good women were forced into opposition.[87] But that's what patriarchy does, it sets women against one another.

11

Post-mortem

When he died in 1973, in a small hospital room, aged 65, of lung cancer, Richard Titmuss had his wife and daughter beside him. Eileen Younghusband died later, older and differently. It was 1981, she was 79, and she was in a car driven by a close woman friend. They were en route to an airport in North Carolina where Younghusband was to board a plane to Chicago; the car plunged off the road and hit two trees. The driver was severely injured, and Younghusband and the third woman in the car were killed. 'Noblewoman Dies in Wreck,' cried the headline in the local paper.[1]

Over a quarter of a century before this, at the very time the Carnegie Experiment was being set up and Richard Titmuss was discovering his difficulties with the women social workers at LSE, Younghusband and the driver in the fatal car crash were exchanging love letters. The car-driver was Martha Branscombe, another internationally renowned social worker, an expert in the field of child welfare; she was Chief of the Social Services Division at the United Nations Secretariat in New York, and in 1943 had helped to found the United Nations Relief and Rehabilitation Administration, an extensive social welfare programme providing aid to war-ravaged nations.[2] Branscombe and Younghusband had first met during the War when Branscombe was dispatched to Britain with a group of other women social workers to help with welfare work. Their contact became closer in 1953 when Younghusband visited the USA to prepare for the Carnegie Course. The tone of Branscombe's letters in the Younghusband Archives is abundantly warm and intimate; the other side of the correspondence presumably was, too, although it isn't there to be read. 'Eileen, My Dear – My so Cherished One', 'My Very Dearest', 'Eileen My Honey': the capitalised Americanisms preface pages of emotions and thoughts, discussions of mutual friends, worries about money and work, the conflict between materialism and spiritualism, and, above all, the progress of social work education in which both women invested so much. There were repeated plans to meet. After one meeting, in 1954, Branscombe writes to Younghusband of, 'the inexpressible meaning of having you so near in all these days and feeling the beautiful and revitalizing force of your love'. She asks Younghusband whether she recalls 'perhaps the more than once expressed desire to push the Atlantic aside … and your "pretty good suspicion" that I was feeling the same desire! I expect then,' she continued, 'that you have a rather clear idea of the uncontrolled direction of thought this evening and the longing to have these notions poured out with your own being absolutely present in the flesh!! Oh yes, you are vitally here and completely visible in the mind's eye.'[3]

This correspondence came as a complete surprise to me when I visited the Younghusband Archives at the University of Warwick. I was going there to find out more about the Carnegie Experiment and the Younghusband–Titmuss relationship. What I found was another story altogether. Housed in the dusty files were not simply these intriguing personal letters, but, much more significantly, evidence of an international network of women social reformers and social scientists who had an enormous impact on the development of the 20th-century welfare state on both sides of the Atlantic. Both Branscombe and Younghusband were members of this network, which was responsible not only for the organisation of social work as a profession but for a much wider self-appointed remit – the sociology and economics of social reform and the translation of scientific study into democratic policy-making. Women members of the network carried out studies of living and working conditions, exposed the policy agendas revealed in these, combined their scientific efforts with practical help for the poor and disadvantaged, and took upon themselves the lobbying and networking needed to bring about effective change. Once change had happened, they did their best to ensure they were put in charge of it. This was a formidable company of 'female institution builders',[4] extending right across the domains of health, education and welfare. The 'girls' network', as they called themselves, made up a sophisticated matrix of 'women welfare-state builders'.[5] But while the boys' network and its products have enjoyed global attention, the history of the girls' network is only just beginning to be written. It is certainly missing from accounts and explanations of what happened when Richard Titmuss went to LSE.

In making as much sense as can be constructed out of surviving records, it's reasonable to conclude that what did happen in Richard Titmuss's Department in the 1950s *was* an example of organisational conflict; it *did* signal a personality clash, a power struggle, and a dispute between class backgrounds – between two empire builders, one of whom had a chip on his shoulder about not having had an empire-building education, and the other of whom was brought up to know absolutely that of course you must build empires. Geoffrey Parkinson, alias Tailgunner Parkinson, a legendary probation officer, writer and 'suburban guerrilla', said of Eileen Younghusband in his *New Society* obituary of her that, so far as he could detect, 'there was not a grain of hysteria or wanton emotion in Dame Eileen's personality. Yet she had a curious ability to provoke it in others.'[6] Titmuss's character and behaviour didn't provide the kind of capable leadership that might have prevented the sparks of the LSE Affair turning into a fire. The material of that fire is also interwoven with real intellectual disagreements. Richard Titmuss was rightly suspicious of what happens when people turn themselves into a profession –

the danger of artificial specialisations of labour, arrogance in the professional–client relationship, and a move away from community-based aid; Eileen Younghusband, with her eyes on tying social work training more closely to university education, imposed demands on his leadership that strengthened these suspicions, and interrupted the Titmuss model of academic social policy. The notion of 'casework', with all its accompanying rhetorical baggage, provided prime collision territory, although, in order to keep crashing, both sides had to engage in caricatures of the other's position. Even Charlotte Towle, who was regarded as importing the casework idea into the LSE curriculum, placed the usefulness of casework in a much broader political context. 'The profession of social work,' she wrote in 1946, 'is concerned with the creation and development of a democratic society'; thus its first purpose is 'the reshaping of social and economic institutions.'[7] She was a realist, applying 'a great deal of commonsense' to all social work doctrines.[8] Her report to the Fulbright Commission on her year in England was marked by the same realism, complaining about the lack of heating and 'stenographic assistance' and the excess of tea-drinking expected of her; more significantly, it drove home the point that the LSE staff hadn't made the best use of her services: 'They thought they wanted change – but as often is the case the experience and the prospect are horses of a different color.'[9] The evidence in the Younghusband and other archives strongly suggests that, beyond these explanations of the arguments about social work at LSE, we need to consider the implications of the homosocial nature of the two worlds of social work and social policy. It was an integral part of the two worlds that the women in the girls' network had women as significant others, and in the boys' network the men connected primarily with other men.

Martha Branscombe, a professionally-suited but cheerful woman in her portraits, trained at the University of Chicago, where she met Charlotte Towle and worked as a research assistant for the magnificently named Sophonisba Breckinridge and the brilliant social economist Edith Abbott (and Abbott had listened to the Webbs in London in the early 1900s, so the trail goes right back there). Breckinridge and Abbott are stars in the firmament of this particular bit of submerged history, the first generation of American women to have trailblazed a way for middle-class women to escape the claustrophobic clutches of the home, dedicate themselves to welfare and its reform, and undertake scientific social research, all at the same time. Both Breckinridge and Abbott were members of Jane Addams' Hull-House reform community, whose research wing inspired the development of Chicago sociology. Breckinridge, who trained first as a lawyer, was a key player in almost all the reforms of the Progressive and New Deal eras. In 1933, she was the first woman to serve as an official US delegate, representing her country at an International Conference of American States in Montevideo. She returned home on one of the first transoceanic flights, and Martha Branscombe wrote that Breckinridge's 'accounts of that journey and her exultation in the experience lead us to speculate that perhaps her delight came in part from the perspective afforded her eyes – a perspective that permitted them to approach a degree nearer to the horizon of her vision'.[10]

The statistician and economist Edith Abbott was a pioneer of scientific social investigation; between 1904 and 1952 she published over a hundred books and papers on wages, pensions, women's employment, child labour, housing, the suffrage, social work education, poverty, health insurance, and crime, many of these based on scrupulous statistical and/or empirical studies. She became an expert on immigration, and in 1935 helped to draft the Social Security Act which established the toned-down American version of the welfare state. It was she who recruited Charlotte Towle in the 1930s to work at the Chicago School of Social Service Administration.[11] This was the first university-based graduate school of social work in the USA, and had been set up by Edith Abbott and Sophonisba Breckinridge in 1920 to combine social research with practical training for social workers and social reformers. Towle's mission was to develop a psychiatric casework curriculum there, but the Chicago casework curriculum, unlike others developing elsewhere in the USA, was 'a reformist and state-building vision of casework'.[12] Edith Abbott herself liked to talk about 'social welfare' not about 'social work', because the former term emphasised 'the public aspects of social service and the development of social policies'.[13] Her 1930 lecture, 'The university and social welfare', is reminiscent (or, rather, prescient) of Richard Titmuss's own 1967 lecture on 'The university and welfare objectives' (although his was much more about the university than about welfare).[14]

Abbott put forward the case for university-based study combining an academic curriculum, 'clinical' social work and social research. Her promotion of the British model of welfare centred on something Richard Titmuss believed in, at least for most of his life: universal benefits rather than stigmatising means tests. Abbott's was also a very modern argument about the use of science to avoid the waste of public money in ineffective enterprises: 'benevolence' she pronounced, 'too often is still considered a matter for the heart rather than the head'.[15]

Edith Abbott's sister, Grace, also features in this history. She was the more practical and administratively minded of the two, serving on national and international committees against the trafficking of women and children, helping to draw up plans for the 1935 Social Security Act, and heading the US Children's Bureau, that 'remarkable experiment in national advocacy for children and families'. The Children's Bureau, created in 1912, was itself a direct result of a sustained campaign by the women's social reform network.[16] Grace Abbott was also responsible for administering the provisions of the Sheppard–Towner legislation of 1921, which first extended public welfare services in the USA to mothers and children. Following the British example established a few years earlier, she carried out the first confidential enquiry into maternal deaths in the USA; every one of the 7,537 deaths occurring in 15 states in 1927–28 was investigated, revealing an appalling record of preventable death. Students at the Chicago School of Social Service Administration referred to the trio of the Abbott sisters and Breckinridge as A^2B.[17] Helen Wright, who worked with A^2B, saw their belief in state welfare provision as so much ahead of its time that it was bound to challenge established opinion in the American social welfare field. Edith Abbott and Sophonisba Breckinridge's founding of the *Social Service Review* in 1927 – a journal still going strong today – created an outlet for their unconventional views.

Addams, the Abbotts and another member of the Hull-House community, Florence Kelley, were the scientific arm of Hull-House's

'Settlement Sociology'. Converted to international socialism in Switzerland, Kelley had translated into English Engels' *The condition of the working class in England in 1844*, and she corresponded with him about her exposure in Chicago to the true and appalling condition of the proletariat. Her researches included government-sponsored studies of the sweatshop system in Chicago's garment industry, and a survey of workers' living conditions in Chicago slums. Once a coalition of lobbyists organised by her had convinced the state government to ban child labour, limit women's working hours and regulate conditions in the sweatshops, Kelley became Illinois's first Chief Factory Inspector.[18] As a divorced mother of three children, she was demographically unusual for Hull–House, most of whose members were single women for whom the place provided a professional training ground and a refuge from restrictive ideas of gentlewomanly idleness: Ibsen's legendary play 'A Doll's House' opened in Boston the same year as Hull–House came into being. The Fabian socialist Beatrice Webb, visiting Hull–House with Sidney on their first world tour in 1898, left us a wonderfully evocative description in her diary: 'The residents consist, in the main, of strong-minded energetic women, bustling about their various enterprises and professions, interspersed with earnest-faced self-subordinating and mild-mannered men who slide from room to room apologetically. One continuous intellectual and emotional ferment is the impression left on the visitor to Hull–House.'[19] The range of issues the Hull–House activists tackled was huge: the vote, women's rights as industrial workers, child labour, the trafficking of women and children, immigration, housing, crime, prison reform, health care, the peace movement. Kelley and another researcher/ reformer, Julia Lathrop, played leadership roles in the Hull–House community. Lathrop took it upon herself to make a special study of county institutions for the mentally ill and disabled, revealing a pattern of inhumane care supervised by incompetent political appointees. As the first Chief of the Children's Bureau, she became the first woman to head a federal bureau.[20]

There are so many 'firsts' in the girls' network. These women broke out of and beyond the traditional categories of social worker, social scientist and social reformer, establishing themselves as a new type of professional expert. They were social engineers, problem-solvers 'who sought an understanding of the entire social system, and a specialised competence to deal with it'.[21] Among their tools was a capacity for organising coalitions among diverse constituencies of women. Another member of the American network was Katherine Kendall, a Scottish émigré who helped to found, and then lead, the body which accredited social workers in the USA, the Council on Social Work Education. Kendall, another of Younghusband's correspondents, carried out the first international survey of social work training for the United Nations. When she went to speak about it at the International Congress of Schools of Social Work in Paris in 1950, she was so nervous that Eileen Younghusband had to take her to a bar near the Sorbonne for a stiff drink.[22] Like many members of the girls' network – although not Florence Kelley, who managed to design a house where you had to go outside to reach the upstairs – Kendall was extremely competent domestically. She was a 'superb cook', knowing 'thirty different ways to cook a chicken'.[23] Perhaps a little more important than chicken-cooking, her survey of social work training convinced the Social Commission of the United Nations to pass a resolution calling for the professionalisation of social work. Kendall was alert to the gendering of the social work world and to its wider implications: 'Social work history and women as leaders are inextricably intertwined,' she wrote in an article comparing and celebrating the achievements of 'three extraordinary leaders' – Alice Salomon in Germany, Edith Abbott in the USA, and Eileen Younghusband in the UK. These women, she said, were great because of their powerful minds, their incurable curiosity, and their scholarship: 'They believed, perhaps naively, that solid facts, carefully amassed and analyzed, would yield rational answers to troublesome questions.'[24] This, of course, is a description of what today we would call 'evidence-based public policy'.

The world of the men during these pioneering days of social research and reform lacked symmetry with the female world because of the hierarchies the gender system brings with it; the men's world exhibited easier and more obvious connections to centres of institutional power. And so, as Richard Titmuss developed his Department at LSE in the 1950s and 1960s, he found it comparatively easy to build a male, rather than female, network: the inner circle was all male, and the women were edged outwards. 'It's very important to be frank' about it, said David Donnison of the growing masculinity of Titmuss's Department: 'The people who were devoted to Richard were in the main men.' [25] The impact of Richard Titmuss's transformation of the Social Administration Department is pictured in two official photographs taken in 1950 and 1971 that head Chapter 9 and this one. In the first photograph, the front row of staff contains nine sensibly dressed women arranged around their serious head, Richard Titmuss. In the 1971 version of the Department, Richard Titmuss remains at the centre of the front row, as you would expect, but now he's flanked by two men: Brian Abel-Smith and Garth Plowman, a psychologist who joined the Department in 1964 and by 1969 had become a professor, which is why he's sitting next to Titmuss in the front row. Next to Abel-Smith and Plowman are Kay McDougall and Zofia Butrym, looking very serious, with their legs crossed in identical attitudes. In that front row there are eight men and five women, including Titmuss's devoted secretary, Angela Vivian.

Writing to LSE's Director, Sydney Caine, in 1960 to argue for more central funds to be invested in the Department, and to complain about his ever-increasing workload (he does seem fond of complaining, but, on the other hand, the administrative burdens of higher education do give one something to complain about), Richard Titmuss observed that he himself was partly to blame: 'The recruitment of a younger, lively and extremely loyal and co-operative staff is rewarding' – but it creates work. [26] In 1962, the Department's 50-year jubilee, Richard Titmuss boasted unashamedly about its success: under his leadership the staff had expanded from 13 to 30 – and this didn't include the loyal administrator Miss Partridge 'who, statistically, should perhaps be represented by two more'; the Department was now the largest of its kind in Europe, equal in size to the largest in the USA, training 37 per cent of all professional social work students in Britain; in the last six years staff in the Department had produced 180 articles and books, including 15 major works based on original research, and there were now 18 research projects ongoing; most importantly, what the last 12 years had demonstrated was that it is possible to teach a large body of social work students and advance 'the true aims of the University' at the same time.[27]

Stories behind and inside stories; what we have here is the triumph of masculine academia as an institution over more grounded and diverse versions of social knowledge. Why did it happen like this? Why was the quelling of the difficult women at LSE part-and-parcel of the rise of the domain of social policy men? The label 'difficult women' plays into a whole tradition of blaming women for behaving with strength, determination and autonomy. Difficult women are women who don't need and/or who challenge men and their perceptions of women. Writing a personal memoir of three such women in his book of that name, the novelist David Plante observed: 'I knew I felt guilt towards, not all women, but difficult women, and I felt guilt because, somewhere in my life, which I could not recall, I had done something, perhaps simply said something, which was wrong, which had hurt them, and the only reaction possible for them to what I had done or said was to be difficult. I had made them difficult.'[28]

Richard Titmuss's encounters with the difficult women at LSE saturated my childhood and adolescence. His stories about these made me meditate in incoherent ways about the whole matter of gender – except that we lacked the concept of gender then. I think now that perhaps the introduction of gender, its differentiation from sex, which followed the publication of my first book *Sex, gender and society* in 1972, could be seen as one legacy of the LSE Affair. I always sensed that there was more to this than met the eye, more than I and my mother were being told, just as there was more to my parents' marriage than an uncluttered choice that she would stay at home and he would go to work. The professional women at LSE, like the teachers at my all-girls' school, offered another possibility: that women could be autonomous and live a life that included the exercise of their minds. None of this was talked about at the time. There were few books that even opened a conversation about why the social positions of men and women were so different.

'It was men he attracted and who became part of his circle,' said David Donnison, looking back at the stage in his own career when he entered Richard Titmuss's Department to resolve the conflict about social work education. 'I think it was partly because men were reared culturally to participate in public debate and to get involved in political discussion and action ... I think there *was* a sexual element in it which nobody would have recognised or thought about or confessed to. But I think your father was a beautiful man and he had an attraction to men that was quite physical.'[29] We know that Richard Titmuss's attitudes to women were ambivalent, and I, as his daughter, knew that most keenly. Roy Parker's diagnosis was that Richard Titmuss was more at ease with men because they were more deferential. 'They admired him, they looked up to him, he was a kind of paternal figure. And the women didn't in the same way.'[30] Some of the women may have been reacting to Richard Titmuss's silent lack of interest in gender as an axis of inequality. This was something on which none of the other Titmice challenged him. David Donnison, looking back, spelt out the basic social policy angle: 'Richard and his circle weren't uncaring about or hostile to women and women's concerns; their hearts were in the right place on all the more important things. But they were more concerned about broader questions of social justice.'[31] One riposte to this is that there can hardly be anything broader than systemic discrimination against half the population. Hilary Rose, a political radical who joined the Social Administration Department in 1964, recalls being invited to a Christmas party in one of the Oakleys' Ealing houses. 'I went to your house and I was sitting there with your mother. I was sitting on the floor, she was by the Christmas tree – and she turned round and she said, "Oh but Hilary, you're really quite nice!" Richard was clearly running me down at home.' Hilary was in Brian Abel-Smith's office at LSE when he received the phone call telling him of Richard Titmuss's death. 'Brian was completely heart-broken.' She wanted to offer comfort, but, conscious of her own heterosexuality and of both Brian's silence about his homosexuality and his great love for Richard, she knew that any physical gesture she might have made to comfort him might have caused him to jump out of the window.[32]

Albertine Winner, who diagnosed my polio in 1949, was a Visiting Lecturer in Richard Titmuss's Department throughout the 1950s, having been recruited by Eileen Younghusband to talk to the social work students about 'Problems of health and disease'. Winner also published the first medical paper about homosexuality in women in 1947. Somewhat curiously, and on what she admitted was an anecdotal basis, Winner distinguished between two sorts of lesbians: women who prefer the society of women, who have strong female friendships 'and only detached relationships with men' and (much more dangerously) 'the promiscuous lesbian' who sets out to seduce weaker women.[33] Winner herself, a robust figure, sidles out of my memory, a definite presence, whether in or out of the Jaguar she was fond of driving. She was an accomplished physician, a specialist in neurology, a Lieutenant-Colonel in the Royal Army Medical Corps during the War and a top administrator in the Ministry of Health afterwards (the first woman to become Deputy Chief Medical Officer of Health in 1962). After her retirement, she worked closely with Cicely Saunders, the pioneer of humane hospice care for the terminally ill. 'She never married,' concludes her *Dictionary of national biography* entry, as do many such entries for the women in this narrative.[34]

Many women social workers and welfare activists on both sides of the Atlantic were in domestic partnerships with other women. Charlotte Towle's 'dearest friend and boon companion'[35] for over 50 years was Mary Rall, an Assistant Professor at the Chicago School of Social Service Administration. Florence Hollis, a Professor of Casework at Columbia University School of Social Work in New York, a 'small, fair, almost in a way, tomboyish' woman who loved talking about theory,[36] and who nearly went instead of Towle to LSE to advise on the Carnegie Course, shared 40 years of her life with Rosemary Reynolds, a social caseworker and teacher of Applied Social Sciences. In Eileen Younghusband's somewhat gender-stereotyped portraits, Rall survives as 'tall, dark and good-looking' with 'essential feminine qualities', but unfortunately a physically weak heart.[37] When Jane Addams established Hull-House in 1889, she did it together with her close friend Ellen Starr. Starr was an exception to the rule of politically reforming women in Hull-House; a disciple of William Morris, she learnt book-binding in England and thereafter produced beautiful books for Hull-House. Starr was later displaced in Addams' closest affections by Mary Rozet Smith, a member of a very wealthy Chicago family, and a consistent financial supporter of Hull-House, 'the great woman behind a great woman'.[38] Addams and Smith thought of themselves as married. Smith paid Addams a monthly allowance, took her on holiday, and tried to stop her working too hard. They slept in the same bed together for more than 40 years; when travelling, they would telegraph ahead to ensure their room had a double bed and not two single ones.[39] They bought a home together in Maine where they enjoyed 'a healing domesticity',[40] and were a perfect example of a 'Boston marriage' – the loving association and co-residence of two women who often shared professional interests as well as their personal lives.[41] In Hull-House too, Florence Kelley and Julia Lathrop established a 'profound' and lasting friendship.[42] Sophonisba Breckinridge formed an intimate alliance with Marion Talbot, Dean of Women at the University of Chicago, but her most important life-partner was Edith Abbott, with whom she shared a 'seamlessly merged' personal and professional life.[43] Mary Richmond, whose 1917 text *Social diagnosis* first laid out the arguments for casework in social work practice, had a close relationship with someone called Gordon Hamilton, whom in my ignorance I assumed to be a man. Amy Gordon Hamilton worked at the New York School of Social Work; her most important contribution to the social work literature was to build on Richmond's text in a book published in 1940, *The theory and practice of social casework.*

And then there was the English contingent: Edith Eckhard, who ran the LSE Department of Social Administration before Richard Titmuss, lived with the suffragist and peace campaigner Kathleen Courtney, an extraordinary woman who fell out with Millicent Fawcett over the women's peace campaign in the First World War and helped to found (along with others, including Jane Addams, Grace Abbott and Sophonisba Breckinridge) the Women's International League for Peace and Freedom at a meeting in the Hague in 1915.[44] Jane Addams' work for peace gained her the Nobel Peace Prize in 1931. Janet Kydd, who did my birthday parties, lived with a close friend called Pat Smith. Nancy Seear, who ran the Personal Management Course in Titmuss's Department, lived with Melrhood Mary Towy Evans, Chief Personnel Management Adviser to the Ministry of Labour. Just before the accident which killed Eileen Younghusband, the car-driver, Martha Branscombe, had been visited by Geraldine Aves from England. Aves was a close friend of both

Younghusband and Titmuss. She and Younghusband had worked together during the war, running social work courses for women from occupied 'allied' countries. The Child Care Course at LSE, set up in 1947, had actually been a joint Aves–Younghusband idea, with Younghusband persuading T.H. Marshall to house it in the Department of Social Administration.[45] Aves, a Cambridge-trained economist, and a 'handsome woman of regal appearance',[46] was Chief Welfare Officer at the Ministry of Health responsible for co-ordinating evacuation and welfare services during the Second World War. She lived with Nancy Rackstraw, an ex-LSE Social Science Diploma student and Child Care Organiser, and enjoyed a close bond with another, Gwyneth Wansbrough Jones, who lived next door.[47]

Eileen Younghusband lived with women, too, sharing a home with Kit Russell of the LSE Department before and after her main live-in partnership with a social worker called Helen Roberts. Younghusband and Roberts lived together throughout the late 1930s and early 1940s in a house in West London owned by the famous epidemiologist Sir Richard Doll. Like Younghusband, Roberts came from a wealthy family, but she dropped the other half of her double-barrelled name, along with the butler and the other servants, and turned to social work instead. She trained at LSE, specialising in psychology. A small, dark, intense woman, Roberts had a special interest in the problems of displaced persons. After the War, she worked in Europe with voluntary relief teams helping in the desecrated areas of Holland and Germany and as General Secretary of the Young Women's Christian Association. This position involved much travel and thus generated a rich, loving and (for my purposes in writing this book) tremendously informative correspondence. Many of the letters in the Younghusband Archives bear exotic addresses – Bangkok, Delhi, Hong-Kong, Karachi, Kuala Lumpur, Rio de Janeiro, Shanghai, Tokyo, Toronto, Trinidad. The letters discuss Roberts' work, and Younghusband's, the welfare of their parents, plans to meet. In one letter, written in 1948 from Geneva, Roberts remembers the anniversary of their first encounter: 'It has been truly wonderful to have you with me – whether in the flesh or in the spirit – during these ten years and I pray that our next decade may bring still richer contact ... God bless and keep you, my beloved.'[48] By the time we get to the 1950s and the incomprehensible refusal of Titmuss and the Director to understand Eileen's position in relation to the Carnegie Course, Helen wants 'to knock all their heads together'.[49]

All these women worked and holidayed together, cared for each other's aged parents, coped together with illness and other difficult life events, made plans, cooked meals, cultivated their gardens, shared visions of a better world, and simply had fun. Describing to her biographer the holidays she and Helen Roberts enjoyed together during the War, Eileen Younghusband reminisced: 'We went to the Lake District ... We went to a farm on Exmoor. We went to Wales ... We went to North Bovey, on Dartmoor. They were all, of course, beautiful, peaceful parts of the country. We used to walk most of the day. We used to take our picnic with us and rucksacks on our backs and books to read and we used to read and talk and sleep in the sunshine.' [50] International connections were quickly made and soon cemented into practical and affectionate liaisons. Thus Eileen Younghusband stayed with Katherine Kendall and Martha Branscombe and/or Charlotte Towle when she visited the USA; on one of Younghusband's visits with Kendall in the late 1950s, Kendall rang up Hollis and Reynolds and asked them to ask Younghusband to dinner, so that was the beginning of yet another new connection.[51] In her year acting as Carnegie Course adviser to LSE, Towle was offered rooms in the homes of Younghusband, Kate Lewis and Geraldine Aves. (Perhaps because of the difficulty of arbitrating between these offers, she chose to stay in a hotel.)

You need a social network map to plot and imagine all these links, which aren't just a matter of personal relationships, but form the material of the women's public achievements and influence. My own imagining of the web of connections is complicated by the misty landscape of my position as Richard Titmuss's daughter. What I remember is only a fragment of what happened. I must have been present, for example, when Charlotte Towle was invited to the Blue Plaque House to meet Barbara Wootton, Wootton's 'charming' husband, and a 'young economist' called Brian Abel-Smith, but I was only 11, and perhaps had been sent to bed.[52] Putting together the archival information with the faded pages of my adolescent diary, I realise that on that famous trip to Europe with my parents and

Brian Abel-Smith in 1956, during which I was much enamoured of both Brian and his posh car, I must in fact have been in the presence of many of the members of the girls' network. When we put the posh car on a ferry from Bonn to Munich, my father was on his way to give a lecture at the Conference of the International Association of Schools of Social Work in Munich. His contribution was to talk about 'Industrialization and the family', a subject with somewhat tenuous links to social work.[53] The location of the conference, in Germany, was an effort at post-war reconciliation; the German social work schools, purged of their Nazi staff, had recently been readmitted to the Association.[54] Did we stay in the hotel remembered by Eileen Younghusband as opposite the bierkeller used by Hitler and his friends, two floors below ground, 'a very sinister place, filled with men drinking and smoking'?[55] My diary has several mentions of encounters with Geraldine Aves, including a rather unbelievable shopping expedition to buy Brian Abel-Smith a goatskin. (Why did he need a goatskin?) Afterwards, the Titmusses and Abel-Smith departed for the Italian Dolomites, and Martha Branscombe and Eileen Younghusband sped off on an Adriatic coast holiday.

This wasn't a world made up of exclusive relationships. It was a world in which women experienced the freedom of being able openly to declare their feelings for one another, and in which they didn't feel constrained by the heterosexual model of the couple. This freedom must to some extent have been aided by the considerable private incomes some of them enjoyed. Sophonisba Breckinridge, for example, maintained a close relationship with her mentor and intimate Marion Talbot, even after the seamless merging of her and Edith Abbott's lives. Jane Addams similarly enjoyed a closeness to Ellen Starr throughout the many years of her partnership with Mary Rozet Smith. Eileen Younghusband's deeply affectionate correspondence with Martha Branscombe overlaps with her continuing intimacy with Helen Roberts. They were all affectionate with one another. Here, for instance, is Kit Russell writing to Eileen Younghusband in 1957 about Eileen's resignation from LSE: 'Darling – it was so good of you to tell me as you did and *very* sweet of you to come last night … To have had you in my life for twenty-five years, been taught by you, worked under you, lived with you and had you as a colleague is something I can never be thankful enough for.'[56]

So the socialising was also harmoniously accomplished in multiples of more than two. In 1958, when she had exited from the LSE dramas, Younghusband spent a month at the United Nations and then had a holiday in New Hampshire with Charlotte Towle and Towle's live-in partner, Mary Rall: Kate Lewis flew from England to join them. They stayed in delightful country inns, especially one called Pinkham Notch, a colonial-style building in meadows sloping down to a river with old apple trees. 'We had a wonderful time, picnics every day, long walks, beautiful drives, wonderful conversation ... a great deal of laughter.'[57] There are little faded photos in the Archives: Charlotte and Mary picnicking in a forest; Mary posed on top of a rock; Charlotte and Kate together; Eileen at her desk in the Pinkham Notch Inn, in a black-and-white dress with a large pink rose. 'Those were wonderful years,' Younghusband said of the period when she and Lewis and Towle 'worked and played so closely together'. In London, Lewis lived round the corner from Eileen; she was another excellent cook and there were lots of parties in her house. Towle's diary for that year records a whirlwind round of parties, dinners, theatre outings and country weekends orchestrated by Younghusband, Lewis, Aves and others in the network.[58] Branscombe and Younghusband enjoyed many holidays together in the USA, England, Ireland and Italy, often built around social work conferences at which they were both speaking.[59]

Meaning is a child of its time, and in our time we are still somewhat transfixed by the idea of exclusive heterosexual bonds: one woman and one man forever and harmoniously fused together. This was the model aspired to in the Blue Plaque House. Beside the monolith of marriage and heterosexual partnership, all other kinds of personal relationships — of parent and child, siblings, extended kin, women or men together, and, of course, the fundamental bond of friendship itself — have been forced to linger in the shadows as topics of study and understanding. Hence the 'never married' terminology of the women's official biographies, ending records of amazing lives on notes of imputed failure. Hence also the widely touted explanation that women's cohabitation with other women was simply second-best, because the men who might have been their mates had been killed by war. Demography may have accounted for some female friendships, but the phenomenon is far too widespread and long-lived to be thus dismissed.

A compelling footnote in Allen Davis's biography of Jane Addams records a conversation he had with Alice Hamilton, a doctor specialising in industrial medicine, and another incumbent of Hull-House, where she ran a well-baby clinic and researched disease in the local community. Hamilton, who became the first woman professor at Harvard Medical School, was in her nineties when Davis asked her about relationships between women in Hull-House. She answered that there was no open lesbian activity, but an unconscious sexuality. 'Because it was unconscious it was unimportant, she argued. Then she added with a smile that the very fact that I would bring the subject up was an indication of the separation between my generation and hers.'[60] Olive Stevenson, a professor of social work, was open about her lesbian relationship with Phyllida Parsloe, another professor of social work, in her autobiography, published posthumously in 2013, but was not so in the 1960s and 70s. 'A kind of social denial was then common,' she wrote, 'such relationships among middle-class women were often tacitly acknowledged by those close to the person concerned.'[61] But physical relationships between women overlapped with a long tradition of female intimacy, a conception of quite proper love, 'beautiful friendship' between women.[62]

Whatever they meant – then and now – the primacy of same-sex relationships was a critical *modus operandi* for both professional and personal fulfilment in the girls' network, among these women whose imaginative methodology managed to knit science and passion, evidence and reform, charity and public service, and personal and public life so closely together that none of the elements seemed logical without the others. Relationships between women were the key to female leadership, reform and policy-making, both nationally and internationally, as indeed they were and are for men. But there's no parallel tradition of a men's community based on co-residence and the merging of intellectual and emotional lives. Relationships in the women's network functioned not only as sources of intimacy and friendship but to provide an informal mentoring system much needed in a male-governed public world. The solidarity of the female community was a backdrop and a resource for women reformers, but they didn't publicly acknowledge it, perhaps because they feared a hostile response: 'It could seem like a bloc, in the old political sense of bloc'.[63] The existence of this community, however, might well have been surmised, and, so far as the LSE Affair was concerned, it could well have rubbed salt in Richard Titmuss's wounds; indeed, it might have upset any (academic) man who wasn't entirely comfortable with the idea that women can constitute an autonomous group. Wendy Posner, who wrote a PhD on Charlotte Towle, pertinently observed that the 'friendship and professional union' between Towle and Younghusband 'served as a shield that may have been as harmful to their goals as it was helpful'.[64] Women's independence from men is a notion with which patriarchal culture has always had some difficulty; a *collective* independence is even more disturbing. It's much easier to ignore it, or fail to give it the attention it deserves. Richard Titmuss doesn't seem to have been at all aware of the operation of the girls' network in the world he entered at LSE. For example, when he tried (unsuccessfully) to prevent Eileen Younghusband accepting the chair of the Ministry of Health Working Party on Social Work in 1955, he was seemingly unable to imagine the influential connections already existing between Younghusband and senior women civil servants. Younghusband's role on the Working Party had already been arranged by her and Geraldine Aves and a woman called Enid Russell-Smith, a senior civil servant in the Ministry of Health, over lunch in the University Women's Club: the official invitation was simply a formality.[65] This was the way things regularly worked in the male world, but it doesn't seem to have occurred to the men that women engaged in it too.

Rose Mary Braithwaite, a supervisor on the first Applied Social Studies Course at LSE, returned to the LSE Affair in 1972 and began a project (like mine in this book) designed to understand what it had really been about. She gathered together a group of people who had been involved in the Carnegie Experiment, and they met regularly for five years. It was clear from the first meeting that a great many people wanted some record made of their feelings and experiences. The aim of the 'Carnegie Resurrection Project', as Braithwaite called it, was to create a record of the genesis, content and impact of this pioneering change in social work education. As one of the group's members said, 'It's part of the history of social work ... if an archaeologist does it later there will be some distortion'.[66] There was some distortion anyway. Even almost 20 years on, the embers were still hot. The Director of LSE refused access to the School's papers relating to the Carnegie Course on the grounds that they were 'strictly confidential'.[67] But there were other papers and archives, and most of all there were people's memories. An Australian social work educator, Alma Hartshorn, offered to write up the Carnegie Resurrection Project's findings, and after 20 rejections from publishers her book, *Milestone in education for social work: The Carnegie Experiment 1954–1958*, was published by the Carnegie Trust in 1982. The final version is a detailed chronological account of events leading up to, and following on from, the introduction of the new Applied Social Studies Course, but the heart of the matter isn't in the book, it's in the correspondence about it in the Younghusband Archives. Hartshorn sent her drafts to many people among the *dramatic personae* of the affair, and others connected with it; she especially sent them for comment Chapter 7, 'The London School of Economics and the beginnings of generic education for social work'.

In the stream of responses she got back, people made observations about Richard Titmuss's 'insensitive leadership', his ignorance and ambivalence about professional social work, his refusal to recognise the close links that existed between Eileen Younghusband and the Carnegie Trust, and his blindness about the fact that the Course depended on very close working partnerships with employment and fieldwork training agencies, including government departments, who therefore saw themselves as equals in the experiment, and who objected to LSE's unilateral action in planning to merge the Course with others and deposing Younghusband and Lewis from their positions of authority over it.[68] Geraldine Aves was of the depressing opinion that 'the whole story really cannot be written until many more years have elapsed'.[69] Alma Hartshorn, replying to one of these letters, made a tantalising confession: 'I know a great deal more than I have included in my writing, and I am sure that there is much more again that I don't know ... Some of the key things which are known to a few individuals cannot be published.'[70] Reg Wright, of the Central Council for Education and Training in Social Work, another reader of the key chapter in Hartshorn's book, had been a student on the Carnegie Course, and his diagnosis was that much of the difficulty stemmed from the problem Richard Titmuss had in accepting conflict and trying instead to please everybody; that Eileen Younghusband was misled by him as to her future prospects at LSE; that Charlotte Towle was a nice woman but merely a technician. His view was that the 'truth' would emerge only if there could be a fuller analysis of Titmuss's role.[71]

Mysteriously, both the tapes and the transcripts recording Eileen Younghusband's own account of the LSE Affair for Kathleen Jones' biography of her can't currently be found in her Warwick University Archives. Richard Titmuss himself wasn't interviewed for the Braithwaite project, because he was already terminally ill. His death forestalled any further dissection of what had happened, prompting instead a quite properly respectful deluge of declarations about his enormous contribution to the world of social science and policy. In view of the legacy of social welfare and social reform that made possible the Department he created at LSE, it's especially poignant to find among the letters kept by his widow one from Katherine Kendall in her capacity as Secretary-General of the International Association of Schools of Social Work. (She had organised that pivotal 1956 Conference in Munich.) Richard Titmuss, said Kendall, was 'a very great man': 'His commitment to causes that we cherish in the International Association of the Schools of Social Work endeared him to us as a comrade in arms for a better world ... there is no-one who can take his place.'[72]

'Comrade in arms' isn't the phrase I would choose after my incursion into this history. The mysteries of the LSE Affair of which I was unaware but suspicious at the time, will remain. They even haunt the corridors of LSE, where women who know about social work were, at least until the late 1990s, liable to be reminded of the problems their predecessors had caused. Eileen Munro, now Professor of Social Policy at LSE, and the author of a respected government report on child protection, recalls that:

The 'LSE Affair' was still vividly in the minds of the older staff members when I became a lecturer in 1995 and I was repeatedly made aware that women social workers were seen as a problematic group (and that I belonged to that group). Indeed, the final closure of the social work courses can be seen as a repeat of the 1950s history to some extent. Though there were some sensible reasons for the closure, the energy to push the decision through seemed strongly influenced by hostile emotions to those 'difficult women'. Some of the women who left the department at that stage were considered highly neurotic by some of the remaining colleagues but I was pleased to see that they all settled into happy working relationships in their new environments.[73]

At the same time, the substantive issues interred in the LSE Affair as regards social work education – the need for both a generic foundation and for specialist training – continue to be fought over on a policy level.

My recent archival excavations uncovered a little neatly typed card dated 1962 from the doubly valuable Departmental Administrator, Pleasance Partridge. Someone (my father?) must have told her I'd been offered a place at Oxford. Such news was communicated by telegram in those days: 'I have never sent a telegram to any of our accepted students,' Pleasance Partridge told me, 'and I think, therefore, they must have wanted you very badly. I can well imagine the entire Selection Committee hurtling to the Post Office after the meeting to get it off at once before you accepted a place somewhere else.'[74] Her exaggeration was comforting. By this time I definitely needed a place somewhere else. Family life had developed new strains as I explored relationships with men of my own age and became politically active in ways that threatened my parents' conventional values. In my new academic abode, with that name 'Titmuss', I was quickly hunted by all the left-wing student societies who wanted my name on their cards. When I left Oxford three years later I had a different surname and I never returned to live in the Blue Plaque House. I had embarked on a complicated process of working out who I was in relation to the legacy of Richard and Kay Titmuss, and all the sagas and dramas of their lives. My aim then was to leave them all behind and develop sagas and dramas of my own. My aim now is to understand more about these stories and about my father's legacy – to the world of social work and social policy, and to the evolution of my own ideas about the uses of a gender-sensitive social science in promoting an effective and just public policy.

12

The Troubles

I was in love, of course, but the marriage, in 1964, was also a relief
to me because it marked a symbolic severance from the culture of
the Blue Plaque House. This is a *post hoc* attribution: I would not
(could not) have put it like that at the time. But turning my back on
the house and all it represented was no simple feat, because of my
admiration for my father's writings and his socialist values, and because
of the pull the legend of our happy family life exerted on my loyalties.
I became a married woman before I finished my first degree; the fact

that marriage required both the permission of my parents and that of Somerville College, Oxford, seemed to me then merely amusing, rather than any kind of serious comment on women's status. I was pleased then to use the excuse of marriage for a name-change. Not so long before, I had consulted Brian Abel-Smith about finding a solicitor to change my name using less traditional means, but I didn't quite have the bottle to go through with it. Struggling similarly at a similar age, Louise Kehoe, daughter of the modernist architect and duplicitous father Berthold Lubetkin, also resorted to the feminine manoeuvre of an early marriage.[1] If I thought marriage or a change of name would enable me to become my own person, I was, of course, wrong. Becoming one's own person is the project of a lifetime. Yet it's also a spurious ideal: the creation of a culture unwarrantably fixed on this notion that everyone's task must ultimately be to find their own separate personhood. We are never separate from the lives that produced us; we carry our childhoods and our genealogy within us always. The only thing that changes is our relationship to these, the stories we tell ourselves and others, our 'reconstructive endeavours'.[2]

However confused I was about the matter of identity, I was clear about my immediate domestic future: I wanted to create a different kind of family from the one I had known until then. I wanted to be enmeshed in warmth, in close physical affection, in clutter and friendly argument. I wanted to live in an untidy house, not a tidy one. Thus I filled our first proper home in Chiswick with colour: a yellow kitchen, orange-flowered curtains, John Lewis's daisy-print in its red and blue versions for the bedrooms, a children's room with a bright turquoise carpet and thick purple curtains (to exclude the light and prevent the children waking up too early – my aesthetics have always had a practical edge). When I see myself in that house now, I remember chiefly my tiredness at trying to do it all. For instance, all those bright curtains were made by me on my maternal grandmother's ancient Singer sewing machine, a most beautiful mother-of-pearl encrusted instrument, with its key tied onto the handle by means of a piece of string cut sometime in the 1890s. I was proud of my housekeeping efforts, having in no sense begun to separate myself from the ideology of female domesticity that reigned in my childhood home.

In the year after leaving Oxford I tried and failed to become a creative writer. A different kind of creativity, motherhood, was the solution to this impasse, but having children was something we both very much wanted to do. One baby was born in January 1967 and the second in May 1968. In a photograph taken towards the end of 1966, a few weeks before the first birth, my father and I are standing together in his greenhouse at the end of the garden overlooking the North Thames Gas Board Playing Fields. We are angled towards one another in slightly strained poses. He wears his usual suit which, despite my mother's efforts to get him professionally tailored, always seemed too big for his bony frame. I am very pregnant in a black corduroy maternity dress. I remember that dress very well (the encasing of one's body in different sorts of clothes could be an interesting way of doing autobiography and social history). We had a cat in Chiswick, a cat I had been allowed to acquire in the Blue Plaque House after much fraught pleading. She was a highly affectionate tabby with very long fur which moulted into that black maternity dress like nobody's business. In the photograph taken with my father I also wear, unusually, a ribbon in my hair. I hardly look like a responsible woman on the verge of motherhood.

When the baby was born my parents came to visit me and him in the hospital. They seemed curiously awkward, and I couldn't talk to them about the savagery of the birth and my apprehensions about being a fit mother to this extraordinarily beautiful and unexpectedly male child. About the female body one could never talk to my father anyway. My mother's story about giving birth to me always reminded me of those descriptions of how Jesus was evacuated from the body of the Virgin Mary 'without a murmur or lesion, in a moment'.[3] Because she was anaesthetised for the delivery, Ann Titmuss's mother wasn't aware of her child slipping (or possibly being pulled) out. According to her story, by the time my mother first saw me I had been washed and dressed, and had my hair brushed so that it stood up in a teddy-boy flick in front. Bombs were falling in London round the hospital: this was, she explained, the reason why I was never breastfed. My parents weren't at ease with the biology of motherhood.

When I told them some months later that I was pregnant again, my mother said 'Oh dear'. But we had planned this second pregnancy and were happy about it. The second baby, a girl, was born at home. These were the days when women who had 'normal' first deliveries weren't expected to clutter up the hospitals. And thereby hangs a tale about parenthood which is painful to this day. I wouldn't wish to infuse it with heavy retrospective melodrama, but it was an episode of inexplicable abandonment, and it sits there, in my head or wherever these mementoes of the past gather (sometimes we feel them in our nerves and our bones).

Having a baby at home is a delightful experience but you shouldn't do it on your own, even as half of a couple. I asked my mother to come to our house for the birth, and she agreed. I made up a bed for her in the sitting room (we had no spare room). When I went into labour in the afternoon I called her and she came. The baby was born about half past ten in the evening; the GP, who had come to assist the midwives if needed (he wasn't), went downstairs to tell my mother, who made a cup of tea for everyone, and then an omelette for me. It was quite possibly the best omelette of my life (and definitely one I wouldn't have got in a maternity hospital). But after that my mother quite shockingly announced that she was going home; she had to go back she said, 'because of your father'. (He was 61 years old, a responsible and healthy adult.) I asked her to stay, but she went. We both asked her to stay: Robin and I were in this together. The midwives showed us what to do if the baby choked and stopped breathing or if I had a postpartum haemorrhage, but they didn't tell us how to do these things and look after a child of 16 months at the same time.

I know now, and must also have intimated then, that the couple in the Blue Plaque House had other concerns apart from the birth of grandchildren and the needs of a daughter in the process of discovering what other people would call *The cultural warping of childbirth, The mask of motherhood*, and so forth, and what she herself would write about under the headings of the filmic *From here to maternity* and the rather more sternly analytic *Women confined: Towards a sociology of childbirth*. This was May 1968, a time of general abandonment, disaffection and trouble in Britain and elsewhere. There were personal troubles in Richard Titmuss's relationships with colleagues – the whole enterprise of the Titmice; tensions in the Titmice's immersion in the politics of the policy-making process; and there were institutional troubles at LSE. In the first draft of her extended and much quoted memoir of Richard Titmuss, Margaret Gowing referred to the difficulties Richard Titmuss also had during this period with his daughter as 'a partial estrangement', a comment that was expunged from the final version.[4]

The straightforward account of my experience as a young mother and emerging feminist and academic appears in *Taking it like a woman*. This records my arrival at a place designed uniquely for women in patriarchy: a place where intense never-ending love coincides with corrosive resentment and despair. Mothers love their children, they almost always love their children, but what you want to do for your children is nearly always more than it's possible for you to do, and doing everything for them isn't the same as doing it for yourself. They call it 'postnatal depression', which is a ridiculous term for many reasons. Who wouldn't feel some distress when dealing with a genitally mutilated body and suddenly exposed to responsibility for the care of a new and totally dependent human being, a condition which imposes the further symptom of sleep-deprivation lasting for months, if not years? I used to leave the colourfully untidy house in Chiswick with a badly packed suitcase and come back an hour later because I had nowhere else to go. My parents were embarrassed. Their sympathies lay with their son-in-law, who had got himself saddled with a deficient wife. They didn't exactly say this, but it was clear from their behaviour. As the months passed, our interactions became increasingly limited and stilted. When we did meet, they talked almost exclusively about my father's work and achievements. Perhaps they didn't know what else to say. Just as I couldn't talk to them about the experience of motherhood, so also the questions that were beginning to grip me about the inequities of gender weren't a permissible part of our dialogue. There were no siblings to buttress these awkwardnesses, and I was ahead of my friends in both having children and discerning the fractures of sex and gender. The 1960s – renamed by one commentator the 'anxious' rather than 'swinging' sixties – entailed, among many other things, a reappraisal of relations between the generations.[5]

In Richard Titmuss's life, the period after his daughter's marriage, which was to be the last decade of his life, brought extra fame and status. He became a Commander of the British Empire, and five universities gave him honorary versions of the degree he never had. Evidence of Richard Titmuss's accelerated fame was carefully harvested by his wife; one component was a fat file of messages, letters and telegrams congratulating him on the CBE. The file makes interesting reading today, because it spells out the many and interlocking networks within which he had learnt to move since he went to LSE. There were, for example, letters from the Vice-Chancellors of the Universities of London and Sussex; the Provosts of King's College, Cambridge, and University College, London; the Master of Corpus Christi College, Cambridge; the Academic Registrar of the University of London; the Professor of Architecture at the Bartlett School of Architecture; Lord Platt at the Royal Commission on Medical Education; and Professors Karl Popper at LSE, O.R. McGregor at Bedford College, and Walter Holland at St Thomas's Hospital Medical School. A long list of organisations sent congratulatory notes: Barclays Bank; the Board of Governors of Hammersmith Hospital; the Council for Training in Social Work; the Industrial Welfare Society; International Voluntary Service; the Local Government Examinations Board; the London Council of Social Service; the National Association for Mental Health; the National Citizens' Advice Bureaux Council; the National Coal Board; the National Council for Social Service; the National Insurance Advisory Committee; the National Old People's Welfare Council; the National Union of Agricultural Workers; the Nuffield Foundation; and the Rowntree Trust. The social workers wrote, of course – Zofia Butrym, Robin Huws-Jones, Kay McDougall, Kitty Slack – and Dr Albertine Winner, who taught on the Carnegie Course. Flowery telegrams appeared from the Prime Minister of Mauritius and the Commissioner for Mauritius in London. From Israel came messages from the Council for Higher Education, the Minister of Economic Affairs, and the Governor of the Bank of Israel. Richard Titmuss's GP and his bank manager wrote, as did my old headmistress from Haberdashers' Aske's girls' school, who could always be counted on for an establishment response; she probably scoured the New Year's

Honours list every year in the hope of spotting someone connected with the school. Some signatories in the CBE file are a bit more mysterious, for example the Principal Medical Officer of 'HJ Heinz Company (57 varieties)'.[6]

In the wake of the Labour Party's 1964 election victory, Richard Titmuss joined leading government commissions – the Community Relations Commission, the Commission on Medical Education, the Finer Committee on the One-Parent Family. He became Deputy Chairman of the Supplementary Benefits Commission (SBC), the body which replaced the old National Assistance Board. His acceptance of this office surprised many, since the SBC was responsible for operating a system of means-tested welfare benefits, to which Richard Titmuss had always been opposed. When invited to join the Community Relations Commission in 1968, he hesitated until he knew that the Archbishop of Canterbury, Michael Ramsey, was to be its Chairman.[7] Prime Minister Harold Wilson wanted to offer him a peerage: he declined, although Peter Townsend's memory is that the peerage was offered to all three Titmice, and that Townsend refused on behalf of them all.[8] When radical fevers gripped student bodies and the world in the late 1960s, Richard Titmuss aligned himself, not with struggling youth, but with property-owners and defenders of rule-bound institutions. There was one exception: his work for the Community Relations Commission and for the body that preceded it, the National Committee for Commonwealth Immigrants, itself established in the wake of a committee Richard Titmuss helped to set up in 1962 to contest a proposed restrictive Commonwealth Immigrants Bill. He wasn't hesitant in the cause of combating racism, about writing headline-worthy letters to newspapers and politicians, even threatening at one stage to desert the Labour Party.[9] (It's always been more respectable to argue about racism than about sexism.) By the late 1960s, Richard Titmuss had decisively become an establishment figure. That establishment loyalty was both cause and effect of the disintegration of the Titmice. There were major arguments with Peter Townsend and with Tony Lynes who, although not strictly a Titmouse, contributed labours without which aspects of their work wouldn't have been possible. John Vaizey, whose liaison with Brian Abel-Smith had been responsible for Brian's introduction to Richard, also came to feel that Richard was a good deal more ordinary and humanly imperfect than appeared from his saintly image.

In the Oakleys' Chiswick house we heard fragments about these professional dislocations and difficulties. We knew (how could we not, when it was all over the newspapers?) that, during the student troubles at LSE, Richard Titmuss stood on the anti-student platform alongside Walter Adams, LSE's new Director, suspected of racist leanings, through his association with Ian Smith's Rhodesia. We heard about the suggested peerage and indicated that it wasn't an idea we liked very much. We knew, and I argued, about my father's position, wearing his SBC establishment hat, on welfare benefits for unmarried women. In his 1950s writings, he had noted the iniquitous practice whereby elderly widows who were found to be cohabiting with elderly (or presumably any) men would have their pensions withdrawn.[10] But as Deputy Chairman of the SBC he supported the notorious 'cohabitation rule' which removed welfare benefits from women discovered by armies of what the media called 'sex snoopers' to be having sex with men. The SBC's 1971 report on the cohabitation rule, largely written by Richard Titmuss himself, was strongly defensive of the administrative need to distinguish between female welfare claimants who were genuinely single from those who were not.[11] The system itself, from its beginning in the 1948 National Insurance Act, demeaningly supposed the generic financial dependence of women on men. This meant that private lives had to be investigated by public officials. The Titmuss solution was better training for the officials who did this, and more efficient professionalised social work services (a point perhaps a little at odds with his earlier distaste for professionalising social workers). Titmuss's position on women and welfare benefits was complicated and contradictory.[12] It embraced at least some of the traditional demonisation of lone mothers long practised by powerful male elites.[13] He disliked sex-snooping, but loved the traditional family. Abolishing the cohabitation rule was tantamount to advocating the abolition of the family – a clarion call that only his feminist daughter was equipped to make. We argued explicitly about this. I remember especially a horrible dispute that happened on the doorstep of the house in Acton. Actually, I suppose the dispute had started before this, but it got worse as I left the house, or I left because it got worse. How could he defend, I pleaded, a system which treats women as prostitutes, earning their keep with sex? My father's counter-argument was that unmarried people can't be treated more favourably than married ones. You see (I said, but he didn't), the real inequity is marriage itself.

It all happened at about the same time: my marriage and motherhood and 'conversion' to feminism; my father's elevations and establishment posts; the fall-outs between and around the Titmice; the disputations of the student and youth movements, and their particular manifestations at LSE. It's as though the politics of the time and the disturbances of power wouldn't leave us alone. It's easy to see how Richard Titmuss might have become an embittered man, and perhaps also not impossible to understand how his own attachment to power might have helped to drive some of the conflicts that embittered him. This must be one reason why the papers and letters relating to the troubles of the 1960s weren't placed by my mother after he died with all the other Titmuss papers in the LSE Archives; why, in fact, they have sat for many years, quietly awaiting their due moment, in box files in a cupboard at the top of my house.

Like the letters to and from John Vaizey preserved in the files, the Titmuss–Townsend correspondence is warm and friendly and mostly quite straightforward, until in 1963 Peter Townsend decides that he wants to move on from LSE to the new University of Essex, which holds the promise of welcome new challenges – more recruitment of students from working-class backgrounds, a common first year, a student voice in academic governance. He's approached by the Vice-Chancellor, Albert Sloman, a man with radical ideas about higher education being an activity which should integrate, rather than divide, teachers and students; Sloman invites Townsend to take the first Chair in Sociology at Essex. Townsend's letter to Titmuss announcing this is so concerned about Richard's reaction ('I have the uneasy feeling that if I decide to accept the chance ... you will be disappointed in me') that it doesn't actually say the decision has been taken.[14] There was a 'very uncomfortable meeting' in the Blue Plaque House during which Titmuss tried to persuade Townsend not to leave LSE.[15] But Townsend wants to work in a place where sociology and social administration aren't so firmly divided as they are at LSE: the Sloman vision is all about breaking down the divisions between subjects and providing students with a good generalist education. Townsend has been promised protected research money. While he knows he's helping to break up the federation of the Titmice, redistribution of their talents would surely mean greater influence for their ideas – the Labour Party and/or the government will find it easier to use them if they don't all belong to one place.[16]

From his new base in Essex, Townsend became a co-founder in 1965 of the national campaigning charity the Child Poverty Action Group. In November 1968, Richard read in the newspaper a report of a speech Peter Townsend had given in Belfast to its Northern Ireland branch. According to the newspaper, Peter accused the SBC of behaving like the old Poor Law in its inhumane administration of means tests and neglect of the principle of welfare rights. Families with children were, he said, especially badly affected, and information on who is entitled to what was still largely secret. As Deputy Chairman of the SBC, Richard Titmuss took these comments very much to heart, and extremely personally. When Townsend sent Titmuss a copy of his speech, he got in return a ten-page (single-spaced on foolscap paper) letter defending the SBC's practices.[17] Titmuss instigated a behind-the-scenes investigation of a case Townsend had quoted, that of a 35-year-old man with epilepsy and a wife and children to support. The Jackson family had their benefits reduced because the manager of the local Social Security Office calculated that they had been overpaid. On behalf of the Child Poverty Action Group, Townsend had argued that this was wrong, and that the family was also being denied exceptional needs payments to cover the purchase of essential clothing, furniture and coal. The behind-the-scenes investigation concluded that recovering the overpayment had probably not been a good idea, but that the exceptional needs payment agreed had taken this into account. The tone of the letter is conciliatory, but officious.

Poorly husbanded correspondence and faded news cuttings are a fragile basis for determining the merits and demerits of such conflicts. But the hurt on both sides jumps out of the spaces between the words. In a last attempt to bridge the chasm that had developed, Peter Townsend wrote at the end of 1971 to ask for Richard Titmuss's help in securing more funding from the Rowntree Trust for his poverty project. He wanted Titmuss, as a past Chairman of the Trust's Advisory Committee, to read some draft chapters. Titmuss, however, was 'suffering from a surfeit of commitments and paper' and wished to be excused this duty.[18] Kay Titmuss's outrage at Peter Townsend's behaviour was almost more than her husband's, but both of them were quite uncompromising about what they read as a betrayal. The betrayal of what by whom was never spelt out. 'My sharpest memory is of a day shortly before Richard died,' wrote Peter Townsend in his diary. 'I took two huge bowls of planted white hyacinth bulbs which he could watch grow and flower. I said I did not want to be invited in and disturb them. At the door neither of them seemed to know how to react – as if they didn't know how to build bridges.'[19]

Richard Titmuss's defence of welfare rights was non-empirical: he never carried out any research of his own which exposed him to ordinary people's lives and experiences. He lacked a background in tramping the streets and politely intruding into people's private domestic spaces in the name of social science. In this he differed from Peter Townsend's extensive experience of qualitative interviewing, and his deeply-felt and acted-on empiricism. A similar dynamic underlay Richard Titmuss's arguments with Tony Lynes about the O'Brien affair. By the time this happened, in 1969–71, Tony had also been away from LSE for some years. He had reluctantly left LSE in 1965 for a temporary civil service post in the Ministry of National Insurance, and was then recruited as Secretary of the Child Poverty Action Group. In 1969 he had taken on the role of Family Casework Organiser (what today we would call a 'welfare rights officer') with Oxfordshire Children's Department. It was in this capacity that he encountered the O'Briens and their financial problems. Mr and Mrs O'Brien had seven children, and not enough money to live on, as neither had a job. Mrs O'Brien had the children to look after, and Mr O'Brien had chronic health problems. The affair that caught the attention of Richard Titmuss and other SBC officials was the matter of how Department of Health and Social Security benefit officers in Banbury, Oxfordshire, interpreted a 'reasonable' level of material help for such a family. Tony Lynes helped the O'Briens with their appeal against what he and they regarded as an unreasonable interpretation. When Richard Titmuss read in the newspaper (again) of Lynes' speech at a housing charity conference citing the O'Brien case, he again sprang into action in defence of the SBC, and wrote to ask for details. Like Townsend, Lynes received a dense ticking-off letter signed by Richard, but drafted by the Chairman of the SBC, Lord Collison, who also wrote an equally dense five-page (single-spaced on foolscap paper) letter to Richard Titmuss detailing all the minutiae of the O'Briens' situation.[20] Much appeared to hang on the fact that Mrs O'Brien didn't want a second-hand cooker. There is something dreadfully depressing about these men discussing the domestic tools of poor women.

Looking back on all this now, Tony Lynes is of the opinion that it must have been hard for Richard Titmuss to have the SBC criticised publicly by someone widely known to be one of his disciples. He thinks the pressure for Richard to defend the SBC came mainly from SBC officials.[21] Lynes' own departure from LSE for a more practical career at the coalface of the struggle for welfare rights fell short of Richard Titmuss's own academic aspirations for him, and certainly deprived him of a valuable aide. Tony Lynes was Richard Titmuss's particular protégée, an indefatigable pursuer of Titmuss/Titmice research questions, and someone whose work contributing to the Titmuss/Titmice influence on policy was much more important than most accounts acknowledge. His original short-term research appointment at LSE in 1958 had transmuted into the title of Richard Titmuss's 'personal research assistant' after Titmuss had complained to the Director about the heavy administrative burden of running the Department.[22] Tony Lynes was a solution to his overload problem. The moment when Titmuss discovered, during the protracted course of the O'Brien affair, that Lynes had booked a room at LSE to give some seminars on supplementary benefit appeals, without telling him, marked the crossing of an invisible line. Lynes says Titmuss was right to be angry but he had booked the LSE room because he still regarded himself as 'part of the LSE set up'. The day was saved by Brian Abel-Smith's mediating skills: he arranged for the seminars to become 'official'.[23]

Like Peter Townsend, Tony Lynes discovered that working on the ground with people the welfare state was supposed to benefit revealed cracks and weaknesses, not only in the mechanics of the system, but in its very conception. Both Lynes and Townsend had entered into the uncertain land between public policy and activism. This wasn't a place with which Richard Titmuss was familiar or in which he felt at home. It was partly an academic question: were employees of universities *supposed* to engage in overt political activity, tying the products of their research and scholarship directly into programmes of reform? The dissensions of the anxious sixties did spark defensive reactions in some quarters, and this was one of them: that universities lie outside the sphere of political action, and whatever is taught and learnt in them should be corralled safely away from any contamination with real-world politics. It was one reason the early social workers eschewed a university connection; they wanted the freedom to carry out their surveys and enquiries and then to promote remedial action without being rebuked for improper institutional behaviour. In the approaching end of the Titmice there were echoes of this historical ambivalence about where universities stand in relation to the national welfare, and about what is political behaviour and what is not. When Lynes started as Titmuss's research assistant, he knew that the Titmice had been working with the Labour Party on national superannuation, but 'I was surprised and perhaps even a bit shocked by the extent of their involvement as members of Crossman's Social Policy Committee ... I thought academics were supposed to maintain a façade of political neutrality. We certainly didn't.'[24]

Because they never worked together, John Vaizey – he who had originally introduced two of the Titmice to one another – could develop a critical position on Richard Titmuss's philosophy without threatening collaborative relationships. They may not have worked directly together, but Vaizey's first book, *The costs of education*, published in 1958, followed a Titmuss suggestion that education was ripe for such an analysis, which would parallel the investigation Titmuss and Abel-Smith had carried out of the costs of the National Health Service.[25] Vaizey and Titmuss were friends, but after 1960 the warm and funny letters from foreign and domestic climes in the box file dry up. What happened? John Vaizey offended many of his friends by eventually leaving the Labour Party, and, although this didn't happen until some years after Richard Titmuss died, his move to the right was obvious much earlier. Having been enthusiastic in the 1950s about the potential of sociology to influence public policy, disenchantment with both sociology and socialism set in. Vaizey said he couldn't support any of the main Labour policies, which were all half-hearted or harmful or both, that the Labour membership was 'swamped by bombastic polytechnic lecturers regurgitating inaccurately the half-baked ideas of sentimental Marxists', and that, in the presence of a culture of corrupted and corrupting institutions, it was best for people to have as much control as possible over their own lives. Hence his embrace of what he called 'Tory pragmatism'.[26]

John Vaizey was a quixotic and volatile figure, with an intellect − 'a mind like quicksilver'[27] − that could well have been too sharp for his own good. He was made a life peer by Harold Wilson in 1976, left the Labour Party in 1978, and became a staunch admirer of Margaret Thatcher, offering his services as her economic adviser. His modestly short volume *In breach of promise* was published in 1983, and is far from immodest in the analysis it offers of Richard Titmuss's contribution to social policy. Along with four other men 'who shaped a generation' − Hugh Gaitskell, Iain Macleod, Anthony Crosland, and Edward Boyle − Vaizey argued that Titmuss failed to come to grips satisfactorily with some of the most fundamental issues of our time. This was despite his brilliance as a demographer and social historian, his accomplishments as 'a backroom ideas man for the Labour Party', and his creation of the new discipline of social administration. He was not an original thinker, and his lack of formal education showed in his inability to follow through the logic of his own arguments about the mechanisms supporting inequality. The particular logic that eluded him was that the goals of social policy must include economic growth.[28] John Vaizey's criticisms of the Labour Party embraced those who, like Richard Titmuss, were unfailingly loyal to it. It looks as though John's own move to the right caused Richard's displeasure, and it was this displeasure, in a man who was doing the same thing in a different way, that brought about another unbridgeable rift.

Among all these troubles were The Troubles themselves. In some accounts they were one trouble, in others two or more. The arguments that rocked LSE in the late 1960s did have two distinct phases, the first in 1966–67, the second in 1968–69, with a quieter intercessory year. Richard Titmuss had been a professor at LSE for 16 years when these Troubles began. From being an upstart in charge of squabbling 'lady midwives', he had firmly taken up residence as a dependably loyal member of LSE's academic governance. LSE was no longer the place it had been, either in its heyday as the infant child of Sidney and Beatrice Webb – the great hope of Fabian socialism – or in 1950 when Richard Titmuss arrived. A survey of student opinion uncovered reports of incompetent and arrogant teaching by academics who treated their posts as sinecures and students as inconvenient intercessors in armchair scholarship (another recurrent problem with academia). The expansion of higher education meant many more students, and the buildings were seriously overcrowded. Far more students came from abroad, especially from the USA. Tuition fees for overseas students had been substantially increased, with resulting protests (and accusations of discrimination) from some students and academics at LSE. When the Students' Union decided in 1964 to boycott South African goods on LSE premises, it discovered it had no power to enforce such a move. There followed demands for more say in the running of the School and more financial support from central funds for Union activities. In 1966, Richard Titmuss, four other LSE professors and eight other members of a specially set-up Selection Committee invited a man called Walter Adams to become the new Director of LSE.[29] Walter Adams had been Secretary at LSE in the late 1930s, and had masterminded the School's wartime decampment to Cambridge. Since then he had acquired a politically awkward pedigree. As Principal of the University College of Rhodesia and Nyasaland (present-day Zimbabwe, Zambia and Malawi), he was running a multiracial institution in a racist society and treading a precarious path between upholding democratic principles in theory and enacting them in practice. He seemed to be fonder of theory than practice, although his reticent manner made it difficult to work out what he *did* actually believe.

The time, the context, and the already pugilist attitude of the Students' Union meant that Walter Adams wasn't a wise choice for the LSE Directorship. The 1960s were years of ferment against war (in Vietnam and with biological and nuclear weapons) and for democratic rights (of black people, workers, women). The student activism at LSE was part of a global dissent movement against the Cold War, human rights injustices and the destructive workings of capitalism.[30] Many young people found their feet and voices in this dissenting world through the politics of the peace and anti-nuclear movements. In Britain, there were annual marches from the Aldermaston weapons research centre 50 miles outside London to a rally in Trafalgar Square, and there were the passive resisters of Bertrand Russell's breakaway Committee of 100. 'Passive protest, massive removal', proclaimed *The Observer* on 30 April 1961, next to a photograph of seated students quietly regarding a mêlée of helmeted policeman in the middle of Whitehall. Richard Titmuss's 17-year-old daughter smiles at the left-hand edge of the photo in her regulation duffle coat and CND badge. It was all great fun, but fun for a great purpose. Hundreds of explanations have been advanced for this international strike against authority, observes Ralf Dahrendorf, another LSE Director, but the point was that it had an 'almost existential quality'.[31] Young people – this was very much a generational conflict – wanted everything now. 'Beware the pedagogic gerontocracy,' declared one of the student banners. They wanted to be rid of the old authoritarianism, and they wanted a legitimate hand in shaping a revitalised social order.[32]

A significant proportion of the LSE student body – some 40% – was involved in the dramas that followed, which centred initially on protest against Adams' appointment. Richard Titmuss sided with those who defended, not only the appointment, but the responsibility of the School to make such decisions without any student consultation. At the end of January 1967 (the very month Richard Titmuss's grandson was born), a student 'Stop Adams' meeting was banned by the existing Director, Sydney Caine, and the School Secretary, Harry Kidd. The Old Theatre in the main LSE building in Houghton Street had been booked for the meeting; its doors were barred by porters, and the Director even had the light fuses removed so the room (which was windowless) became pitch black. Some students decided to ignore their exclusion and pushed past, holding candles to provide light. One of the porters fell over and others came to his aid, including one, Edward Poole, who was 64 and close to retirement. He had a heart attack and died. 'The death of a college porter in front of a student mob at the London School of Economics,' announced *The Times* imperiously, 'brings into our midst a nastiness that many people supposed could only be found abroad.'[33] Poole was known to have had a weak heart, but had it been a normal day and had he gone home as usual, he might have had a longer life.[34]

In the aftermath of the Old Theatre fracas, a Committee of Inquiry was set up, several students – 'not dishonourable young men', according to their tutors – were disciplined, and two were suspended.[35] These were David Adelstein, President of the Students' Union, and Marshall Bloom, President of the Graduate Students' Association. Under *The Guardian* newspaper's headline of 4 February 1967, '124 of LSE teaching staff condemn student behaviour', Titmuss is mentioned as the first distinguished signatory of a strongly worded public statement condemning student criticisms of Adams' appointment. When the LSE authorities refused to lift Adelstein and Bloom's suspensions, a mass student boycott of lectures and a sit-in followed. It lasted eight days. There was no violence, in fact a good deal of fun was had by all: 'The lobby and corridors of the main building were filled with students sitting on the floors, holding seemingly endless discussions … reading, singing, eating, or just sleeping. The blackboards normally displaying neatly written notices of school functions bore boldly drawn slogans, and banners were draped from the walls.'[36] In the face of this disturbing (dis)order, the suspended students were allowed back, and Adams crept in quietly and took up his post. There were a few minor changes, including the departure to the much more suitable locale of an Oxford college of the School's Secretary, Harry Kidd, who had played a key anti-student role. Kidd's book, *The trouble at LSE*, is a decidedly one-sided account. The copy in my possession carries the dedication 'for Richard Titmuss with gratitude for many acts of kindness', and in the file is a letter from Titmuss to Kidd congratulating him on a 'most elegantly written account', 'a judicious blend of wit, tolerance and firmness'.[37]

In this letter Richard Titmuss asserts that he wasn't nearly as engaged in this Trouble as many of his colleagues. He played a more obviously prominent role in phase two which began in October 1968. There was to be a national demonstration against the war in Vietnam, and the Students' Union proposed offering LSE as a sanctuary for medical aid and political discussion during the demonstration. Walter Adams decided to close the building. His action was viewed as inflammatory, and the South African dimension was re-ignited when it came to light that a number of LSE governors held South African investments. At a meeting with the Students' Union, the new Chairman of the Governors, the right-wing economist Lionel Robbins – a man about whose sympathies Richard Titmuss had long complained, but with whom he now joined forces in objecting to the students' actions – was also interrogated about a series of seven steel 'security' gates that Adams had had installed to exclude 'unauthorized access' to School buildings.[38] These were embedded in concrete, a serious business. In his letter to the Students' Union, Adams took an unpersuasively bureaucratic line in quoting fire regulations and the need for special access after events such as student dances as reasons for the gates' appearance.[39] The Students' Union declared that the gates must be taken down within seven days, or they would do it themselves. They weren't, so they did, with instruments variously described as one or several pick-axes, sledgehammers and/or crowbars, and crucially with a pneumatic drill loaned from strikers at the Barbican.[40] The police were called, the School was closed and the hundred or so students who had repaired to the bar were asked to come out one by one so that the perpetrators could be identified by staff. A few weeks later the Board of Governors issued a dictate that the School would take disciplinary action against any students who deliberately disrupted lectures, and that it was the staff's continuing responsibility to identify by name any and all of them. In Richard Titmuss's Department, one of his staff sent a memo to her colleagues offering to attend their lectures in order to assist with this provocatively burdensome duty.[41] The School was closed for 25 days, 30 students were arrested, injunctions were taken out against 13 of them, and two lecturers were disciplined. One of these, Nicholas Bateson, said that tearing the gates down was required in order for proper solidarity to be shown with Rhodesian Africans, Thai guerrillas and Palestinians Arabs. The other, Robin Blackburn – a more theoretically minded man – called the gates 'the material expression of class oppression'.[42]

Richard Titmuss used his position on the Standing Committee of the School to mount a vehement attack on the students and the dissenting lecturers. He wrote to the School's Deputy Academic Registrar in May 1969, with a story about his own personal experience. He had attended a lecture given by the political economist Professor Alan Day and had been appalled at the heckling behaviour of some students: Day had been forced to stop through sheer physical exhaustion. Titmuss said that he and Hilde Himmelweit, Britain's first Professor of Social Psychology at LSE, tried to reason with the students, but were similarly shouted down.[43] He also wrote to Robin Blackburn: 'the last time this happened to me was in the East End of London in the 1930s, when I tried to speak against the Mosley invasion'. He emphasised his belief as a socialist in freedom of speech and conscience and asked Blackburn to do what he could to preserve those freedoms at the School.[44]

Blackburn and Bateson were sacked, and their appeals against this did not succeed, since the whole appeals process was, according to Blackburn, partisan and improper, as you would expect from 'the entire clique of self-appointed capitalist manipulators' who ran LSE.[45] It was 30 years before he was able to get another academic job. Even Townsend, trying to recruit him for the excitingly radical University of Essex, was stymied in this plan by the legacy of the Troubles: Vice-Chancellor Sloman vetoed the appointment.[46]

Events at LSE were part of a widespread questioning by students of institutional authority, and by young people generally of the pro-war and anti-democratic tone of government and public policy. University campuses became battlegrounds for political change, not only in Britain, but in Brazil, Czechoslovakia, France, Germany, Italy, Jamaica, Japan, Mexico, Poland, Spain, and of course the USA. The LSE version was actually relatively mild. Ted Short, the Secretary of State for Education and Science, spoke in the House of Commons at the end of January 1969, about the LSE Troubles, wanting to reassure the public that most students were law-abiding. The main problem, he declared, was the Americans: 'These gentlemen [sic] are clearly not here to study. They are here to disrupt and undermine British institutions. This small group are the thugs of the academic world'.[47] Short was wrong: it wasn't an American conspiracy, although one of the two students suspended in phase one of the Troubles, Marshall Bloom, had been involved in American civil rights protests before he became a graduate student at LSE. After the LSE Troubles were over, Bloom returned to the USA. On being called up for military service in Vietnam, he committed suicide.

Less dramatically, at ex-Titmouse Peter Townsend's Essex, there were peaceful sit-ins around the idea of a 'free university'. Three students were suspended for demonstrating against a visiting scientist from the government germ warfare outfit at Porton Down. Like most of that University's staff, Peter Townsend was in favour of a full inquiry, during which the students could put their side of the story. Because he was misquoted in newspaper reports, he found it necessary to write to the other two Titmice to put the record straight.[48] He already knew that in LSE's disputes with its unhappy students, Richard Titmuss wasn't as sympathetic to the student viewpoint as he was. A news cutting about events at Essex in Richard Titmuss's files has passages marked in red biro about the university administration there being viewed by students as repressive and distant, and discontented students reacting with violence against university property. This was something else Titmuss and Townsend couldn't agree about. Under the caption 'The case of two superbrains who didn't hit it off to a T', the *Daily Mirror* reported at the end of 1970 how the gulf between Titmuss and Townsend had been gossip in left-wing circles for some time. Townsend's active campaigning against the Labour Government's poverty policy was proof that he had supplanted Titmuss in power and influence: 'The guru has had to give way to his vigorous disciple'.[49]

When Tessa Blackstone and Roger Hadley in Titmuss's own Department, and with the help of two statistical colleagues at LSE, undertook to find out by asking the students about the extent of their support for the Troubles, the finger was pointed, not at the Americans, but at students of social science who were considerably more likely than their peers in other disciplines to have taken part in the boycott and the sit-in. Sociology and anthropology produced the most troublesome students; geography the least. This high profile of social science as a disciplinary base for student protest reflected an international pattern, and so did the theme of student dissatisfaction with the neglectful behaviour of academic staff towards them.[50]

Another social scientist at LSE, another David, did for the Troubles what David Donnison did for the LSE Affair. David Downes, a criminologist, sent his account of the Troubles to Richard Titmuss for comment. Richard Titmuss complained that because of the Troubles he had been forced to withdraw proposals for a course on community relations, which had been one of the most difficult decisions of his life. So he wasn't in the mood to comment on Downes' piece, except to object to his characterisation of the School as 'profoundly authoritarian'. What were Downes' criteria for saying this? Was he making a statement about how LSE compared to other universities here and abroad, and, if so, what was his evidence? Titmuss ended by saying that, in approaching retirement himself, he was still not clear about how to combine academic freedom with centralised decision-making about the allocation of resources and the maintenance of standards in teaching and research.[51] From his daughter's vantage point, elsewhere in the university Richard Titmuss knew intimately, this remains a gravely unsolved problem.

The day after Richard Titmuss died, Walter Adams wrote to his widow:

> Perhaps it helps a little for you to know how all of us at the School admired Richard and were so proud of him – his imperishable contributions to … the betterment of our national life … his brilliant teaching, and the shaping of thousands of men and women who were his students, colleagues and disciples. He was a giant who made all life seem greater and nobler … But for me it is his friendship that was the most precious gift. From the moment I returned to the School he gave me an affection that was inspiring and of immense help … I was too shy to tell him that I worshipped him and loved him … Richard's great spirit cannot die.[52]

13

Dusting his bookshelves

Abolish the role of housewife
AND THE FAMILY!

To read Dr Ann Oakley's analysis of housework and her portrait of the housewife, is to go on a voyage into despair.

John Allan, Staff correspondent in London, reviews two books due in Australia this year.

Almost all housework is disliked by almost all housewives, Dr Oakley has found. The housewife herself is a victim of our male-oriented and dominated culture, programmed to accept her victimisation.

From this pattern of treadmill labour, passive acceptance, largely inarticulate resentment and the loneliness of the home emerge non-persons prone to unsourced dissatisfactions and undiagnosed depressions treated by unsympathetic doctors with tranquilisers and sleeping tablets.

lished last November, and Housewife, originally the 10 central chapters of The Sociology of Housework, published last October.

Dr Oakley, a slim, calm and gentle-voiced mother of a boy, 8, and a girl, 6, is 31 and lives with her husband in a grey street in a lower middle-class area

What we inherit from our parents – their treatment of us and the shaping of this by the conditions of their own lives – is a multilayered gift or burden. People who reduce it to a simple formula, a common feature of profit-driven celebrity memoirs, are deceiving themselves as well as us. At my school we sang a hymn which opened with the invocation 'Let us now praise famous men'. As a female child, standing there in the school hall with some six hundred other girls and a staff of women teachers, I found this odd: why were we praising famous *men*, where were those men, who were they, and what exactly were they supposed to have done for us? This cryptic celebration of masculinity was one of many taken-for-granted habits of the time in girls' education.[1]

I couldn't have emerged from childhood as the daughter of Richard Titmuss without being a socialist of some kind. I understood from very early on that the point of being on this earth is to work for the public welfare, not for private aggrandisement. I learnt that this means supporting public sector institutions like the NHS and state-funded education. By a process of permeation rather than direct appreciation, I saw that gross inequalities of income, resources and life chances are morally wrong and corrosive of a healthy society. My induction into socialism was a matter of emotion rather than reason. The reason came later. And with it, because I was a woman, came the additional perception that from the pursuit of class equality you cannot reasonably exclude equality between the classes of men and women. The problem was – I now see but didn't then – that the politics of post-war reconstruction in which our family was embedded drew the social classes but not the genders together. The democratic ideal of one nation took as its binding ideal The Family as the nub of The Community. Equality for women meant complementary difference, not self-governing autonomy.[2]

There was no moment of sudden revelation, and not much revelation at all until after I stopped living in the Blue Plaque House and became a discontented suburban housewife. Then I was absorbed into a process of epiphany which embraced no less than the discovery of gender, the academic study of women's labour, and the politics of feminism. My nuclear family and I moved from the colourful Chiswick house, driven out by cacophonous neighbours, to a small tower of a house in Ealing, still within easily reachable distance of my parents, but with the advantage of standing absolutely on its own. We bought the house from a now famous conductor and his family, who took all the doorknobs with them. In the new quiet house Robin and I both had book-lined studies, but he, a proper teaching academic, had more books in his than I had in mine. I was still hovering on the edge of fiction and fact, uncertain whether I should go on trying to be a novelist or should turn instead to social science. In this hovering period, I wrote two unpublished (but not unpublishable) novels and many short stories; resorted to market research as a source of income; researched higher education for a friend of my father's and the careers of medical graduates for a doctor in Edinburgh; trekked bemused round London schools as a researcher on a project about how they treated 'immigrant' children (badly); was commissioned to produce several scripts for children's television; marked A-level sociology examination papers (resigning when they introduced different codes for female and male candidates); and tried my hand at converting my father's social history of the Second World War into a children's book – a project the publisher and I amicably agreed to abandon, since it was obvious to both of us that my heart wasn't in it.

In this interregnum between the end of university and the beginning of what people today think of as Ann Oakley, I also did some interviewing for another of Richard Titmuss's projects – the Institute of Community Studies. We had to write the kind of entertaining descriptions of homes and the people in them that the Institute staff could turn into readable, but not necessarily very scientific, books. 'The flat is in the basement with a dark and dingy front door ... Mrs L took me to a room at the back, which has a kitchen leading off it. Both were very poorly furnished ... Mrs L is a small woman with glasses and an apparently timid manner. She speaks very quietly and appears shy, but in fact she does have very strong opinions. Her hair, which is frizzy, is parted in the middle and pinned back either side and forms two wings either side of her face.'[3] In pre-electronic days, these observations had to be inscribed long-hand in notebooks and then typed out at home on foolscap paper, carefully interleaved with sheets of shiny black carbon paper.

It was perhaps partly the equation between men and intellectual talk that kept me hovering for so long. This insight is derived from reading other women social scientists' accounts of their careers. A background of politically radical male talk, such as I experienced, seems particularly likely to generate indecisive daughters.[4] Most of the talk about equality in my parents' house *was* done by men, by the quietly radical R.H. Tawney, the passionate Peter Townsend, the blue-eyed nobleman Brian Abel-Smith, the too-clever economist John Vaizey, and by the politicians who wanted to do as well as talk: Peter Shore, Richard Crossman, the men from Mauritius. 'Let us now praise famous men' – the school song was right after all. Removing the men from one's head – undoing the unwritten equation between intellectual talk and masculinity – is hard, even for the most determined feminist sociologist.

A prime feature of memory imposes itself on all my recollections of those years – that scenes are remembered with the self within these, so that one gazes down as an outsider on the inside past. I wrote about a particular moment in *Taking it like a woman*, a moment when I realised how badly sociologists had treated the domestic labour of women; I described a scene in which I watched myself dusting my husband's bookshelves and taking down a study of factory workers called *Alienation and freedom*. This newly dusted volume said that women could never be alienated in the paid workforce because they were so intrinsically satisfied with their labours at home. I certainly read that book and many others like it, but I can see now how the creative, rather than sociological, imagination may well have been at work in producing that account of a revelationary moment. There she is, dusting the bookshelves, while the little children clamour round her feet and their father is away at The University teaching people how to understand the social world (but not, yet, her place in it). There she is, including everything she will become – the doyenne of *The sociology of housework*, the discoverer of gender, the interviewer of women, the purveyor of stories about childbirth, the closet novelist, the sociologist of methodology, the biographer, the autobiographer, even the unpopular advocate of experimental social science and evidence-based policy. The stories of our lives have to be condensed and elliptical because otherwise they're boring and the central themes get lost. We must convince ourselves as well as others of logic, linearity, evolutionary progress: it *was* like this, it *must* have been, because it's such a good story.

Richard Titmuss never wrote about housework, just as he never did any. He played to the old stereotype of the absent-minded professor, whose head is so much in the clouds of abstract thought that he doesn't notice the odd socks he's put on, the train that's going to the wrong place, the leg of a study table smouldering from its proximity to an electric fire. These events and many more were enthusiastically recited by my mother as evidence of my father's domestic incapacity. It was her way of justifying her own role. *Her* domestic management was an essential pre-condition of *his* intellectual prowess: indeed, without her, he would scarcely be alive. The lesson a daughter learns from this is that intellectual and domestic work inhabit completely different spheres. The busy housewife looks after the thoughtful man, and they talk about equality without knowing what they're talking about. I didn't read what the thoughtful men who talked in the Blue Plaque House wrote then, but, when I did, I was floored by the conundrum that they, too, seemed to assume the *Alienation and freedom* line – women's labour ties them to a natural world of love and care, whereas men exist in an historically contingent material place which is also the domain of public policy.

'Few subjects are more surrounded with prejudice and moral platitude than this,' noted Richard Titmuss in 1952, when I was eight, of the 'conflict' between women's 'roles as mothers, wives and wage-earners'.[5] The result was a whole new set of social problems. He didn't elaborate on these, except to point out that the biggest growth in women's employment was among married women who were also mothers. Changes in industrial employment were affecting men's attitudes to the home, he said; thus, alienated husbands might be becoming more domesticated, more willing to play with the children, help with the shopping and even visit the launderette.[6] I wonder how he knew?

I wonder, too, whether he saw the division of labour in his own home as a matter of prejudice and/or conflict. Maybe he saw his own daughter as a social problem when she began a doctoral research project on women's experiences of housework. Like most social scientists at the time, Richard Titmuss saw housework as a non-sociological topic. British sociology was occupied in the 1950s and 1960s by a complacently masculine model; the social world was divided into topics – stratification, deviance, industry and work, the family and marriage, political institutions, and so forth – none of which recognised their masculine bias, and all of which excluded any kind of focused gender analysis. 'We are, for practical purposes in a male world,' commented an anthropologist, with that important outsider vision.'The study of women is on a level little higher than the study of ducks and fowls ... a mere bird-watching indeed.'[7] When the sociologists Alva Myrdal and Viola Klein put forward their analysis of *Women's two roles: Home and work* in 1956 – one of the first publications to take the issue of women and the social structure seriously – they had to break through an attitude of condescending male hilarity. The eminent male sociologist who edited the *International Library of Sociology* at the time, Jack Sprott, referred to their manuscript as 'On les girls' and rejected it.[8] This was a thoroughly 'gentlemanly social science' in sociologist Mike Savage's phrase, biased in class as well as gender terms. It was gentlemanly in three ways: in assuming both men's domination over women and the domination of trade and empire over industry and manufacturing, and in depending on an élite infrastructure of gentlemanly schools, universities and labour markets.[9] The centre, the focus, the anchor, the energy of gentlemanly social science in the 1950s and 1960s in Britain was LSE, just as earlier it had performed the same function for gentlewomanly social work.

My own initiation into academic social science repeated the pattern of Daddy's men which had dominated my teenage years. Hence the escapades into the higher education research, textbook-writing and the fabulous world of the Institute of Community Studies. When I registered for my PhD, it was at Bedford College, where my husband taught sociology, and where my father's friend and ally in university business, O.R. McGregor, ran a sociology department. The man who agreed to supervise my PhD had achieved his own only with the support of my father, who had been one of his examiners, and who had successfully fended off the criticism of the other one. I managed my PhD with the help of a postgraduate studentship from what was then called the Social Science Research Council. My father had been a founder member of this. Among his papers is a photograph of the SSRC's very first meeting on 21 January 1966: 17 men and two women, one of them a secretary, earnestly peering at the camera from behind a large octagonal desk sprinkled with clumpy glass ashtrays.

One of the SSRC's rules for postgraduate studentships was that married women should get less money than married men or unmarried people. This is the direct parallel of the Supplementary

Benefits Commission's treatment of women. Richard Titmuss concurred with the view that marriage entailed a state of dependence for women. Marriage had physically liberated his daughter from dependence on the Blue Plaque House, but had thus replaced this with another form of internment.

The effort of recalling that time brings the usual visual images, but these drag along with them an unexpectedly strong current of feeling. The images are static: fixed figures in a landscape of West London interiors: me in the little towered house in Ealing with its recovered doorknobs – the blue tiles on the kitchen wall; the sound of the Underground beyond the allotments beyond the garden where I grew crooked carrots to teach the children where food comes from; our daily routines of school-taking and fetching; the production of meals and children's clothes on that faithful mother-of-pearl-encrusted sewing machine: all that labour which means nothing because women do most of it and yet it's the most important labour in the world. On the margins of these pictures the couple in the Blue Plaque House plough on with their own regime of gender-specific tasks and roles, her anxious about her own health, but determined not to let it show in her housekeeping, in the orchestrated miserliness of her dinner parties; him, gaunt and sage, advising governments, amassing data for his book on altruism and social policy, despairing at the return of a Conservative government in 1970. I flit between these still-lifes in my head, but what remains constant is a naive indignation, a sense of disbelief and distress that there could be so much of a gulf between my experience of the world and the theory of the good society within which, and to which, I was brought up. Such dislocations between the lives of parents and their adult children are common, even expected and part of the 'normal' pattern. An important feature of my own position was, however, just this term 'social science'. Were we – my father and I and our respective academic colleagues – not scientists, fact-gatherers, pursuers of evidence about the working of social systems, and did these efforts not reveal an extraordinary tendency, so extreme as to suggest a plot, to devalue the lives and experiences of women? Sexism, patriarchy, whatever you called it, was (is) simply a question of evidence. The evidence was (is) there for anyone to see, but first it must be identified, excoriated and hung out to dry.

As my father struggled to recover from the aftermath of the student rebellion at LSE, and enjoyed a heightened access to the corridors of political power afforded to him and the other Titmice by the Labour government, I joined the women's liberation movement, sold my heavy gold wedding ring, and lost and found myself in late-night consciousness-raising sessions with other like-minded women in West London. Sisterhood was powerful – for a while. Flaky copies of some of the literature we generated repose in my attic – the weekly newsletters, the *Spare Rib*s, the media coverage. The front cover of *The Sunday Times* magazine on 12 September 1971 carried a youthful Germaine Greer laughing in a yellow bikini. Inside were pieces on the housewife's day, pay inequality, obstetric surgery, the argument about misogyny between Kate Millett and Norman Mailer ('What Katy Did to Norman' rather than 'What Norman Did to Katy'), and a reference guide to what was dismissively known in media circles, and so by nearly everybody else, as 'Women's Lib'.

The best questions are the simple ones, but the answers can be complex, especially when the social context is, and there's nothing simple about patriarchy. Why is it assumed that men win bread and women make it? Why does maternal love mean cleaning other people's shit off lavatories and watching out for their delicate egos all the time? I trundled round West London with my old-fashioned tape recorder in a shopping basket relentlessly excavating women's experiences and perspectives, and wrote it all up with the help of what I later learnt was called 'quantitative malestream social science'. I quite possibly wanted my father to admire my chi-squares. On the other hand, I was amazed by their story-telling power, especially since there had been no inkling of this in the dull mathematics teaching at my girls' school. Women, I realised, can easily see themselves as incompetent because launching oneself into masculine zones can be such a frightening business.

It all began to seem very peculiar to me, this cultural and material separation between people who mostly look after homes and families and people who mostly don't. A huge anthropological and historical project therefore got tacked onto the collection of contemporary urban data about women's domestic labours. How do other cultures organise all this? Where did modern Euro-American ideas about the gendering of housework come from? It was wonderful to have a legitimate reason for sitting in libraries, since in libraries it's possible to imagine being a real scholar. Redrawing the lines of the division of labour in my own home, I guarded extremely carefully the prize of one day a week in the University of London Library, in that pale iced cake of a building which Adolf Hitler fancied for his London headquarters and which inspired the Ministry of Truth in George Orwell's *Nineteen Eighty-Four*. Senate House Library suffers quite inexplicably from winds whose howling penetrates the stacks on the upper floors. I've always found it comforting to shelter there, safe from the storms outside and imperviously locked in the quiet reaches of the mind. In those days I would return from the windy heights of truth in the evenings to Ealing on the Underground, a vantage point from which it was possible, because our house was directly and horizontally visible from the train, to see the window of the children's room. The point of this was to observe whether or not the blue blind had been pulled down over the window: a solid blue rectangle meant I could safely return home without having to take over putting-to-bed duties; an empty rectangle was a warning. It sounds calculating and it was. But it was easier for the children, who didn't have to make the Daddy–Mummy transition when they were tired and cranky. It was what women have to do. We have to be calculating because otherwise things fall apart.

I can't tell now whether it was the power of these domestic negotiations or the analysis women in the housework study offered me, but the difference between men helping and women always keeping the responsibility seemed an aspect of domestic life that other people (including Richard Titmuss in his observations about the changing family) hadn't noticed. He 'helps' her with the children or the housework, but the children and the housework remain hers. Such a simple distinction between responsibility and help hadn't apparently been made before. It 'ultimately proved to be an analytically powerful entry' into women's experiences of their labour.[10]

Then I got diverted from writing up the PhD by my first real writing commission, a short book in a series called 'Towards a New Society' which was the brainchild of Paul Barker, the editor of the mildly left-wing social science/policy journal *New Society*. My book

Sex, gender and society, articulated the conceptual distinction which had until then eluded the comprehension of most people (except for grammarians and a few esoteric medics) between the nature of our material bodies, which are sexed, and our cultural selves, which are gendered. The immediate response to the book was a bit puzzled and uneven, but time quickly saw it migrate into 'the standard for most sociology',[11] and 'a feminist primer',[12] enabling a materialist account of women's oppression,[13] by usefully replacing the sociologically jaded language of 'sex roles'.[14] The message spread beyond social science by successfully introducing the term gender into the lexicon of ordinary discourse.[15]

Sex, gender and society was the book my father laid aside without comment when I gave him a copy. Perhaps he didn't think it a serious book. Chapter 1, 'The biology of sex', exposed the reader to explicit diagrams of sexual organs; he wouldn't have felt comfortable with those. Yet this was precisely what social science meant to me: the laying aside of easy judgements, the difficult unearthing of sometimes culturally troubling facts. I was my father's daughter in believing that facts do exist; but we departed from each other's ways of thinking in his preference for micro-level analysis and mine for tangling with concepts and ideologies and beliefs and how these are shaped by social conditions. He did use sociological concepts, but with 'a distinctly poetic licence'.[16]

My book about gender was in the vanguard of that long-drawn-out and unfinished business: the de-masculinisation of social science. This called for fresh methodologies and conceptual tools, much as the women's liberation movement – its political parallel – demanded that women act and organise together in new ways. The conjunction of academic and political/policy enterprises – the reshaping of social science and women's position – was actually absolutely in the tradition of British social science. It ought therefore to have been at least understood, if not embraced, by British social scientists; but the subject was women, so that was that. Reframing the subject as gender, as in my *Sex, gender and society*, made very little difference. Over time, in the 1970s, gender became a pseudonym for women, and then it was eventually returned to sex, so that non-acculturated fetuses and even sperm have gender, which makes them quite unbelievably prescient. I can't emphasise enough the significant failure of both public and academic understandings to grasp that gender is about men as well as women. That's the whole point. I spelt it all out years later in a book called *Gender on planet earth*. My American publisher gave it a pink cover featuring a high-heeled shoe, which said it all.

What happens to texts and ideas and conceptual devices once they're placed in the public domain is beyond the deviser's control. It may be ingenuous, but I didn't anticipate how *Sex, gender and society*, and its two successors, *Housewife* and *The sociology of housework*, would be hailed as 'classic' feminist texts. I didn't write them as political ammunition; they really had the character of what I've written so many of since – research reports. The more academic reviews understood this; they hailed the housework books as 'a fresh and challenging account', replete with 'acute perceptions', although, predictably, some complained that I had underplayed the positive side of home-making.[17] (Housework is always called 'home-making' when people want to beef it up.) The problem with housework is that everyone considers themselves an expert on it; in reality few people are. (My next book will be called *The science of housework*.) The front cover of the women's magazine *Nova* bore a picture of a woman with a cabbage instead of a head, and the script, '"The time has come" the housewives said,/ "To talk of many things:/ Of pay and hours and nursery schools/ Of cabbages and ABOUT TIME TOO!"'[18] We also had, inevitably, 'Kitchen stink',[19] 'Housetrap',[20] 'A dirty business',[21] and, of course, 'A broom of one's own'.[22] The reliably demeaning *Daily Express*'s by-line was 'How Mrs Oakley learned to stop burning beefburgers and live'.[23] Journalists were preoccupied with getting shots of me standing in my own kitchen – much more fun than a serious woman behind a desk. Housework was suddenly media-newsworthy: women had been out of the news for so long, it was safe to let them in slightly for a while. Even Jilly Cooper thought my account made 'pretty good sense', opening her review with: '"I'm going to write about housework this week," I said, "but you never do any," said my neighbour tartly'.[24]

I had forgotten *The sociology of housework*'s dedication until I picked it up today: 'To the memory of my father Richard Titmuss in recognition of a great personal debt, and because, more than twenty years ago, he first drew attention to the sociological neglect of the position of women'. Now I read it I can remember writing it in the hugely emotional aftermath of his death, the tears in my eyes.

The early 1970s, when I was finding my own social science feet and publishing these first books, were years of great personal trouble for my parents. In October, 1971, Richard's sister Gwen, she with the scarred face, errant husband and failing heart, collapsed and died at the age of 65. Their mother, 'The Evil one', who lived with Gwen, was brought to the Blue Plaque House when Gwen became ill, but after a week she was removed to a nearby nursing home. Here she, too, died three months later. That was January 1972. The next month my father developed acute pain in his arm and shoulder, which was diagnosed as muscular-skeletal and treated with physiotherapy. In October, lung cancer, with bone secondaries, was offered as a much more plausible explanation of the pain.

A great deal happened in the 1970s: a revitalised opposition to war and authoritarianism; economic recession and the oil crisis; a new prominence for terrorism and fundamentalism; earthquakes and Margaret Thatcher. It was a busy time for social science, which dutifully spawned new 'sociologies of'. These included the sociology of health and illness, previously known as medical sociology and social medicine. Richard Titmuss wrote about medical sociology, about medicine as a social service, and Ann Oakley started her journey as a sociologist of health and illness with studies of maternity care. His interest was in the NHS as an organisation, in the development of destructive 'organizational fetishes',[25] but he also saw the effect on both providers and users of health care of increasing science and specialisation, the disappearance of whole-person medicine, and the therapeutic importance of courtesy and sociability. Her focus has been on the absence of science from many health care practices, on the risks and long-term impact of intervention. We would, it occurs to me now, have made a good team.

As the sociology both of health and illness and of gender developed, it became increasingly common for social scientists to deploy as data stories from their own lives. Their own lives have always creatively inspired or depressed them, but for a long time the legacy of gentlemanly social science made it impossible to admit this. The told story, the story fixed in a particular place of public issues, can have enormous persuasive power. Richard Titmuss's posthumously published account of his radiotherapy treatment for cancer is a stirring defence of the principle always close to his heart of equal access to 'free' treatment at the moment of need.[26] It makes the point much more memorably than the statistics of which he was so fond. Perhaps if he'd been born later and lived longer he, like his daughter, would have secured a reputation as a 'qualitative' social scientist.

Another note of his hospital experiences that year survives, hand-written and incomplete, wistful about the London landscape he would soon leave behind, and mindful of those labours nourishing his last vision of it:

> It's 9.15 p.m. and all is quiet in the long corridor of the Edgar Horne Ward on the third floor. The busy, ceaseless, complex traffic of the hospital has come to a stop. The consultations and the seminars are over for one day, the decisions, about life, death, pain and peace have been made; the lady with the mobile vacuum cleaner sometimes homesick for Barbados ("it comes over me sometimes like a wave, dear") has returned to Camberwell; the handsome, friendly young man from Mauritius who brings me *The Times* every morning is watching the telly in a crowded room; and all the others who bring me water, food, messages, mobile shops, mobile libraries, flowers, and friendliness are now busy with their own affairs. On the ward only the nursing staff are still with us. They may not be visible as one struggles onto the bridge to have a last look at the Thames.[27]

14

Vera's rose

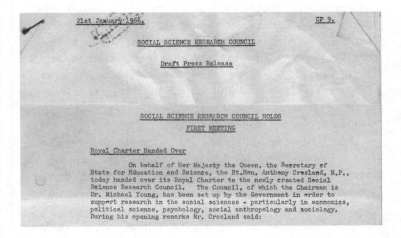

21st January 1966.   CP 9.

SOCIAL SCIENCE RESEARCH COUNCIL

Draft Press Release

SOCIAL SCIENCE RESEARCH COUNCIL HOLDS
FIRST MEETING

Royal Charter Handed Over

On behalf of Her Majesty the Queen, the Secretary of
State for Education and Science, the Rt.Hon. Anthony Crosland, M.P.,
today handed over its Royal Charter to the newly created Social
Science Research Council. The Council, of which the Chairman is
Dr. Michael Young, has been set up by the Government in order to
support research in the social sciences - particularly in economics,
political science, psychology, social anthropology and sociology.
During his opening remarks Mr. Crosland said:

The physical landscape of trees and fields and hedges with their
interruption of stone cottages is wrapped in a soft grey mist. This is
autumn now, with the hues changing from bright to muted green,
curled brown leaves lying on the grass. It takes a long time to write
a book, all the time from spring to autumn and then the whole of
another year's seasons. Outside the window, beyond the space where
I write, bright bursts of lime green, chrome yellow and a dark–bright
red interrupt the message of decline and disappearance. Ambiguity
and ambivalence are part of nature. There are purple sloes still in the
hedgerows and fat blackberries high up where no one can reach
them. My magic apple tree throws its fruit casually, in abundance,
on the ground. The green globes lie in the wet grass. If I don't shift

them, they decay into it, transforming themselves into dark brown crystallised balls. Nature is profligate and self-indulgent. When I walked out there this morning, I saw that several crops of mahogany fungi had appeared on the lawn overnight. They look most appealing as breakfast food, fried in a little butter, but I know better than that. If I had my life over again I'd learn the safe way to pick mushrooms.

If I had my life over again, I'd be much more mindful of the lives around me, open to the meanings that stretch across the permeable barrier between the public and the private. If I had my life again I'd talk to Richard Titmuss and his wife about what drove them really, and why they had a child and how they turned her into me. I'd sit down with Kay Titmuss and her husband and ask them gently why she seemed so unhappy and why he seemed to have such difficulty with the idea of women as equal human beings. It's because we 'know' marriage and family life too well that we know particular marriages and family lives not at all: they hide so successfully under the enormous cloak of brand image.[1]

To the side of the inviting fungi sprouting on the lawn is Vera's rose. It's a Charles de Mills rose, a spectacular old variety with deep crimson blooms containing delicate tessellations like petticoats. The flowers are an absolute queen among roses, or perhaps it would be more appropriate to compare them with the demeanour of a mature woman, secure in her views, comfortable in her petticoats, and quite without any stridency. There's nothing strident about Vera's rose, although there is a mystery about its identity which no rose historian has yet been able to solve to everyone's satisfaction. It's a Gallica rose; it made its first appearance under the name 'Bizarre Triomphant' in 1803 in the catalogue of a French firm that supplied the Empress Josephine's rose garden.[2] There was once a rose dealer called Charles Mills Blyth in Nottinghamshire, not far from where I write, so perhaps the rose's modern name is a hybrid of its origins. Vera Seal, whom I met in her little house with purple velvet curtains in the New Forest when she was eighty-nine, asked if she could give me the mysteriously-named rose. She and I were working together on a biography of her great friend Barbara Wootton. Vera and I became friends, too. At the height of biography-writing, letters from Vera would arrive almost daily, adding a few new observations, an additional memory or two, enclosing a page from my typescript with Vera's thoughtful annotations in the margins. But these gifts weren't enough. She wanted to give me something that would endure without always staying the same.

With the end of summer flowering, the blooms are brown and dry and drooping now. They resemble the papers I've been reading of meetings that took place fifty or sixty or more years ago, meetings that Richard Titmuss attended or apologized for not being able to attend, of the Social Science Research Council or the Institute of Community Studies or the British Sociological Association or the London School of Economics, all those stalwarts of the last century's social science. I had very little idea, until I came to examine these remnants, how central he had been in the institutional story of British social science. It isn't just a paper trace of a paper member or titular chair of the executive committee or the advisory board of this or that: his engagement is active, probing, calculating, cajoling, critical, analytical, remonstrative. He dreams up schemes and sucks people into them, holds séances in his LSE office, pens research grant applications, is vociferous in committee meetings, talks to publishers, manages the entire world of social science and men in the public eye. The pages which tell me all this smell of dust and dead skin cells, disputations and agreements, the airless smoky rooms wherein their texts were composed. The reader breathes in the scent which isn't at all fragrant, but more like the odour of a hare being chased by hounds across a hunting ground. The tracks in the papers are those we social science detectives have to follow.

Bits crumble off the edges of the brown papers when I touch them, like the desiccated petals of Vera's rose. The bits stick to my clothes and I brush them off with an irritation they don't deserve. These are the records of the past, evidence of events that happened, or conversations that flowed or faltered, of people positioned with their intersecting, argumentative, influential lives. All such records are liable to be partial because there's no methodology in the world of social science research or anywhere else that can promise an exact substitute for experience. Take letters, for example: the letters we use, that I use in this book, as a guide to the past, are 'simply what the letter writer chose to commit to paper that happened to survive'.

And that 'happened to survive' isn't usually random. The daughters of
C. Wright Mills, my sociologist hero, for instance, putting together a
book of his letters and autobiographical writings, found themselves
with the conundrum of a wholly positive correspondence between
him and his mother, while they knew from their own experience
that the relationship was an ambivalent one. All evidence to this
effect had presumably been discarded.[3] Memory, experience and
interpretation perpetually shift and metamorphose, resisting the tidy
template of a jigsaw puzzle.

Vera Seal knew Richard Titmuss; Richard Titmuss was a colleague
and friend of our joint heroine Barbara Wootton; almost every name
I come across in these collections of letters and brown papers is a
name I already know, a name that instantly delivers a mental picture,
the sharp flash and click of an old Brownie camera. The mind's eye
conveys the image with an automatic precision; we don't have to
scurry around in the back of the mind looking for these things. But
they tend to arrive without dates or proper locations. I knew these
people but when and where? What did they mean to me, compared
with what they meant then, when they lived in those brown papers?

Take the name 'Don Howard'. I found his name in the Eileen
Younghusband Archives; on one of her American trips she's going
to see him, to be met by him at Los Angeles airport: she's looking
forward to it. Don Howard lives in California, where he's Dean of
the School of Social Welfare in Los Angeles. The camera of the mind's
eye blinks, and there's Don Howard lined up with his family and
three Titmusses outside a ranch in the Saint Gabriel mountains in
California on the Titmusses' second trip to the USA in 1962. He met
us at the airport, too. The colours of the photographs in the album
have blurred into a strange brown–purple tone which dims the bright
Californian sunshine, but you can see it, nonetheless, in our squinting
eyes. There are the Howards and in front of them Professor and Mrs
Titmuss with Ann Titmuss squashed in between them, clothed in a
most unbecoming brown jersey. I fall over the Howard name again
when going through yet more files of crumbly papers. In 1967 Don
Howard tries to persuade Richard Titmuss to take a job in California.
Life is better in this 'Eden-land', he urges. Not so, replies Titmuss:
London and England offer me far more than any university in the

USA could possibly do (and by the way, he adds, I've refused four other such offers in the past year).[4]

As Wright Mills said, the good writer tries to enrich private life by making it publicly relevant, and to humanise public affairs by giving them personal meaning. I hope I've done some of that in this book. I realise that no one can hope to expose the falsity of legends with impunity. When Nigel Nicolson decided to reveal private aspects of his parents and their marriage – politician Sir Harold Nicolson's racism, writer Vita Sackville-West's conservatism, and the homosexual behaviour of both of them – he wrote, 'Let not the reader condemn in ten minutes a decision which I have pondered for ten years'.[5]

How I wish I could write straightforward books, uncontroversial ones, solid academic ones. They wouldn't be interesting, though: their writing wouldn't interest me. It's complexity, overlapping worlds, the decay and rebirth of themes, flowers and seasons, that holds my attention.

15

This procession of educated men

Richard Titmuss came late to academic life. At 43 when he joined the staff of LSE, this was his first formal membership of any higher education institution. His daughter, on the other hand, entered higher education by going to an élite university at the conventional age of 18 – the élite bit being quite consciously chosen by her to create ripples of parental pride in the Blue Plaque House. The degree was followed by an almost unbroken pursuit of university-based social research (49 years and still counting). Thus, father and daughter both accomplished much of what they are most known for within the institutional structures and strictures of academia. But their experiences differ, not only through the divergence in their interests, but because academia is at heart a patriarchal business – commercially, politically and ideologically.

The original title of Virginia Woolf's essay *Three guineas*, published on the eve of the Second World War in 1938, was *On being despised*. Conceived as a sequel to her much-quoted *A room of one's own*, and building on ten years' research, it's an extended critique of the power relations linking gender, aggression, authoritarianism, higher education and the whole superstructure of the patriarchal state. Woolf's underlying project in writing *Three guineas* was to understand the social forces that produce fascism. Her beloved nephew Julian Bell, 'a young Achilles', had recently been killed in the Spanish Civil War. He had enlisted as a non-combatant, driving ambulances, a choice that satisfied the Bloomsbury set's commitment to pacifism, while also permitting that ultimate proof of manhood, participation in war.[1] Because of its subject-matter, readers of *Three guineas* might have expected as textual illustrations pictures of soldiers, battles and desecrated and damaged bodies splayed on bloody fields. Instead Woolf chose five photographs of men in military, religious, legal, heraldic and academic uniform. The men in these pictures are weighed down with gowns, mortar boards, wigs, medals and swords. Their presence in the text is quite shocking, precisely because it disturbs the reader's expectation. To some eyes, the men appear so worthy and important; to others they look simply ridiculous – mere boys in fancy dress clothing.

Woolf didn't find them ridiculous: she found them appalling. To her the figures depicted a destructive symbiosis between the weight of tradition, the state of masculinity and the project of war. 'Now we are here to consider facts,' she urges, replying to one of three requests for the contribution of a guinea to a good cause – the 'three guineas' of the book's title:

> ... now we must fix our eyes upon the procession – the procession of the sons of educated men.
>
> There they go, our brothers who have been educated at public schools and universities, mounting those steps, passing in and out of those doors, ascending those pulpits, preaching, teaching,

administering justice, practising medicine, transacting business, making money. It is a solemn sight always – a procession, like a caravanserai crossing a desert. Great-grandfathers, grandfathers, fathers, uncles – they all went that way, wearing their gowns.[2]

So solemn is this procession that, when women join it at the end, as they are beginning to be allowed to do when Woolf is writing, it's important to ask the question, where is it leading us? Woolf's view is that it's not taking us in any direction we want to go. 'The professions have a certain undeniable effect upon the professors,' she contends. 'They make the people who practise them possessive, jealous of any infringement of their rights, and highly combative if anyone dares dispute them. Are we not right then in thinking that if we enter the same professions we shall acquire the same qualities? And do not such qualities lead to war?'[3]

Three guineas was one of the most unpopular of Woolf's books. Friends and literary critics tended to ignore it completely or called it 'nasty' and 'preposterous'.[4] The connections she made between the institutions of the nation state and the state of masculinity stretched the imagination too far. The reaction of one of her (many) biographers, Nigel Nicolson, who was also the son of her lover and close friend Vita Sackville-West, was typical. He contrasted how 'charmingly' Woolf had made the case for equal rights in *A room of one's own* with the unacceptable stridency of *Three guineas*. She had a right to be angry, yet she had, he said, very little really to be angry about. The flowering of *her* genius had never been thwarted by convention or ill-treatment. Yes, she had been deprived of a university education, but that meant only that she lacked the intellectual discipline that might have prevented the 'hyperbole' of *Three guineas*.[5] 'Exaggeration not meant to be taken literally' says the dictionary about 'hyperbole'. The seriousness with which Woolf intended the message of *Three guineas* is probably not unrelated to her history of childhood abuse, her breakdowns, mental health problems, treatment at the hands of doctors and eventual suicide, plunging into the River Ouse at the age of 59 with stones in her pockets.

Every woman who writes or speaks about this 'system of social structures and practices in which men dominate, oppress and exploit women' – alias patriarchy[6] – is liable to be called angry, or inconsiderate, or emotional and, of course, man-hating. Joan Smith, who wrote a book of essays called *Misogynies*, considered it ironic that she had written a book about men's hatred of women only to be accused herself of hating men. (The ease with which men take the academic analysis of patriarchy personally is remarkable, by which I mean it's well worth noting as a symptom of the condition itself.) Nobody accused Richard Titmuss, in his dealings with the difficult women at LSE in the 1950s, of giving in to patriarchal tendencies, yet his co-option of Eileen Younghusband's project, his networking with male colleagues to ensure that neither she nor any of her female colleagues got promoted to senior positions, and his clever inveigling of less senior men into his department, are all recognisably inegalitarian moves. As Hilary Rose, appointed to the Titmuss Department in 1964, observed of her new working environment, 'there were bright young academic men who needed approval, support and promotion but there was no parallel concept of bright young academic women ... We were supposed to be like the women in the social policy we taught – the self-sacrificing, disembodied and non-competitive partners of men'. During the Troubles, the women staff on short-term contracts who supported the students were quietly 'let go'.[7] Today equal rights legislation has supposedly put an end to this; indeed, it would have done, if we didn't live in a patriarchy, but we do, so it all still goes on (see later in this chapter). The main point about patriarchy is that it's *systemic*. It isn't restricted to individual behaviour; it's 'not casual but structured, not local but extensive, not transitory but stable, with a tendency to self-reproduction'.[8] Hence the patriarchal family tends to replicate itself in the patriarchal university, the faculty, the department. Internal rivalries are structured by gender and generation. The pattern of the paterfamilias, the head with his dependent wives, children and servants, reappears in academic interactions and especially where there's competition for resources, which is almost everywhere these days.[9]

'You asked me what it was like to be a woman member of staff at LSE,' said Eileen Younghusband to her biographer, Kathleen Jones, of her earlier years in what would become Richard Titmuss's Department. 'Do you know, I don't think we thought about it in those days. I think there was still such a hangover of Victorian attitudes about women. It certainly never occurred to me that I was being kept down because I was a woman. I think I probably had grown up with the whole attitude that women were inferior to men. It was never said, it was just part of the atmosphere.'[10] To call Richard Titmuss's own behaviour patriarchal would have been quite foreign to the mood of the time. But, according to several people recalling its history, he did run his Department like a Victorian family. Junior staff saw him as an austere and detached figure, protected by 'an awesome secretary who ... made him tea or coffee and kept people at arm's length'. He had the habit of holding court at lunchtime in the senior common room, where the junior lecturers would gather round and listen to pearls of wisdom. 'You had to pay court to Richard,' remembers one of them; they sat round him and he took charge of the discussion. David Donnison felt a little uneasy about all this, particularly when he had helped to recruit people who were then somewhat dismayed to find themselves in a place 'where the principal figure was a bit like an old testament prophet'.[11]

In the 1950s women stayed at home or left it only politely and unobtrusively. Woolf's *Three guineas* had faded from memory, and the next great feminist text was only just starting to infiltrate the British cultural and academic consciousness. Simone de Beauvoir's *The second sex*, 'a delayed time bomb',[12] was published in 1949 but not available in English until 1953. A two-volume exposé and critique of women's secondary status throughout history, and especially in French and American bourgeois culture, its translator was a retired American professor of zoology, Howard Parshley. He corrected de Beauvoir's biology and cut ten per cent of the text, under instruction from the publisher who wanted to reduce costs. Parshley had one heart attack during the translation and another fatal one soon after; de Beauvoir remarked that, without her book to work on, his life had lost all meaning. The origins of *The second sex* are attributed to an observation made by de Beauvoir's long-term companion, Jean-Paul Sartre, that she had been brought up *specifically* as a girl.[13] Another observation is that the book owes its driving logic of women as the 'other' to de Beauvoir's reading of a work by a male social scientist, Gunnar Myrdal's *An American dilemma: The negro problem and modern democracy*, published in 1944. (It's also, of course, possible that de Beauvoir thought of *The second sex* all by herself without the help of any man.) In Appendix 5 of Myrdal's book, 'A parallel to the negro problem', Myrdal noted that Black slaves imported into colonial America had simply been given the same legal status as women, servants and mules possessed at the time.[14]

Richard Titmuss and his wife knew Gunnar Myrdal and his wife, Alva, another highly competent social scientist. She was Principal Director of the United Nations Department of Social Affairs, Director of the UNESCO Department of Social Sciences, Swedish Ambassador to India, an MP, a social researcher, policy analyst and author, and winner of the Nobel Peace Prize, but she also did much of Gunnar's typing. Her sociological work has been strangely neglected, even though she was the first social scientist to put forward a theory of social-democratic citizenship that wasn't gender blind, in contrast to the later one universally admired, which belongs to T.H. Marshall at LSE.[15]

In the late 1960s, when women were finally allowed to teach English at Columbia College in New York, the American literary critic and English literature academic Lionel Trilling, who is unlikely to have read *The second sex*, commented about the admission of women lecturers: 'This is not at all a good idea. Older men should teach younger men, and younger men should then go out and encounter women as the Other.'[16] This was the university whose 'treehouse gang' and 'old–boy secrets' the English literature scholar Carolyn Heilbrun endured for many years before retiring early to save her sanity. During her uncomfortable sojourn at Columbia, Heilbrun wrote detective stories about academic murders using a pseudonym and adding a blanket disclaimer that of course they were purely products of her imagination. The duplication of the discrimination story in other cases elsewhere isn't a matter of anyone's imagination: 'The Skocpol affair', for example, which dragged Harvard University into the annals of disreputable employers in 1980–81, involved the denial of tenure to one of the 20th century's leading political scientists, Theda Skocpol, who just happened to be a woman, and who took the University through a costly legal case at the conclusion of which they had to admit their mistake.[17]

Recalling her own career as an academic sociologist interested in feminism, Olive Banks goes back to a moment in her girlhood in the late 1930s when she left school and applied for a job in a public library, only to be told that the library service was closed to girl applicants. In 1947 Banks went to LSE to study sociology, where she was equally disappointed to find no sensible trace of gender as a structural principle or anything else in what she was taught.[18] That was about the time when the social workers at LSE were finally moved off the separate salary scales reserved for women 'tutors' (not lecturers) – they were historically treated, in Eileen Younghusband's words, as 'the lowest form of life'.[19] In 1961, 87 per cent of university staff in the UK were men. I didn't really notice this when I went to Oxford in 1962, partly because I landed in the protected enclave of a women's college, but also because I was far too excited by my first encounters with the possibilities of the sociological imagination. Although I did own a copy of *The second sex* – a prophetic gift from my first boyfriend – I hadn't read it (neither had he). Chelly Halsey, a friend of Richard Titmuss's, who taught me sociology at Oxford, was much more interested in class than gender (although gender can be considered a form of class). In his history of British sociology published a few years ago, Halsey wrote of the post-war period that British sociologists headquartered at LSE 'provided a comprehensive description of British society, its demography, its ethnic composition, its education, its religion, industry, crime, and its class structure'.[20]

Not so. There was no sociology of gender, of reproduction, of domestic labour, of personal life, in those sociological analyses of education, industry, crime and class: they all took as their subject men's experiences. The trick was to do what medical research had done for so long (and still does) – ignore women because their bodies and experiences are so different (from the norm, which is male). Where gender did put in a fleeting appearance, it came in a sociobiological/evolutionary/functionalist guise: in the family, men headed households and women performed their labours of love, so naturally there had to be differences in their public roles. This was the way gender was treated by the sociological theorists when Richard Titmuss joined LSE in 1950, and it was substantially the sociology I learnt from Chelly Halsey at Oxford in the early 1960s. Sociological theory was dominated by a man called Talcott Parsons who purveyed an approach known as 'structural functionalism', according to which the systems which make up society do so because they are functional for it. Thus, the normative white middle–class family of American society in the 1950s, the family system Parsons knew best, and one which was especially notable for limiting women's opportunities, became the model for all families worldwide. Men's role in the family was labelled 'instrumental' and women's 'expressive'.[21] This was the conceptual model in the heads of most male university professors. When Tessa Blackstone applied in the early 1960s for an LSE scholarship to do a PhD on nursery education, Richard Titmuss was not impressed. Recalling his reaction, Blackstone told me: 'Your Dad ... obviously had the view that nursery education was peripheral to any aspect of social policy. My interpretation was, "women should look after their children".' A few years later Blackstone was appointed to Titmuss's Department at LSE as a temporary substitute for one of the male staff who was going off on leave. She gave birth to her second child shortly before the LSE term started: 'I remember thinking ... that I mustn't let the fact that I'd just had a baby stop me starting at the beginning of term because otherwise it'll damage my later chances and I'd be letting down other women.' So when the baby was two weeks old, she took herself on the train from Enfield to Holborn, 'and I remember walking down Kingsway thinking I'm not going to get to the bottom'. When she got there, another new member of staff, a man who specialised in industrial democracy, asked her how she could possibly justify employing someone to look after her children.[22]

When I came to publish the outcome of my PhD research on housework, I wrote an introductory chapter called 'The invisible woman: sexism in sociology'. 'A way of seeing is a way of not seeing,' I objected. Functionalism in particular was 'rampant sexism'. What could possibly be non–instrumental about cleaning homes and throwing out rubbish, and whose needs did this kind of family serve anyway? All this sexism was not, I argued, unconnected with the views about women the founding fathers of sociology held and practised in their private lives. This was at a time when it was regarded as quite improper to insinuate in any academic work that the private and the public might actually be connected.[23]

By this point, 1974, second-wave feminism was under way, and books such as Shulamith Firestone's *The dialectic of sex*, Germaine Greer's *The female eunuch* and Kate Millett's *Sexual politics* (the latter based on another PhD) had begun to disturb even academic complacency about women. The history of feminism's infiltration into the academy singles out this same year, 1974, as its starting point.[24] The British Sociological Association Conference that year was on the theme of 'Sexual divisions and society'. It was organised by a group of feminist sociologists, and took place in the cold environs of an Aberdeen spring, with excursions to local fisheries organised on the side. I gave a paper on housework and was accompanied by my husband (with his mother kindly looking after the children during a power cut in London). In my memory he came with me purely because of his companionate interest in gender, but flicking through *The sociology of housework* just now I see, buried in a footnote, that he too submitted a paper, one with a suitably masculine-sounding title, 'Comparative perspectives on gender as a structural principle'. My not remembering this is one of many salutary lessons about the sociology of memory I've learnt while writing this book.

I do remember the hostile climate, both meteorological and academic, of Aberdeen. There was much political excitement among the women: an all-female caucus gathered behind closed doors to plot the global transformation of the social sciences had to endure sociological men banging on the doors clamouring to be allowed in. That's how we feel all the time, we whispered. It was the first academic conference I'd ever been to, and the other thing I remember is the sexual pairing that happened after hours: I was told it was customary at such events, but I felt shocked, particularly because the conference was seriously about sexual *divisions*, not sexual *connections*. The next BSA conference on this theme had gender in the title, which is what the first one ought to have had, and that would have cleared up this particular confusion.

In 1968, when I was beginning to consider academic research as an occupation, and Richard Titmuss was trying to recover from the student disturbances at LSE, only 16 per cent of university sociologists in Britain were women.This figure climbed slowly to 26 per cent in 1997.Women also began to publish more, and the strange convention of journal articles carrying only initials before men's surnames but full first names for women had started to wane.[25] When Chelly Halsey asked eight sociologists to write brief essays as an epilogue to his *A history of sociology in Britain*, I was one of two women. We both commented on the importance of sociology coming to terms with 'gender issues'. Using Halsey's own data, I noted that 100 per cent of the important mentors named by the 216 sociology professors in his survey were men (as were 81 per cent of those asked to take part in the survey).[26] David Glass, sociologist, demographer and LSE professor, got the most votes; Richard Titmuss came next. 'Women are seldom named,' lamented Halsey. 'In almost every case there was no more than one vote.' A second question – which 20th-century sociologists have contributed most to the subject? – achieved the same result: Max Weber, Emile Durkheim,Talcott Parsons, Robert Merton, Erving Goffman. The list even included Karl Marx who wasn't a 20th-century figure: the 'learned professors' got their dates wrong.[27]

The business of academic social science expanded hugely in the 1960s and '70s, the era when Richard Titmuss's Department at LSE became a place for young men to do policy research powered by the charisma of the Titmice. Harold Wilson's Labour government was a key driving force.The new political administrators saw good research as the basis of effective policy, and the research–policy loop as lubricated best by close contact between academics and politicians. Institutional support for social science in this period included the formation in 1966 of the Social Science Research Council, the first publicly funded system for financing social science research; the creation of the Office of Population Censuses and Surveys in 1970, as a new national body co-ordinating and standardising statistical data; and an influx of new social science and policy journals as much-needed outlets for research findings. In an orchestration written mainly by the male academic and policy network, the unified study of the social became a symphony of different socials.

Other universities followed LSE in dividing sociology and the other 'socials' off from social work.Theory remained the province of men, with women asking increasingly awkward questions, and often trying to answer these through empirical research, which condemned them to the subordinate role of 'contract researcher'. To do anything that reeked of feminist research was to risk one's academic reputation.[28] One of the referees to whom Policy Press sent my proposal for this book asked for more about my 'conversion to feminism'. But, since feminism isn't a cult, there was no conversion. As Juliet Mitchell argued in her signal *New Left Review* article in 1966, 'Women: the longest revolution', feminism and women's solidarity with it is an ever-present possibility: the conjunction of the two merely depends on conducive historical moments. The same circumstances that produced the student dissidence with which Richard Titmuss had to deal at LSE pushed women as a group to re-frame their own situation. The result was the Women's Liberation Movement, 'second-wave feminism'. This, unlike its tidal predecessor, swept into the world of academia a whole new set of debates and terminologies and demands, many of these formalised as 'women's studies' or, later, 'gender studies'. For academic women who discovered their sympathies with all this, the ideology, politics and practice of organised feminism provided a playground away from the university, a sounding board, and, above all, a comfort blanket. It's just a small example, but when I overcame my lifelong dislike of public speaking sufficiently to accept a seminar invitation sometime in the early 1970s, I chose Glasgow on the grounds that I wouldn't know anyone there; when I returned to London, my entire women's liberation group was waiting for me at the airport.

Just as he was unsympathetic to the radical students, so Richard Titmuss wasn't comfortable having a politically radical daughter. My association with feminism was treated by both my parents rather like a mental disorder. The fact that a feminist political understanding had implications for the business of knowledge – how it's created by whom and for what purpose – and thus for the public world of Richard Titmuss's work, probably seemed a further breach in the canons of civilised behaviour.

Looking back, we may see it differently from the way it was. The way it was can be captured only in a particular kind of episodic memory, when incidents/events/scenes with especially strong emotional significance have the capacity to explode with fiery detail.

So I remember, watching myself in the moving frame of memory – which is how this episodic recall works – many small experiences in and with the institutions of academia which relay a story of conflict and confrontation, a different kind of story from the one Richard Titmuss owned in his passage through the territory of difficult women and troublesome students.

I'm getting off a train in Gloucestershire in 1974, wearing a long skirt, as one did in those days; my husband is at the station to meet me. He's taken the children to stay with his mother, and that's where we're going, to her bungalow, perched on the edge of a reclaimed gravel pit, with a small boat so the children can travel across it. I'm exhausted from a four-hour PhD viva, during which I had to defend my study of housework in front of two men who kept lapsing into masonic arguments with one another. It bemused me, their preoccupation with the territories of their own minds and careers, their stubborn reluctance to take my project seriously, despite the 434 pages and 83 tables of my thesis. 'You're going to get your PhD,' they said at the beginning of this ordeal, 'but you're going to have to persuade us; you must defend every word you've written.' The *viva voce* examination – an oral defence of a piece of academic work – is, like other academic practices, a species of combative and competitive behaviour, in short just the kind of exercise Virginia Woolf criticised in her *Three guineas*. The people waiting for me in the house by the reclaimed gravel pit that evening wanted to celebrate my success, but I didn't feel at all sure that it *was* a success. I don't mean that I doubted I had got my PhD; I mean that the process of getting it was very disturbing. My supervisor was, like many senior male academics of that period,[29] fond of his identity as a sexually predatory male. It was talk rather than action in my case, but I never knew where to look. It's hard to participate in an institution of which you disapprove. But in this sense universities are no different from families, which must be lived in and adapted to more humane forms.

A little further on in my life as an academic woman I was interviewed for a job at Bedford College, a place with a strong history in the argument for women's education, located in the middle of Regent's Park, by another boating lake. This interview wasn't for just any job, it was a job I'd created for myself by successfully applying for a research grant from the Social Science Research Council to study 'social and medical aspects of first childbirth'. Academic protocol (which often forgets its own purpose) required the holding of a formal interview. At this I was asked what I intended to do, were they kind enough to give me my own job, about the care of my children. I was speechless, which was just as well. Of course I would know what to say now.

These were lonely times for women in academia. It's always lonely being an outsider. The eminent sociologist Margaret Stacey (one of my own mentors, despite her absence from Chelly Halsey's list) felt 'very lost, afraid and alone' emerging from a decade of nappy-washing in the unfriendly atmosphere of Swansea University in the early '60s. She wrote to Barbara Wootton, herself an extraordinarily successful woman, to congratulate the latter on her autobiography *In a world I never made*, and especially on its title, which was taken from a poem by A.E. Housman:'I, a stranger and afraid/In a world I never made'.[30] When Stacey later (in 1974) went to the University of Warwick as a professor, she was accompanied to her first Academic Board meeting by the eminent sociologist John Rex. 'I've brought a lady,' explained Rex to the all-male assembly. For Stacey, the ensuing silence took her back to a moment in her London war work when she entered a men's lavatory by mistake.[31]

Another decade or so later in my own life, by which time the Sex Discrimination Act had come into existence, and I had written an article about it for the *British Journal of Law and Society*, and thus had made an intensive study of it, which would later prove to have been a very good idea, I am sitting at a large dark polished conference table in a large dark polished office somewhere debating something of academic importance with a dozen or so men and one other woman. By then a friend, Dale Spender, had begun to publish her studies of how men and women speak – differently, reflecting the limitation of women's semantic spaces in 'man-made' language. The topic of men's speech patterns was a salient one at this meeting, whose rationale and location I've forgotten. The only thing I remember about it was how the men kept using sporting metaphors. The language of innings and goal posts was completely foreign to me and the other woman present: we consequently couldn't understand the points the men were making, and were unable to take part in the conversation. So she and I had a word about it, and at the next opportunity we introduced a gender-balancing metaphor derived from the making of béchamel sauce. The trickiest part of this, as every reader will know, is the bit where you put the egg yolk in and the whole thing is liable to curdle. (For culinary experts, this isn't the classic béchamel sauce, which is eggless, but the version used in Greek cuisine and/or in the cheese sauce for a lasagne.) When we mentioned the béchamel recipe, the men were silent, uncomprehending. We found it easier to let them get on with their games. Tessa Blackstone recalls that when she joined the Cabinet Office in 1975, she was bemused by the phrase 'taking a short canter round the course'. She eventually worked out that it meant trying something out.[32]

The next memory of an academic ordeal is an institutional as well as a personal one. It's also of much graver proportions, which is one reason why it's set out in some detail below. I tell it not because there are still accounts to be settled – it was all a long time ago and life has moved on – but because it's such an excellent demonstration of how discrimination in academia works. It also echoes that uncomfortable lesson of the LSE Affair: the capacity of women as well as men to be keepers of patriarchal customs.

In January 1985, I gave up being a contract researcher (for a while, I came back to it later). I took up the post of Deputy Director of the Thomas Coram Research Unit (TCRU) at the Institute of Education in London. TCRU is a social policy research unit set up in 1971 with money from the English Department of Health to study the social, educational and health needs of young children and families. Its location then, near the historic Thomas Coram Foundation in Bloomsbury, was in a 1930s building above a day nursery which was intended to serve as a research laboratory for the TCRU psychologists until the nursery withdrew its support. The Unit was reached via an external metal staircase with extremely noisy rungs whose annunciative voice I can still hear today. It had been set up by Jack Tizard, a child psychologist and professor at the Institute of Education. The Director of the Unit when I joined it was Jack Tizard's widow, Barbara, herself an academic researcher of repute. There were few women heading research units at the time, so it was another lonely business. Barbara was paid less than Jack had been because she was a woman. She was also in some ways a reluctant Director. She felt that she had to take the post to ensure TCRU's survival after Jack's premature death, but she didn't relish the management duties that went with it.[33] At first, she welcomed me as someone who could relieve her of some of this management burden, and I tried to do so, but matters in the Unit were complicated. There were tensions and unhappinesses I didn't understand – some the legacy of past situations, others the result of professional disagreements and competition for resources. Like families, every research unit has its own special way of being unhappy.

Another few years passed, during which I enjoyed TCRU as a secure base for doing some innovative research on social support, and other more prosaic studies of family health care, continued with my work for WHO, helped to set up an association to advance contract researchers' rights, spent my annual leave writing a pseudonymous novel at the Rockefeller Foundation Centre overlooking Lake Como, negotiated a legal separation from my husband, and began a long-term relationship with a friend of Barbara Tizard's who had joined the Unit's computing support team. In 1990, she announced her retirement and I applied for her post. Barbara herself had told me when I joined the Unit that she was looking for a successor; my appointment was part of a plan. However, more recently she had made it clear that I could no longer count on her support. Her change of attitude puzzled me: I could only suppose I had proved a disappointing stand-in for her as Director, with my more cooperative line on staff 'management'; there had also been a minor professional technical disagreement between me and the Unit statistician, and my relationship with her and his computing colleague seemed a cause of some displeasure to both the statistician and Barbara. But I'm only guessing. Six of us were interviewed for her job – four external candidates, myself and another internal candidate – by a Committee of six, including two Institute of Education professors, two other professors with Institute connections, the Director of the Institute and a representative from the Department of Health. The interviews were surprisingly short for such a senior post, only about half an hour each. One of the Committee asked me whether I thought that, given the tension in the Unit (about which he was unspecific), it would be better for an external candidate to be appointed. I replied that surely this was a matter for the Committee itself to decide. Another member of the interviewing panel said he thought I was an extremely busy person and I would need to give something up if I became Director of TCRU. He then referred to my novel-writing in a rather disparaging way (I had published my novel *The men's room* two years previously but it wasn't on my academic c.v., which the Committee had in front of them). None of them asked me any questions about my intellectual contribution, past, present or future, to TCRU's work, nor about my international work for the World Health Organization, which at the time was substantial.

The following morning I was telephoned by the Institute of Education's Director, who told me that the job had been offered to someone else.

And so I faced continuing to work as Deputy Director of TCRU under, and I did think that it would be under, a man who was less qualified to run the Unit than I was. However Richard Titmuss had got his own university job, and however he had managed to recruit all his bright young men, by 1990 the behaviour of university departments had been cleaned up – in theory – by equality legislation and formal guidelines. In selecting someone for a job, the only salient criterion is supposed to be the person's fitness for the job in question. Particular criteria – usually labelled 'essential' and 'desirable' – have to be spelt out. Then it's a matter of seeing how each applicant matches up to these criteria. An important element in academic job applications is usually candidates' records of research and publications. In this case, the successful candidate's c.v. listed nine externally funded research grants, one sole-authored book, seven sole-authored chapters and five sole-authored peer-reviewed papers. The comparable figures on my c.v. were thirteen, nine, forty-one and twenty-seven. The job selection process ought also to include a clear record of each candidate's score against the specified criteria, and the basis on which the selection panel decides who is to be the favoured candidate. But it transpired that no one had kept a record of how the decision not to appoint me (or the other four rejected candidates) had been made. In the post-hoc version hastily cobbled together by the personnel department, the successful candidate had scored half a point more than me for his 'leadership potential'.

'It is important to examine the institutional practices within universities, as there is no reason to believe that women academics are less able than men, and therefore there can be no reason other than sex discrimination to account for their inferior status within universities.'[34] Sometime in the ensuing few days, one of the TCRU staff who commiserated with my lack of success in achieving the Directorship, a woman with some legal training, asked me if I thought I had grounds for challenging the appointment. Conversations with a solicitor, with the Women's Legal Defence Fund, and with the Equal Opportunities Commission, all followed. When the Chair of the Selection Committee took me out to lunch at the local Chinese and suggested I apply for a job elsewhere, and when I told him I was considering challenging the decision of his panel, there was another one of those uncomprehending silences.

A few days later I handed the Director of the Institute of Education, the person ultimately responsible for my non-appointment and the man who had rung me with the news, a document called a 'Section 74' questionnaire. This asked for information relating to the appointment which was needed to establish whether or not discrimination had taken place. Sometimes patriarchy does what we expect and fear it will; but sometimes it surprises us. The Institute Director accepted my Section 74 questionnaire with good grace, although he did look a little stunned, and then he went on to suggest that it might be possible for me to set up a new research unit of my own somewhere else in the Institute. Various departments subsequently made pleas to house me, seeing this as a useful way of strengthening their gender base. The incoming Director of TCRU, worried about competition, laid it down as a condition that 'my' unit could not have equivalent standing to his. This was, of course, another aspect of injustice, for who authorised him to have such power?

The Social Science Research Unit (SSRU) formally came into existence in October 1990 as an item in the Department of Policy Studies at the Institute of Education. We were housed in a series of attics that no one else wanted with genuinely sloping roofs on the fifth floor of a building in a Bloomsbury square. The solipsism of 'I' in this account isn't a fair representation; four people left TCRU with me in a move of giddy suddenness one week after its new Director took over, and we were joined by two other researchers, creative individuals who were the remnants of another sociological research unit. The name 'Social Science Research Unit' was devised by me in the same manner as I dreamt up the titles of all my books – in the bath. The term 'social science' seemed important, in view of what Margaret Thatcher and Keith Joseph had by then done to what used to be the Social Science Research Council.

The new SSRU was given virtually no resources, apart from our attics and some second-hand furniture. We took with us two old computers, but we had no telephones until I and a colleague deposited ourselves in the office of the man responsible for these things and refused to move until he gave us some. My salary was covered, and half a salary for an administrator, both for a limited period: all other staff had to be funded on external research grants. Had I been a man, I would have insisted on proper resourcing from the start (had I been a man quite probably none of this would have happened). I wouldn't have had to write endless memoranda about the need for photocopiers, or computers or more rooms, as the research grants flowed (were dragged) in, or the desirability of having some form of heating in the offices, and also windows that opened, so that staff would neither freeze nor suffocate. I wouldn't have had to go on and on about somewhere to park the bicycles – we were early advocates of the cycle-to-work campaign – and a sign for the front door so that people could find us. I was perpetually made to feel that these requests were beyond the pale, the outcry of an unreasonable woman, instead of statements about the minimal resources required for any such operation to succeed.

One of the people who left TCRU with me was doing research on gender and perceptions of pain. In her small attic office, which was the first one you reached when you arrived breathless at the top of the stairs, she had pinned up on the wall pictures of people in terrible pain – Edvard Munch's silent 'The Scream', Frida Kahlo's impassively revealing 'The Broken Woman', Gerrit van Honthorst's horrible 'Saint Sebastian'. Ironically, those daily climbs up the stairs and all the hassles involved in setting up SSRU coincided for me with the menopause. My mind and body were both stressed with change, thereby proving what patriarchy assumes, that women are always at the mercy of their unstable bodies. I could never be sure whether the institution or my hormones were the cause of my extreme fatigue and changes of temperature. I did, however, find a good use for the latter, talking about the hot flushes openly in academic meetings as a way (like the béchamel sauce metaphor) of silencing masonic masculine dialogue.

As a postscript, I did apply for the other job recommended to me after my unsuccessful attempt at the directorship of TCRU. This interview, by eight men and one woman, was much more taxing, largely because the discussion was led by a sociologist who specialised in theories about post-modernity and was not remotely interested in what I had to offer. Someone rang me up afterwards and told me they had decided not to make an appointment at all. A few weeks later an academic friend of mine relayed a different story: after the interviews, the post-modernity man had asked my friend's brother-in-law to apply. He got the job.

But this story does go on and on. In 1991 the Karl Mannheim Chair in Sociology at the Institute of Education fell vacant. Karl Mannheim was another sociological theorist, who had taught at the Institute for six years in the 1940s. People advised me that, at 47 with a track record of successful research and publications and management experience, I ought to be a professor. My initial response was to feel that this was something my father was, not something I aspired to for myself. I just wasn't able to excise from my memory all those moments when, as a small girl at that dreadful girls' school, we sat in rows at cramped ink-stained desks addressing envelopes for our end-of-term reports, and I had to learn how to spell professor (one 'f', not two), which nobody else had to do. It was a patriarchal identity in every sense. In any case, the title 'Dr' worked perfectly well for exacting good service from garages. Nonetheless, I applied for the Karl Mannheim Chair (these were the days when I seemed to be permanently writing job applications). The application required considerable creative ingenuity as I had to argue that my work fitted under the umbrella of 'the sociology of education' – it did, of course, quite well, once you got away from the narrow institutional meaning of 'education'. And then one day I caught the Institute Director and Deputy Director leaping into a taxi to attend the inaugural lecture of a colleague elsewhere in the university whom they told me they hoped could be persuaded to assume the Karl Mannheim mantle. As a way out of the fix – their fix, not mine – they encouraged me to apply for what is called a 'personal' chair. A 'personal chair' involves acquiring the title of professor as a recognition for work done. An 'established chair' is a job of professor to do or be this or that, and the job exists independently of the person who holds it. Established chairs are higher status than personal ones. My personal chair was delivered with amazing speed in time for me to withdraw my Karl Mannheim application. On hearing I had become a professor, another one in the Institute rang me up and said that he hoped my chair would be a comfortable one in the traditional sense, meaning that I would be able to sink back into an oblivion of academic inactivity. I asked the Director if becoming a professor meant a salary increase; he told me that this was a matter of a 'gentleman's agreement'. The language of merit I understand, but I've not had any opportunity to learn how gentlemen behind closed doors deal with one another.

'This is not a vulgar feminist conspiracy,' said one member of SSRU interviewed for a piece in *The Times Higher* in 1993 entitled 'Unique unit where men are in a minority'.[35] No, it wasn't any kind of simple conspiracy. At this point I could write a triumphal narrative – the millions of pounds raised, the numbers of jobs funded, reports and papers written, conferences and meetings spoken at, literature citations, policy impact, and so on – but such incantations are tedious to read, and the evidence exists for anyone who wants to find it.[36] Behind most successful men are wives at home; behind most successful women lie stories of failure and disappointment. I know I'm seen as a successful woman, a woman who's stormed the citadel, shot through the glass ceiling, etc, etc. But if we decline to be honorary men, we must also critique the idea(l) of the exceptional woman. Let us return smartly to the lesson of Virginia Woolf: what kind of world is this that we're asked to aspire to? What strains does it impose, what forms of combative behaviour does it foster and depend on? And what, anyway, are the realities of women's place in it?

Most women who work in the patriarchal academy are secretaries or cleaners, not professors, mentors or contributors to the history of any academic subject. Of course there has been progress since the 1960s: a huge increase in female higher education students, less tokenism for female staff, advances in pay and promotion opportunities. But the rule for women's jobs is the same as elsewhere in the occupational system: women's achievements don't match their educational success: there's a 'broken chain'.[37] The gender pay gap in British higher education is still a masterful 13 per cent. Eighty-one per cent of professors and 72 per cent of senior management are men. The highest proportion of women – 92 per cent – is found in the category of secretaries, typists, receptionists and telephonists.[38] The American writer Adrienne Rich put it exceptionally well some years ago: 'The university is above all a hierarchy. At the top is a small cluster of highly paid and prestigious persons, chiefly men, whose careers entail the services of a very large base of ill-paid or unpaid persons, chiefly women.'[39] This is a formula with multiple manifestations. For example University Vice-Chancellors in Britain, mostly men, are 'the new breed of fat cat'; they reward themselves handsomely – pay rises in the order of 20 per cent or more in 2013 – while their academic staff take inflationary cuts, and the people who clean universities and do all the support work, mostly women, are outsourced to cost-cutting private companies which refuse even to fund sick pay.[40] Whatever country you look at, gender and academic status are systematically related: more women in the lower grades, more men in the higher. This is a pattern that's changed very little over time, the main reason being that the 'gender stereotypes' sustaining it are themselves extremely resistant to change. Because ideas about what men and women in the academy do best are so all-pervasively grounded in everyday perception and values, it's very difficult for them to be seen as discriminatory.[41] This is a matter of 'ordinary, everyday, unspectacular behaviour', even 'right' behaviour, performed 'moment by moment and day after day'.[42] Discrimination is ordinary. When Barbara Bagilhole interviewed a group of women academics, she found that three-quarters reported discrimination in their higher education institutions, and two-thirds had experienced it personally. Many of their reports were of ordinary, everyday behaviour:

'There's an in-group of men who all know each other. A lot of discussion goes on in unplanned meetings where decisions are made and if you're not in that you're not part of the decision making.' [Senior Lecturer]

'There is no understanding of the way women are put down. Women say things in committee meetings and they are ignored until a man says them.' [Senior Lecturer]

'My work on gender is trivialised and dismissed ... I often make a point and then it's ignored, then a male colleague takes it up and it becomes his point.' [Lecturer][43]

Women form the bulk of contract researchers, widely recognised today as 'second-class citizens' in the university policy process.[44] Like the social workers Richard Titmuss found at LSE in 1950, contract researchers have historically not been treated as academic staff at all. They inhabit a 'culture of impermanence'.[45] In Britain, regulations ensuring equal pay and conditions for contract researchers weren't enacted until 2002.

The story of what happened to women in the academic world of social science when Richard Titmuss worked in it, and as his daughter is still doing, is really quite simple: what has changed is all on the surface of our understanding; what has not changed continues its monumental oppositional pull underneath. Feminist scholarship, women's studies and gender studies programmes haven't brought about the enormous changes that were anticipated. Knowledge per se is still constructed out of, and leads us into, a universe of gender-skewed perceptions and experiences; the other sort, that gets the label 'feminist', is corralled, like women historically, into a special place of its own.

Virginia Woolf practised what she wrote about in *Three guineas* in refusing all ceremonial honours. 'If we are offered offices and honours for ourselves, we can refuse them,' she said, 'how indeed, in view of the facts, could we possibly do otherwise?'[46] She turned down an honorary university degree; she refused to be made a Companion of Honour by the Crown; she regarded prestigious university lectures as obsolete practices inherited from the Middle Ages which only pander to academic vanity and encourage warlike competition.[47]

In another much more recent episodic memory I'm standing at a lectern in the mock Italian Renaissance décor of McEwan Hall at Edinburgh University, having not taken Woolf's advice, being made an Honorary Doctor of Science in Social Science of that University. I'm wearing a glorious robe of heavy orange-red silk, and a black draped hood lined with deep turquoise which I'm handed in an Ede & Ravenscroft bag to take home afterwards (dressing-up clothes for the grandchildren?). The University choir sings something called 'You know how this is', and the organist plays the Music for the Royal Fireworks: the ceremonial procession of the sons and daughters of educated men swings pompously down the central aisle of the hall. The men look more interesting than academic men usually do because their robes add colour. In my speech of thanks for this honour I mention that the academic head-dress was designed for men and it makes women look like mushrooms. Tempted to extend this into a metaphor of women constituting a sort of general university fungus, I say instead that this is quite possibly the first case of an academic father and his academic daughter both being honoured by the same university.

Without its contradictions and paradoxes, life just might be unbearably boring. Evidently, the honours of a patriarchal academy still mean something to me; I am still proud to be my father's daughter.

16

Telling stories

'This memoir,' wrote social work professor Olive Stevenson in her autobiography, 'is a particular kind of journey ... The journey passes through some very dark places, in my private life and working life (which cannot be separated), and it does not lead to a comfortable resting place'.[1] Every book is a story, with a narrator or narrators, a subject or subjects, and a text; to conclude with a comfortable resting place is often an artefact. Complexity is inherent in the relationship between the person telling the story and both what the story is about and its purpose: to entertain, educate, inspire, galvanise into action, to prove the facts of something. Truth-telling, which sounds such a noble enterprise, is itself the most complex of acts. This book has been a personal and intellectual journey across various terrains: the rocky land of family history, the seductions of cultural legends about people, the convoluted passages and by-ways of different versions of the social: producing descriptions of it, inventing theories about it, making policy to change it. All this is the landscape of my growing up and of my adult work as a social scientist.

The science fiction writer Joanna Russ admits that the content of her books becomes clear to her only in the act of writing them. Starting with something of personal importance to her, she then attempts to follow 'the four dimensional, misty, half-glimpsed, supercomplicated, overdetermined network in which my first preoccupation is suddenly visible as only one knotted strand'.[2] So it has been with this book. What began as the prompting of memories caused by the intervention of English Heritage in affixing a blue plaque to the wall of my childhood home turned into an excoriation of layers of history and biography, with many deviations and mini-excursions along the way. As I said at the beginning, memory is about identity. We remember what fits with the ideas we have grown about ourselves. To be challenged with reminders of what we've forgotten, or perhaps never knew, is to prompt a powerful struggle for understanding.

The American sociologist C. Wright Mills, who has already appeared in this book, published his *The sociological imagination* in 1959. I read it five years later, in 1964, the year I left the Blue Plaque House. 'Blossom and sunshine' I wrote on the flyleaf under my name. It's a book I've often quoted since, because it convinced me that it *is* possible to combine the two activities that have always interested me the most: the practice of science in studying the social, and the use of the imagination in understanding the results of this. Wright Mills' emphasis is on the three elements of biography, history and social structure as all essential. (On the exact meaning of 'imagination' he is a bit less clear.) In his Appendix 'On intellectual craftsmanship' – an excellent portmanteau of advice to aspiring social scientists spoilt only by the normal (for the time) assumption that craftspeople are men – Wright Mills offers the following often quoted and highly plausible set of instructions:

Do not allow public issues as they are officially formulated, or troubles as they are privately felt, to determine the problems that you take up for study ... Know that many personal troubles cannot be solved merely as troubles, but must be understood in terms of public issues – and in terms of the problems of history-making. Know that the human meaning of public issues must be revealed by relating them to personal troubles – and to the problems of the individual life. Know that the problems of social science, when adequately formulated, must include both troubles and issues, both biography and history, and the range of their intricate relations.[3]

The wall between the public and the private has governed many kinds of story-telling, from canonical biographies of great men and women to hygienic accounts of social research which omit any sense of researchers' own motives or the ordinary problems of collecting and interpreting data. These stories are much less interesting than the other kind, because they jar with the reader's own experience of reality as more complicated. 'The personal is political' was a credo of the 1970s Women's Liberation Movement, and it was largely the infiltration of feminism into the academy that queried the conventional political distinction between public activity and private concerns. My own work has often disinterred the one from the other, for example in showing how the unpaid labour of women in the home is a public issue, in talking about social support as a taken-for-granted and therefore neglected therapeutic intervention, or in providing a critical view of mechanical textbook models of social research interviewing. So I have been complicit in that methodological transformation which allows books like *Father and daughter* to be written, with all their messy travelogues of personal experience and public record, their excavation of secrets, lies and silences.

It used to be thought that biography is science. The diligent biographer respects 'his' subject, unearths facts, traces an unequivocal journey from the cradle to the grave. Autobiography, on the other hand, is usually a confessional and self-indulgent exercise. When people tell stories of their own lives, their motivations, in a world which values the public over the personal, are always suspect. Yet once you see these two, the public and the private, as symbiotically joined, the authorial voice reframes itself as sociological rather than narcissistic: it has a real story-telling purpose. *Father and daughter* has drawn on memories, interviews, material in personal and public archives, scholarship on the history of social science and social work, and on discussions of what is now sensibly called 'life writing'. There are many ways of writing stories about lives; there's even now something called 'autoethnography', an exercise in which the authorial eyes are turned wholly inward, so that the subjective becomes the only proper reality. I would never go so far as that, but the interpretative challenge of archival documents and other people's memories encountered in writing this book has been no small matter. What to make, for example, of the emotional letter from LSE Director Walter Adams to Richard Titmuss's widow (at the end of Chapter 12), or of the extravagantly romantic correspondence between the difficult women, or of the letter from American social work expert Charlotte Towle (in Chapter 10) labelling Richard Titmuss and his 13-year-old daughter as schizophrenic? Much is talked in the social science methods literature of something called 'triangulation' which can be applied to 'qualitative' research data in order to establish credibility. The term comes originally from broadcasting, where it relates to the use of directional antennae in deciding where a radio signal actually comes from. As a reader of hundreds of research grant applications, I've always been very suspicious when reading in them that the data will be 'triangulated', because it usually means that the researcher doesn't have a clue what to do. Nonetheless, the useful element in the idea of triangulation is that, when different sources are telling you the same thing, this is more likely to be the case than when they speak with different voices. So, with respect to Walter Adams' letter, I'm inclined to say that, even in the strictest patriarchal code, men are allowed the occasional lapse into emotion, a flood of singularly salty tears. Of the women's correspondence, it's reasonable to conclude (there's much other evidence to this effect) that women may write to each other lovingly with or without the background of heterosexist genital-sexual technique.[4] The fact that they have so written, for centuries, and about everything, has simply escaped the masculinist history of human communication. About Charlotte Towle's allegations, an unfortunate aspect of social work's professionalisation has been its apeing of medicine in making judgements about mental health and disorder: Richard Titmuss wrote most convincingly about this (even as he momentarily became a victim of it).

'Parents die. Heroes and symbols do not,' writes son Greg Bellow of his father, the award-winning novelist Saul Bellow.[5] The blue plaque event which provided the starting point for *Father and daughter* shouts legendary and symbolic status. In order to be thus commemorated, a person has to have been dead for 20 years or more, have been of significant public standing and had an exceptional public impact, made some important contribution to human welfare or happiness, and be considered eminent by most in their profession.[6] Richard Titmuss was a legend in his own time, revered by many, hailed as the founder of social policy and/or a scion of the welfare state, revealing to us secrets about the social division of welfare, and mapping for us the inequitable allocation of benefits and risks in an irresponsible society. His daughter grew up puzzling about the celebration of legendary men, its place in relation to the achievements of ordinary people. Greg Bellow's motive for writing a memoir of his father was to present a more complete picture of Saul than existing biographies, which focus on his extraordinary talents as a writer, and don't confront the toll his behaviour took on his family and friends. Reading his father's obituaries, Greg also felt that 'dozens of self-appointed sons and daughters were jostling in public for a position at the head of a parade that celebrated my father's life'. There was, he decided, 'a scholarly need' for a portrait 'by a loving son' that revealed Saul's complex nature. This is about the desire to reclaim territory – he was *my* father.[7]

Richard Titmuss wasn't a saint, and he was my father. The contradictions evident in his philosophy of welfare played out in his private life. Juxtaposed with the legend – today 'a rallying point and grounds for hope to an increasingly embattled enclave of collectivist and egalitarianly minded scholars'[8] – are critical observations about the man and his scholarship. One of the Titmice, Peter Townsend, commented on his 'unpredictability', 'instability' and 'insecurity', on how the measured calm of his demeanour hid more than the usual clutch of human inconsistencies.[9] Some of Richard Titmuss's intellectual direction reflected the interests and abilities of younger men, especially the brilliant Brian Abel-Smith. Richard Titmuss adopted conservative positions on universalism versus selectivity in welfare benefits, on the student rebellions and the new radical movements of the late 1960s, on the presence of women in academia, on the creation of the new universities.[10] He feared the new and defended the old, was more comfortable in the establishment than against it. He *enjoyed* the establishment, partly because he started out as an outsider to it. The true story of the proffered life peerages in 1964 – to whom among the Titmice these were suggested, and who actually turned them down – may be unknown, but the letter written in his last illness by Richard Titmuss to ex-Prime Minister Harold Wilson is not. If he recovered, he said in the letter, and if (as he expected) Harold Wilson would lead the next government, he was prepared, after all, 'to serve in the House of Lords'. In reply, Wilson recorded his appreciation of the suggestion and promised to keep it in mind.[11]

Richard Titmuss's fondness for establishment links served the Titmice well, but it didn't endear him to everybody. Some of his behaviour brought criticism – that he was 'a snake in saint's clothing' (this from Michael Oakeshott, a right-wing LSE colleague, although it's said that other people agreed with his description[12]). It was observed by some that he had failed his Department in not delineating more clearly the subject of social administration and in allowing the social work side to lapse in favour of policy research. Kay McDougall noted that he never gave a single lecture to the professional social work courses in his whole time at LSE, and that if he'd really seen a connection he would have wanted to give social work more of his attention. McDougall did ask him once to give a talk but he didn't prepare it and it wasn't a success: 'He wasn't a marvellous lecturer in any case.'[13] His style of measured delivery from a prepared typescript didn't suit everyone. McDougall's view was echoed by Adela Nevitt, a housing policy expert, who was a student in the Social Administration Department at the time of the LSE Affair and who returned in 1962 as a research officer. She was one of the people interviewed by Margaret Gowing, who compiled the British Academy memoir most widely drawn on in secondary accounts of Richard Titmuss's life. Gowing's memoir did not reflect Nevitt's comments. I found them for the first time a few months ago in one of the small notebooks Gowing deposited in the Titmuss Archives in LSE.[14]

Interpretation is always key. Consider photographs, which, unlike words, don't speak for themselves. The meaning inheres in the viewer's gaze. Photographs, the kind that nestle inside old archives, are often intentionally artful, a composed iconography of the happy family, for example, the splendid plump-cheeked well-dressed child, the serious young woman, the bearded patriarch, men discussing important subjects round a polished table. Some years ago I corresponded with a French economist, Philippe Fontaine, who was interested in my father's work on blood donation. He had many questions about my father's life and interest in altruism, and then he asked me for a photograph of my father. I have a cupboard full of these, mostly posed and edited professional portraits, like the one on the cover of this book, but the photo I sent Philippe Fontaine for some reason was a deliberate lie. The photograph that appears on the glossy cover of *Isis*, the journal in which Fontaine published his piece, shows Richard Titmuss in his book-lined study (which isn't incidentally where he wrote his books) with his left hand resting apparently affectionately on the mound of fur that was my cat – the cat that moulted into my black corduroy maternity dress.[15] My father hated that cat, and I can't imagine what persuaded him to pose with her like that, but there he is, a benign cat-loving professor.

Maintaining the enclosure of legendary figures safely within their legends is an artifice, an act of continuing composition. Different biographies of the same person can tell different stories, upholding images of heroes or alternatively of more ordinary people. One example is Leslie Stephen, Virginia Woolf's father, who appears in the first biography by his friend (and relative), the medieval historian Frederick Maitland, as a sensitive and congenial man,[16] and in a later biography by Noel Annan as someone whose outrageous behaviour to the daughters of the household was part of a much more flawed personality. At home, Stephen was 'insensitive, egotistical and … tyrannical. In the family, which he worshipped as the sacred entity on which the whole edifice of society and ethics is built, he revealed

... what was hidden from his friends: the inner core of his nature.'[17] Closer to home, to the intellectual circles surrounding Richard Titmuss, are the Swedish couple Alva and Gunnar Myrdal, whose three children all published stories about them, and particularly about her. The son, Jan Myrdal, portrays his mother as cold and calculating, uninterested in children except as laboratory experiments,[18] while the daughters, Sissela Bok[19] and Kaj Fölster,[20] compose more sympathetic stories around the theme of the difficulty inherent in trying to be a mother and a human being. Memories are genuinely different, as the writer Carolyn Heilbrun discovered when her adult children told stories about their childhoods at a family celebration. Not only did the stories told by different adult children clash, but Heilbrun and her husband could hardly remember any of the events and occasions they described.[21]

Documentary evidence – letters, manuscripts, notes of all kinds – can be laid aside, as Gowing did with her notes on Nevitt's 'evidence' about Richard Titmuss. It may simply not be looked at, so that the stories it contains aren't part of any official record. In the famous partnership of Simone de Beauvoir and Jean-Paul Sartre, de Beauvoir is commonly seen as illustrating his existentialist philosophy in her life and writing. Yet their posthumously published letters and diaries show that the direction of cause and effect was sometimes the other way round. Her novel *She came to stay*, considered an application of his philosophy, was read by him before he wrote *Being and nothingness;* it was one of the sources of his ideas, rather than a reflection of them.[22] Then there are bonfires. One arch-arsonist was Sigmund Freud, who started burning things when he was 29, convinced that psychoanalysis would only be seen as a science if he destroyed all evidence to the contrary.[23] The Settlement Sociologist Jane Addams was a ruthless sorter of her correspondence with Mary Rozet Smith – she burnt much and sent a selection to her nephew, James Weber Linn (who wrote the first biography of her), with the injunction 'Please read – destroy!'[24] Charlotte Towle culled her papers, abandoning much of her personal correspondence – there's hardly a trace of her long-term relationship with Mary Rall, for example, in Towle's University of Chicago Archives. One of Eileen Younghusband's executors, Nona, Countess of Essex, wanted to dispose of all Younghusband's correspondence, but was persuaded not to by another executor, Robin Huws-Jones. This near-miss event is recorded in the Younghusband Archives because Phyllis Willmott, who was writing a biography of Geraldine Aves, wanted to read the Aves–Younghusband correspondence. In a letter to the librarian at the National Institute of Social Work, Huws-Jones highlighted a big problem about accessible records: Younghusband and Aves had corresponded very little. 'They met often and telephoned even more. Transcripts of these [conversations], had they been available, would have been enthralling.'[25] Eileen Younghusband herself wasn't expecting to die on that American trip, and so hadn't prepared her papers for the trials of post-mortem scrutiny. Richard Titmuss's papers were thoroughly overhauled by his widow, who made a distinction between those that should be deposited in the LSE library and those that shouldn't. That's why I still have some of the letters and diaries and records of meetings this book has drawn on, and how I knew before I opened them that the files relating to the arguments about social work and troublesome students and the fallouts with the Titmice might not altogether show my father in a good light. For why else would my mother have kept them, except to safeguard the legend of her husband as a saintly man? The legend – well, most of it – rests in the public archive; the story of Richard Titmuss as an ordinary man is the skeleton in the cupboard.

Richard Titmuss's work continues to attract the admiration of social policy scholars, especially those who worked with him and who 'fell under his spell'.[26] What they admire is the Titmuss 'framework' which linked together moral, political and economic strands of the argument that welfare depends on effective government intervention to respect and service what Eileen Younghusband's friend Charlotte Towle called 'common human needs'. But a framework isn't a theory, and the consensus among Titmuss scholars is that he never managed to draw his ideas together into a convincing composite theory of welfare;[27] that his strong moral sense produced a misleading idealism about the capacity of social policy to create the good society;[28] that his work reflected an untoward romantic fondness for a sense of national identity,[29] that he held 'a rather blinkered view of power, vested interests and market forces'.[30] Even his magisterial account of wartime services, *Problems of social policy*, which I once tried to turn into a children's book, has been subject to a re-evaluation which argues that Richard Titmuss was wrong about the wartime foundations of the welfare state: the heightened government awareness of welfare during the war didn't produce greater solidarity.[31] His work, the Titmuss paradigm or 'semi-paradigm', is described as riddled with contradictions, for instance on the question of how far people are responsible for their own poverty and whether the dysfunction of families can be blamed on inadequate maternal behaviour.[32] At the heart of his approach beat the idea of the welfare state as 'the politicisation of good conduct',[33] and a rather mystical and hazy vision of the human capacity for goodness, 'full of muffled resonances of the idealist discourse of the Victorian age'.[34] He could never make up his mind about whether the welfare system ought to be viewed simply as the rational operation of social policy, or whether it was something beyond and above this: an embodiment of social integration and community spirit. He argued powerfully against social inequality but couldn't entertain the idea of class conflict any more than he could face the conflicts of gender.[35] For a student of welfare such as him, the neglect of informal welfare – the domain of (mostly) female labour in the home and the family – was astonishingly remiss.[36] He was 'compassionate but elitist and deeply undemocratic';[37] he found criticism unpalatable, on both personal and public levels.[38] His commitment to welfare was practised in countries whose policy-makers had never heard of him.[39] The claim that he and the other Titmice were architects of the welfare state is hard to prove.[40] But having said all that, 'Richard Titmuss was one of a kind. It is impossible to situate him in the standard division of academic labour'.[41]

Reading these critiques I find myself wanting to defend my father, not because he was right and they're wrong, but because the position of being his daughter gives me a particular awareness of his vulnerability, his human incapacity, which we all share, to be and do everything. He was a child of his time. We all are. His work and mine, the views attributed to us and the labels we're given, the ways in which we behaved and the ways in which we're seen to have behaved, position both of us in relation to the intellectual and ideological conflicts of our age. Richard Titmuss's mild-mannered socialism had to entail a defence of the state as a centralised provider of welfare, just as my own attachment to gender analysis inevitably yields a repertoire of observations about inequality between men and women. The comment about the impossibility of situating Richard Titmuss's work in the standard arrangement of academic labour rings true – of both of us.

While legends inform us about the cultural hunger for heroes and mythologies, they obstruct our ability to see beyond the landmark of the individual to the geography of the landscape. In taking a closer look at the legend of Richard Titmuss, I can also see how the reaction – my reaction – against the masculinist social science his work represented has become the substance of another legend, a legend about me as a social scientist who stuck her neck out to challenge establishment social science about its demeaning dismissal of half the social world. 'She was seen as emblematic of the new approach of emphasising subjectivity and qualitative perspectives,' says sociologist Miriam David of my work in the 1970s and '80s.[42] Thanks to the UK Data Service, an ESRC-funded mechanism for accessing many collections of secondary data, there's now a website called 'Pioneers of Qualitative Research'. This offers the material of interviews with 34 20th-century social scientists, 22 men and 12 women, all born between 1901 and 1948, 23 of them still living. Richard Titmuss isn't there because he didn't do any qualitative research, but Ann Oakley is, not because she ever claimed to be a qualitative researcher, but because this is the legend she's become.[43] Those of us who show how scholarship has been a singularly biased pursuit are called 'feminist' or 'qualitative' or both, and thus placed in a special room of our own. The clamour of our voices in that room is indeed like that famous quotation from George Eliot's *Middlemarch*: 'If we had a keen vision and feeling of all ordinary human life, it would be like hearing the grass grow and the squirrel's heart beat, and we should die of that roar which lies on the other side of silence'.[44]

Legends about individuals are also children of their time, which is why the interrogation manifest in *Father and daughter* of the Richard Titmuss legend has meant extending long probes back into history. Many histories of (stories about) social science have telescoped and twisted its long, intricate and gendered history in the interests of engineering it into particular frameworks: the evolutionary march of all science; the gentlewomanly mission of social reform; the rise of grand theory in the gentlemanly precincts of academia; the engrossing progression and regression of arguments about methods. The story of *Father and daughter* has settled on two small moments in this convoluted history: the separation during the 1950s and 1960s in Britain of social policy from the older linked traditions of social administration and social work; and the emergence, since the late 1960s, of gender analysis. The first moment is associated with the legend of Richard Titmuss, the second with the legend of the 'feminist pioneer', his daughter, Ann Oakley.

Both moments have their own special histories. 'Settlement' social science as practised in Jane Addams' Hull-House and the other five hundred or so Settlements established by 1920 was an important prelude to the conflicts that took place between social work and social policy three decades later. The reason why Settlement social science happened outside the universities was because it was largely the province of women, who weren't welcome inside them. This didn't prevent, and may actually have encouraged, its capacity to be enormously influential both as an engine for social reform and as an inspiration for university sociology. The international character of Settlement social science extended its reach. When the American Edith Abbott spent a year in London in 1906–07, she lived part of the time in St Hilda's Settlement in Bethnal Green, taking courses at LSE in statistics, mathematics, economic history, municipal government, public finance and sociology, including one taught by Sidney and Beatrice Webb on 'Methods of social investigation'. The term Abbott took it, Sidney taught it, but the model didn't vary: social science is a matter of hypothesis-building and -testing, a science like any other. Returning to Chicago, Abbott launched a similar course there.[45]

Not quite coincidentally, Edith Abbott also took back with her to Chicago Beatrice Webb's habit of smoking: 'Let men beware of the smoking woman,' urged Webb once, considering it 'a far more fatal power' even than the vote.[46] This was a time when smoking was a sign of female emancipation, and when resources for social research, apart from private philanthropy, were non-existent. Most social research was funded by private bodies, particularly the big American foundations. Social statistics was in its infancy, social work was unrecognised as a professional occupation, and nobody quite knew what sociology was. Qualitative work was the domain of men; women were responsible for the empirical study of contemporary society using quantitative and survey methods. When Edith Abbott and her colleague Sophonisba Breckinridge taught their Chicago courses, their teaching style contrasted with that of the male sociologist there, Graham Taylor; whereas he lectured in a casual manner, making much of personal stories, Abbott and Breckinridge adopted a rigorous, formal and theoretical approach: social problems were for them a matter of scientific investigation rather than 'emotional generalisation from a limited field of observation'.[47]

Histories of social science talk about 'a pattern of denying the methodology and intellectual impact' of Settlement work, about its 'intellectual burial', especially among the male founders of Chicago sociology, who called the women's social science 'social work' and downgraded it – if they acknowledged it at all – to little more than reporting 'the feelings and sentiments' of slum-dwellers.[48] The men's elision of the women's social science into social work was a clever strategy, but it depended on denying the symbiosis between social work and social investigation. Jane Addams herself pointed out that the work of the Settlements antedated by three years the first sociology department in universities, and by ten years the first foundations for social research.[49] Perhaps the Chicago men really didn't know what the women were doing, and perhaps this helps to account for the origin myth of social science methodology – that the women started out doing the qualitative work, and the men came along and built their quantitative and theoretical empires to tower disparagingly over the lesser empire of feelings and experiences. So-called 'qualitative' research or 'qualitative' sociology is the poor relation of quantitative social science; it's the view from outside the ivory tower, the science of the outsider. It's a label, a designation, a value-judgement, and, since the launch of second-wave feminism, it's been part of the hermeneutics of gender.[50] Hence its disposal on my shoulders, where it wears me down with the tedium of having perpetually to engage with it. Paradigm warfare isn't nearly as lethal as the really killing kind, but it's unproductive in the same way: it can't and doesn't settle the question. The question is: What is the question this research is trying to answer, and what kind of method is it therefore appropriate to use? Propelled into the world of social science by a childhood of listening to men arguing about social policy and insinuating the innate female hysteria of social work, I've certainly tried to respect and listen to feelings and experiences in all the research I've done. Yet most of the 74 research projects listed on my *curriculum vitae* involve numbers, percentages, statistical tests, questionnaires, surveys, systematic reviews of huge literatures, and even something as unrepentantly quantitative as randomised controlled trials. In the legend of Ann Oakley the pioneer qualitative researcher, these are conveniently forgotten, or misunderstood, or (most frequently) taken as evidence of some peculiar 'conversion' experience.[51]

Voices, experiences, the subjectivities of others – the need for these to be researched and represented is acute in structures whose logic of power relations systematically silences some voices while privileging the sound of others. The German sociologist Norbert Elias, an outsider within a culture and a traveller between cultures, was asked in his 87th year how he felt about his success: 'I still have the fantasy that I have long had,' replied Elias, 'that I am speaking into a telephone and the voice at the other end says, "Could you speak louder, I can't hear you," and then I start to shout, and the other voice keeps saying, "Speak louder, I can't hear you".'[52] The outsider's fantasy, of eventually being heard, has always been a call to political action. So it was with feminism, whose entry into the academy in the 1970s required an ideological reaffirmation of the qualitative social science project: an exposure of the quality of women's discourse, women's ways of knowing, the subjective experiences of women reconstituted as the (submerged) objective reality. Talking about that women's realm of social work, Charlotte Towle anticipated the crux of the feminist critique in pointing out that social amelioration calls not only for 'the informed head' but also for 'the informed heart'.[53] Towle saw the early women social scientists such as Jane Addams, and Mary Richmond, whose *Social diagnosis*, published in 1917, launched the concept of casework into the social work community, as having developed 'the social dimension' of political democracy through their focus on the forgotten realities of life among the disadvantaged. 'Social diagnosis' was a term also used by Beatrice Webb in her explorations of the methodology of social science.[54] Seen as the poor relation of social science and social policy, the social reform and welfare activities of these women actually enabled the fields of academic social science and policy to develop a broader basis: the social welfare background was a strength, not a weakness. This depended, however, on a relatively peaceful co-existence in the same institutional setting. It wasn't always like this, particularly in the USA, where social welfare energy was redirected to the theory and practice of casework. The 'study of social ills and public remedies' was dropped later from the British social work tradition and picked up by the field of social administration. It wasn't the welfare state which prompted the study of social administration, but the heritage of social work effort and education.[55] More or less the same argument can be made for the history of sociology: that its post-war development was altogether shaped by the links between social reform, social work and social research facilitated by the international project of the 'girls' network'.

Quite possibly the notion of 'the case', a central plank in qualitative ways of knowing, entered sociology from social work. Indeed, one of the early LSE social workers, Sibyl Clement Brown, gave a paper in the late 1930s on 'The case study as a method of social research' to an interdisciplinary group set up by a Cambridge anthropologist to discuss social research methods.[56] The early Chicago sociologists certainly made much of 'case-study method' in their claim that the essence of scientific sociology was empirical research and sticking as closely as possible to the data.

What is clear is that many stories about the development of sociology sideline as subsidiary all other activities, including the social investigations of women social reformers, even when they weren't. 'That is the perspective one expects when groups write their own history.'[57] It makes the celebration of pioneers doubly suspect, because usually the pioneers are taking forward something that has already been thought of: that's how science, including social science, works. Through their work charting the miseries of urban Chicago, Jane Addams and her co-workers regarded themselves as sociologists, although Breckinridge herself, wanting distance from patronising male sociology, stressed that she shouldn't be considered a member of 'the sociological group'.[58] British sociology, centred on LSE, was different from American sociology, but both shared the same urge to disentangle themselves from their reformist roots. The original head of Richard Titmuss's Department, E.J. Urwick, had offended no one when he called sociology 'the science of social work', but those days were long gone.[59] In the Titmuss era, the LSE sociologists referred to the Social Administration Department as 'the Department of Applied Virtue'.[60] The criminologist David Downes, who joined the Social Administration Department in 1963, described the condescending attitude of the sociologists, 'one of whose lecturers … said something like, "well, these lectures are for sociologists, not for people who are going on to administer public lavatories"'.[61] Presumably the sociologists and the Titmice didn't sit at the same tables in the senior common room, just as the social workers and the new breed of social policy staff kept themselves apart. Even as late as the mid-1960s the 'academic' staff professed no interest at all in what the social workers were doing, and everyone considered this a normal state of affairs.[62] It does have to be said, as did several of those interviewed in 2013 for the Department's history, that this distancing was partly a consequence of the social workers' own belief that no one without a social work background could possibly have anything valid to say about it.[63] Sociology wasn't a label Richard Titmuss himself used; indeed, once the political radicalism that infested LSE in the 1960s arrived contaminated by sociology, he became particularly anxious not to have anything to do with it, and even found himself making liaisons with the economists whose right-wing views hadn't previously appealed to him.[64]

With the famous wisdom of hindsight, two paradoxes stand out. The first is that it was the administrative creation of Titmuss's own Department as an enterprise distinctly separated off from sociology – sociologist T.H. Marshall's attempt to relieve himself of the burden of managing the social workers – that helped to drive apart the reformist works of social policy and social work, on the one hand, and the more theoretically minded business of sociology, on the other. The second paradox is that the more social work focused its attention on procedures of professionalisation and the specialist language of psychodynamically informed casework, the easier it became for social policy and sociology both to cast off any recognition of their joint familial relationship. The use of casework to unite different social work fields – the essence of the experimental Carnegie Course which nearly shattered Richard Titmuss's Department – was the key tool in defining social work as more than a technical matter of helping to administer public sector social services. But instead of returning social work to its previous incarnation as social reform, it emphasised the individuality of need and the social workers' specialist psychological knowledge. The social policy world was then quite right in insisting that none of this had to do with reformist (or any kind of) policy-making.

In fact, the study of social policy benefitted directly from social work's earlier and then progressively abandoned twinship with social reform. The 'psychologising' of social work was led by female social work educators and opposed by male social administration academics.[65] We are thus returned to the observation about homosocial worlds, a step that re-connects us to the theme of gendered ways of knowing. The existence of men's networks and women's networks is easily mistaken for the old doctrine of separate spheres: women with their special sensitivity and aptitude for caring operating in an autonomous domestic domain, men populating the public world of industry and politics and scholarship with their 'detached objectivity'.[66] The divorce of social work, of female social science, from institutionalised sociology, allowed sociology to repeat all the mistakes of male socialisation.

It's a bewildering history, with all these interconnections between gender, method, and concepts of the social. The story isn't a linear one, and it isn't the same on both sides of the Atlantic. Sociology took longer to become institutionalised in Britain, which meant that the Schools of Social Science, Sociology or Social Study that proliferated in the early 20th century as a forum for women social workers occupied their separate sphere for longer. By the time we come to the 1950s and 1960s there's a strong interest from non-feminist social scientists in qualitative research, community studies and the whole general strategy of immersion in the lives of the disadvantaged as a basis for formulating policy. This was the rationale for the Institute of Community Studies, which Michael Young, Richard Titmuss's PhD student, founded in an East London settlement in 1954, in alliance with the sociologist and writer Peter Willmott, and with Peter Townsend, who was to become one of the Titmice. Like Sophonisba Breckinridge, but for different reasons, they were careful to differentiate themselves from the sociologists, an insecure bunch as Peter Willmott recalled them, protagonists of an infant discipline struggling to fill it with theory and science.[67]

The sultry heat of a Greek summer saturated the lecture hall when Richard Titmuss addressed his audience at the Twelfth International Congress of Schools of Social Work in Athens in September 1964. In the front row was his daughter, wearing a pink-and-white-striped poplin dress and sitting next to her about-to-be-husband, who looked smart in a linen jacket and polished shoes. Richard Titmuss's subject was 'The relationship between schools of social work, social research and social policy'. His text exhibited no fondness for research: 'Research workers retire to cultivate their ten square inches of social phenomena for much the same reasons as caseworkers continually re-examine their feelings about dominant mothers and passive fathers,' he declared. In both cases they're looking for security and neutrality. He did conclude that social workers ought to concern themselves some of the time with social policy research, although 'theoretical and methodological advances in the social sciences' meant that they could no longer do so without specialist social science help. Ergo, social workers weren't social scientists and shouldn't pretend to be.[68] This rather damning message escaped me at the time. I noted in my diary only that the lecture was dull, and that before it Robin Huws-Jones, Director of the National Institute of Social Work, and one of Eileen Younghusband's literary executors, but then to me simply a cheerful friendly Welshman, came and said hallo to me. Lectures and social work experts must have seemed insignificant indeed to a young woman in love and recently hypnotised by the glories of Greece – the Parthenon and the Agora golden in the sun, a boat ride to a tiny island full of donkeys and ripe figs. I remember, looking at the conference photograph now – which is in black-and-white, but transposed in my mind to accommodate the sticky pinkness of that dress – that my main concern at the time wasn't with theories about the proper intersections of social work, research and policy, but with the practical discomfort of a urinary tract infection brought on by the heat, too much sex and too much sedentary labour helping my husband-to-be collect economic statistics in the offices of the Ionian Bank. Stories about lives are also stories about bodies, and bodily sensations are part of memory.

Various puzzles remain in what is still a substantially untold history. Why did Richard Titmuss's moral imagination, so keenly alert to the importance of altruism, not notice how important the early women social workers were in acting out what he believed in, participative citizenship? Why did he not query the intrusion of the state into this process, the interruption of the welfare state in the community-mindedness of its citizens? It was E.J. Urwick who argued that the state's increased role in providing welfare would destroy the transformative potential of community-based social work.[69] This was something Richard Titmuss's wife Kay knew about from her own background as a volunteer social worker, so the question there is why she didn't involve herself more directly in the arguments he was having about the role of social work. Alma Hartshorn, who wrote the book about the Carnegie Experiment, sent her a copy when it was published in 1982, a decade after Richard Titmuss's death; Kay responded, remembering the 'stresses and strains' of those years, and reminding Hartshorn of her own seemingly still-vivid social work history.[70]

Richard Titmuss's transformation of the Department of Social Administration at LSE into a Department of Social Policy was no foregone conclusion. Had the internal disputes been handled differently, the Department could have become a national centre for social work research and training staffed with a cadre of able social work professors, as happened elsewhere, for example in Bristol and Aberdeen. This strategy would have overcome the problem that the social policy courses had to subsidise the social work ones, because of the latter's greater fieldwork costs.[71]

The answer to the question as to why so many key women social scientists have dropped out of the wider story is of course obvious: all histories have holes through which minority groups fall to a lower and darker place. Women disappear, or are given special rooms of their own. But we know much less about the mechanisms and strategies which cause this disappearance or unwanted specialisation. We're quite ignorant about the connected histories of women 'practical intellectuals', who combined learning, action and public policy. We don't know the extent to which interlocking networks of women reformers/researchers/social scientists/practical intellectuals have operated in different countries at different times and with what consequences. For example, the Swedish social researcher and reformer Kerstin Hesselgren was trained as a sanitary inspector at Bedford College in London in the early 1900s (having already learnt nursing and home economics and, most extraordinarily, acquired a certificate as a barber–surgeon). She practised her passion for research-based social reform by being one of the first Swedish women MPs, the first female factory inspector in Sweden, the instigator of many social investigations, a prime mover in the first social workers' union, and a network-builder for women across political parties and classes. When the Swedish government set up a Committee on Women's Work in the late 1930s, Hesselgren was its Chair, and another social scientist/reformer/politician, Alva Myrdal, was its Secretary.[72] Networking, especially women's networking has, like friendship, been neglected as part of the story of 20th-century social science.

A childhood exposure to the social science of the Blue Plaque House taught me four enduring lessons. The first is the lesson about how lateral thinking is much more productive than stubborn disciplinary allegiances. It matters not at all (or only in an 'academic' sense) whether what we're doing counts as social policy or social administration or sociology, whether it belongs in the field of education or health or welfare or in the more amorphous land of public policy. The questions override territorial enclosures. Richard Titmuss specialised in seeing that. Secondly, I understood that what I would later encounter as 'the crisis in epistemology' of Western culture – the suspension of belief in any kind of stable objective reality – is simply a trick of the mind invented by theorists who've got nothing better to do. Reality does exist, and so does the real stress and pain that derive from a completely non-random (unfair) distribution of life-chances. Thirdly, I learnt that one way to make a

258

difference is to argue on the basis of evidence rather than opinion about the need for change (which is not to say that evidence plus opinion, in the kind of clever networking Richard Titmuss and his disciples were so good at on 'their Holborn stage',[73] isn't the most effective option of all). Lastly, you don't need to hold all this in your head so long as you know where to find it. Back in the 1950s we really did have door-to-door salesmen who tried to offload copies of the 32-volume *Encyclopaedia Britannica* on us. I was a sucker for their sales technique, but my financially prudent social accounting father was not. He told me to get on a bus and go to the library. Richard Titmuss would have loved the democratic epistemology of the internet (although his wife would probably have needed to operate the computer for him).

Notes and references

In the notes below 'TP (AO)' refers to Richard Titmuss and Kay Titmuss's papers in the possession of Ann Oakley, 'TP (LSE)', to Richard Titmuss's papers deposited in the Archives of the British Library of Political and Economic Science at the London School of Economics.'OP' are papers, in her possession, relating to Ann Oakley's life and work. 'YP' refers to the papers of Eileen Younghusband in the Modern Records Centre at the University of Warwick; 'YP Tapes' to the box of unlabelled tape recordings held there. Where the notes say 'YP Tapes', the information comes from my listening to the tape in question; 'YP Tapes, transcript' refers to the box of (partial) transcripts in the Archive. At the time I read them, these had not been ordered or catalogued. The full reference for both tapes and transcripts is MSS.463/EY/Z/1-2. 'CTP' indicates the Charlotte Towle Papers deposited in the Special Collections Research Center at the University of Chicago Library. 'CI' refers to the series of interviews with social workers conducted by Alan Cohen and held in the WiseArchive, Modern Records Centre, University of Warwick, www2.warwick.ac.uk./services/library/mrc/explorefurther/subject_guides/social_work.'LSE HDSP' refers to an oral history of the Department of Social Policy at LSE with interviews conducted by Sonia Exley, data to be deposited in the British Library of Political and Economic Science and the UK Data Archive.

Notes

Chapter 1, Daughter of a Blue Plaque Man

[1] F.C. Howard to R.M.Titmuss, 21 September 1951,TP (AO).

[2] Wright Mills, C. (1959) *The sociological imagination*, New York: Oxford University Press, p 225.

[3] Miller, S.M. (1987) 'Introduction: the legacy of Richard Titmuss', in B. Abel-Smith and K.Titmuss (eds) *The philosophy of welfare*, pp 1-17, at p 16.

[4] Crossman, R. (1973) 'Tribute', *Professor Richard Morris Titmuss: A thanksgiving*, St Martin-in-the-Fields, 6 June (unpublished paper), TP (AO).

[5] *The Observer* (1950) 'Welfare professor: Richard M.Titmuss', *The Observer* profile, 22 March.

[6] Elias, N. (1994) *Reflections on a life*, Cambridge: Polity Press, p 14.

[7] Lomas, P. (ed) (1967) *The predicament of the family*, London: Hogarth Press and the Institute of Psychoanalysis.

[8] P.Townsend, Diary, 21 August 1997, copy of unpublished ms given by PT to AO.

[9] M.Vaizey, Interview by AO, 11 February 2014.

[10] Douglas, K. (2010) *Contesting childhood: Autobiography, trauma and memory*, New Brunswick, NJ: Rutgers University Press.

[11] Steedman, C. (1986) *Landscape for a good woman*, London: Virago, p 44.

[12] Gordon, L. (1990) 'What is gender blind is gender obscuring: the new feminist scholarship on the welfare state', in L. Gordon (ed) *Women, the state and welfare*, Madison, Wisconsin: University of Wisconsin Press, pp 9-35, at p 30.

Chapter 2, Falling into the bog of history

[1] Jephcott, A.P. (1942) *Girls growing up*, London: Faber, p 22.

Chapter 3, Memory and identity

[1] Miller, N.K. (1991) *Getting personal: Feminist occasions and other autobiographical acts*, London: Routledge, p 14.

[2] Wootton, B. (1959) *Social science and social pathology*, London: Allen & Unwin, p 322.

[3] de Beauvoir, S. (1960, originally published 1949, trans. and ed. H.M. Parshley) *The second sex*, London: Four Square Books, pp 25-6.

4 Abel-Smith, B. and Titmuss, K. (1987) 'Preface', in B. Abel-Smith and K. Titmuss (eds) *The philosophy of welfare*, pp ix-xvi, at p xii.

5 Titmuss, R.M. (1960) *The social division of welfare*, Eleanor Rathbone Memorial Lecture, Liverpool: Liverpool University Press. Reprinted in Abel-Smith and Titmuss (1987) *The philosophy of welfare*.

6 Styron, A. (2011) *Reading my father: A memoir*, New York: Scribner, p 154.

7 Styron, p 183.

8 Douglas, M. (1966) *Purity and danger*, London: Routledge and Kegan Paul.

9 Bell, A.O. (ed) (1984) *The diary of Virginia Woolf, vol 5 1936–41*, Orlando, FL: Harcourt Brace Jovanovich, entry for Monday, 30 September 1939.

10 Woolf, V. (ed. J. Schulkind, revised H. Lee) (2002) *Moments of being: Autobiographical writings*, London: Pimlico, p 125.

11 Dickerson, E.R. (n.d.) 'Richard Titmuss CBE – teacher, counsellor, thinker and friend', unpublished ms, TP (AO).

12 *Acton Gazette* (1973) 'Over 1,000 pay last respects to Prof. Titmuss', 14 June.

13 Ball, D. (1978) 'The quiet saint who gave us the blessing of his inspiration', *Health and Social Service Journal*, 29 September, pp 1108-12.

14 E. Leach, quoted in Halsey, A.H. (2004) 'Titmuss, Richard Morris (1907–1973)', *Oxford dictionary of national biography*, Oxford University Press.

15 Rosen, A. (1973) 'A personal remembrance of Richard Titmuss', *Social Work Education Reporter*, Council for Social Work Education, 21 (3): 10.

16 Halsey (2004).

17 Dasgupta, S. (1973) 'Richard Titmuss: the man and his mission', *International Social Work*, 16: 49-52, at p 51.

18 Hennessy, P. (1973) 'Professor Richard Titmuss', *Times Higher Education Supplement*, 20 April, p 2.

19 B. Wootton to K.C. Titmuss, 7 April 1973, TP (AO).

20 Crossman, R. (1973) 'Tribute', *Professor Richard Morris Titmuss: A thanksgiving*, St Martin-in-the-Fields, 6 June (unpublished paper), TP (AO).

21 Gerth, H.H. and Wright Mills, C. (1947) *From Max Weber: Essays in sociology*, London: Kegan Paul, Trench, Trubner & Co., Ltd, pp 245-52.

22 H. Rose to K.C. Titmuss, 27 April 1973, TP (AO).

23 Randall, W.L. and McKim, A.E. (2008) *Reading our lives: The poetics of growing old*, Oxford: Oxford University Press, p 9.

24 Cited in Randall and McKim, p 40.

25 Rose, S. (2003) *The making of memory: From molecules to mind*, London: Vintage, p 363.

[26] Marris, P. (1996) *The politics of uncertainty: Attachment in private and public life*, London: Routledge, p 24.

Chapter 4, Family and kinship in London and other places

[1] Woolf, V. (1993, ed. R. Bowlby) *The crowded dance of modern life*, London: Penguin, p 21.

[2] Gowing, M. (1975) 'Richard Morris Titmuss', *Proceedings of the British Academy*, 61: 401-27.

[3] R. Pinker, Personal communication.

[4] Grundy, F. and Titmuss, R.M. (1945) *Report on Luton*, Luton: Gibbs, Bamforth.

[5] Inventory of the possessions of William Tyttmus, 1685, Hertfordshire Wills.

[6] *Bedfordshire Advertiser and Luton Times*, 14 July 1905.

[7] Bedfordshire and Luton Archives, WW1 AC/OP/2/132, CC/X17, CC/X22, JN792/14, JN793/3.

[8] *Luton Times and Advertiser*, 10 April 1908.

[9] Bedfordshire and Luton Archives, CC/X17, CC/X22.

[10] *Luton Times and Advertiser*, 10 June 1904 and 8 March 1907.

[11] Szreter, S. (1992) 'Mortality and public health, 1815–1914', *ReFresh* 14): 1-4.

[12] Silverman, M.E. (2002) 'D. Evan Bedford: master cardiologist and bibliophile', *Clinical Cardiology*, 25: 250-1.

[13] Townsend, P. (1958) 'A society for people', in N. MacKenzie (ed), *Conviction*, London: MacGibbon & Kee, pp 93-120, at p 112.

[14] Rose, H. (1981) 'Rereading Titmuss: the sexual division of welfare', *Journal of Social Policy*, 10 (4): 477-501.

[15] Rose, H. (1995) 'Speaking volumes', *Times Higher*, 23 June.

[16] Wilson, E. (1980) *Only halfway to paradise*, London: Tavistock, p 65.

[17] Frankenberg, R. (1976) 'In the production of their lives: men (?) ... sex and gender in British community studies', in D.L. Barker and S. Allen (eds) *Sexual divisions and society: Process and change*, London: Tavistock Publications, pp 24-51, at p 43.

[18] Institute of Community Studies Advisory Committee, Minutes of 4th Meeting, 21 June 1956, TP (AO).

[19] 'Lord Young of Dartington', *The Times*, 16 January 2002, p 19.

[20] R.M. Titmuss (n.d.) Note attached to unpublished ms, 'Housewives and equality', TP (AO).

[21] Stacey, M. (1969) 'The myth of community studies', *British Journal of Sociology*, 10 (2): 178-92.

[22] Young, S., 'A view from the cage', unpublished ms, OP.

[23] Mogey, J.M. (1956) *Family and neighbourhood: Two studies in Oxford*, Oxford University Press, p 156.

[24] P. Townsend to R.M. Titmuss, 5 September 1956, TP (AO).

Chapter 5, Mrs Titmuss's diaries

[1] R.N. Maini to K.C. Titmuss, 23 June 1978, TP (AO).

[2] K.C. Titmuss to 'Agatha', 25 November 1975, TP (AO).

[3] K.C. Titmuss to R. Crossman, 10 November 1973, TP (AO).

[4] Baker, A.P. (2004) 'Glass, Ruth Adele (1912–1990)', *Oxford dictionary of national biography*, Oxford University Press.

[5] Simey, M. (1996) *The disinherited society*, Liverpool, Liverpool University Press; M. Simey to A. Oakley, 24 November 1996, OP.

[6] M. Simey to K.C. Titmuss, 8 November 1976, TP (AO).

[7] Lord Collison (1973) 'Prof. R.M. Titmuss', *The Times*, 12 April.

[8] P. Townsend, Diary, 21 August 1997, copy of unpublished ms given by PT to AO.

[9] Lewontin, R.C. (2004) 'Sex, lies and social science (a book review with subsequent correspondence)', in C. Seale (ed) *Social research methods: A reader*, London: Routledge, pp 182–92, at p 190.

[10] Mills, K. (ed) (2000) *C. Wright Mills: Letters and autobiographical writings*, Berkeley, CA: University of California Press, p 255.

Chapter 6, Love and solitude

[1] Raine, K. (1956) 'Vegetation', in *The collected poems of Kathleen Raine*, London: Hamish Hamilton, p 39.

[2] Södergran, E. (1985, trans. S. Katchadourian) *Love & solitude: Selected poems 1916–1923*, Seattle: Fjord Press, p 23.

[3] Södergran, E. (1918) 'Introduction to Septemberlyran', quoted in S. Katchadourian, 'Introduction' to *Love & solitude*, p xi.

[4] Maitland, S. (2008) *A book of silence*, London: Granta, p 49.

Chapter 7, The story of the Titmice: an alternative version

[1] Sheard, S. (2013) *The passionate economist*, Bristol: Policy Press. The term 'Titmice' was also applied to social policy scholars trained by Richard Titmuss. See Mann, K. (2008) 'Remembering and rethinking the social divisions of welfare 50 years on', *Journal of Social Policy*, 38 (1): 1-18, at p 1.

[2] H. Glennerster, LSE HDSP, 2013, p 21.

[3] Smith, C.S. (1991) 'Networks of influence: the social sciences in the UK since the war', in P. Wagner, C. Weiss, B. Wittrock and H. Wollman (eds) (1991) *Social sciences and modern states*, Cambridge: Cambridge University Press, pp 131-47.

[4] Delisle, F. (1964, originally published 1946) *Friendship's odyssey*, London: Delisle Ltd.

[5] Oakley, A. (1991) 'Eugenics, social medicine and the career of Richard Titmuss in Britain 1935–50', *British Journal of Sociology*, 42 (2): 165-94.

[6] TP (LSE), TITMUSS/3/436.

[7] R.M. Titmuss to J. Morris, 29 October 1959, Titmuss Papers (AO).

[8] J.Vaizey to B. Abel-Smith, 14 August 1952, Abel-Smith Papers, 6/9, quoted in Sheard (2013), p 71.

[9] Vaizey, J. (1983) *In breach of promise*, London: George Weidenfeld & Nicolson Ltd, p 75.

[10] Sheard (2013), p 71.

[11] Sheard (2013), p 486.

[12] P. Townsend, Diary, 21 August 1997, copy of unpublished ms given by PT to AO.

[13] B. Abel-Smith to AO, 12 April 1995, OP.

[14] B. Abel-Smith to AO, 14 May 1995, OP.

[15] J.Vaizey to R.M. Titmuss, 4 February 1959, TP (AO).

[16] Kanter, J. (2004) 'Clare Winnicott: her life and legacy', in J. Kanter (ed) *Face to face with children: The life and work of Clare Winnicott*, London: Karnac, pp 1-94; Kahr, B. (1996) *Donald Winnicott: A biographical portrait*, London: H. Karnac Books Ltd.

[17] Kahr (1996), p 45. This story is contested by some on the grounds that Clare Britton, Winnicott's second wife, declared her regret that she had never had his baby (D. Donnison, Personal communication).

[18] Kahr (1996), p 87.

[19] Kahr (1996), p 60.

Chapter 8, Meeting Win

[1] Davidoff, L. (2012) *Thicker than water: Siblings and their relations 1780–1920*, Oxford: Oxford University Press, Chapter 4.

[2] Davidoff, L., Doolittle, M., Fink, J. and Holden, K. (1999) *The family story: Blood, contract and intimacy 1830–1960*, Harlow, Essex: Wesley Longman Ltd, p 5.

[3] Strathern, M. (2005) *Kinship, law and the unexpected: Relatives are always a surprise*, Cambridge: Cambridge University Press, p 11.

[4] Davidoff (2012), p 4.

[5] Smart, C. (2007) *Personal life: New directions in sociological thinking*, Cambridge: Polity Press, p 45.

[6] Titmuss, R.M. (1970) *The gift relationship*, London: Allen & Unwin, p 15.

Chapter 9, Harem in Houghton Street

[1] Pinker, R. (1995) 'The place of freedom in the concept of welfare', in E. Barker (ed) *LSE on freedom: A centenary anthology*, London: LSE Books, pp 229–45, at p 235.

[2] Prochaska, F.K. (2006) *Christianity and social service in modern Britain: The disinherited spirit*, Oxford: Oxford University Press.

[3] Davis, A.F. (1973) *American heroine: The life and legend of Jane Addams*, New York: Oxford University Press; Lasch, C. (ed) (1982) *The social thought of Jane Addams*, New York: Irvington.

[4] Addams, J. (1961) *Twenty years at Hull-House*, New York: Signet, p 98.

[5] Plummer, K. (ed) (1997) *The Chicago School: Critical assessments, Vol. II, Theory, history and foundations*, London: Routledge.

[6] Fitzpatrick, E. (1990) *Endless crusade: Women social scientists and progressive reform*, New York: Oxford University Press; Freedman, E. (1979) 'Separatism as strategy: female institution building and American feminism, 1870–1930', *Feminist Studies*, 5 (3): 512–29; Shoemaker, L.M. (1998) 'Early conflicts in social work education', *Social Service Review*, 72 (2): 182–91.

[7] Harris, J. (1989) 'The Webbs, the Charity Organisation Society and the Ratan Tata Foundation: social policy from the perspective of 1912', in M. Bulmer, J. Lewis and D. Piachaud (eds) *The goals of social policy*, London: Unwin Hyman, pp 27–63, at p 42.

[8] Harris, J. (1992) 'Political thought and the welfare state 1870–1940', *Past and Present*, 135 (1): 116–41, at p 137.

[9] Irving, J.A. (1948) 'The social philosophy of E.J. Urwick' (Preface), in E.J. Urwick, *The values of life*, Toronto: University of Toronto Press, pp xi–lxv.

[10] Harris (1989), p 44.

[11] Stocks, M.D. (1970) *My commonplace book*, London: P. Davies, p 82.

[12] Attlee, C.D. (1920) *The social worker*, London: G. Bell & Sons, Ltd, Preface (no p no), p 221.

[13] De Vesselitsky, V. (1917) *Expenditure and waste: A study in war-time*, London: G. Bell & Sons.

[14] Tawney, R.H. (1916) 'Introduction' to V. de Vesselitsky, *The homeworker and her outlook*, London: G. Bell & Sons, pp xiii-xvi; Vesselitsky, V. de (1927) *'Up or Down?' A play in one act*, London: Stepney Skilled Employment Committee.

[15] Jones, K. (1984) *Eileen Younghusband: A biography*, London: Bedford Square Press, p 23.

[16] Russell, K., Benson, S., Farrell, C., Glennerster, H., Piachaud, D. and Plowman, G. (1981) *Changing course*, London: LSE, Chapter 2.

[17] Dahrendorf, R. (1995) *LSE: A history of the London School of Economics and Political Science 1895-1995*, Oxford: Oxford University Press, pp 298, 517.

[18] Reisman, D. (2005) *Democracy and exchange*, Cheltenham: Edward Elgar, p 273.

[19] Davidson, J. (2010) *A three-cornered life: The historian W.K. Hancock*, University of Sydney: New South Wales Press Ltd, pp 193-4.

[20] Tawney, R.H. (1950) 'The War and the people' (review of R.M. Titmuss, *Problems of social policy*) *The New Statesman and Nation*, 22 April, pp 454-6; Marshall, T.H. (1973) 'Richard Titmuss - an appreciation', *The British Journal of Sociology*, 24 (2): 137-9, p 138.

[21] Marshall, T.H. (1973) 'A British sociological career', *International Social Science Journal*, 25 (1/2): 88-100.

[22] D. Donnison, Interview, 17 April 2013.

[23] K.C. Titmuss (n.d.), Note on C. Marsh, TP (AO).

[24] Vaizey, J. (1983) *In breach of promise*, London: George Weidenfeld & Nicolson Ltd, p 67.

[25] Halsey, A.H. (1996) *No discouragement: An autobiography*, Houndmills, Basingstoke: Macmillan, p 216.

[26] Dahrendorf (1995), p 382.

[27] Pinker, R. (1989) 'Social work and social policy in the twentieth century: retrospect and prospect', in Bulmer et al, pp 84-107, at p 84.

[28] Willmott, P. (2007) 'Russell, Katherine Frances (1909–1998)', *Oxford dictionary of national biography*, Oxford University Press.

[29] H. Rose, Interview, 16 July 2013.

[30] Thomas, J. (2004) 'Winnicott, (Elsie) Clare Nimmo (1906–1984)', *Oxford dictionary of national biography*, Oxford University Press.

[31] Pinker (1989) p 95.

[32] Chesterton, J. (1962) 'At last some FACTS about Those Working Mothers', *Daily Herald*, 19 May.

[33] 'The real reason why wives go out to work', *Daily Mail*, 17 May 1962.

[34] Jephcott, P. (1962) *Married women working*, London: George Allen and Unwin Ltd, p 162.

[35] Turnbull, A. (2004) 'Jephcott, (Agnes) Pearl (1900–1980)', *Oxford dictionary of national biography*, Oxford University Press.

[36] Smith, M.K. (2008) 'Pearl Jephcott, youth and the lives of ordinary people', www.infed.org/thinkers/pearl_jephcott.htm.

[37] P. Jephcott to R.M. Titmuss, 14 August 1961, TP (AO).

[38] Turnbull (2004).

[39] A. Carr-Saunders to R.M. Titmuss, 20 February 1957, TP (AO).

[40] Strebel, I. and Jacobs, J.M. (2013) 'People and buildings: Pearl Jephcott and the science of life in high flats', *Candide*, no 7, October, pp 13-36; Strebel, I. and Jacobs, J.M. (2014) 'Houses of experiment: modern housing and the will to laboratorization', *International Journal of Urban and Regional Research*, 38 (2): 450-70.

Chapter 10, Difficult women

[1] 'Tailgunner' Parkinson (1981) 'Obituary, Eileen Younghusband', *New Society*, 11 June.

[2] Oldfield, S. (2001) *Doers of the world: British women humanitarians 1900–1950*, London: Continuum, pp 6-9.

[3] CI, no 26, p 7.

[4] CI, no 26, p 5.

[5] Burnham, D. (2011) 'Selective memory: a note on social work historiography', *British Journal of Social Work*, 41: 5-21, at p 14.

[6] YP Tapes.

[7] YP Tapes, transcript.

[8] R. Parker, Interview, 27 November 2013.

[9] D. Donnison, Interview, 17 April 2013.

[10] Marshall, T.H. (1973) 'A British sociological career', *International Social Science Journal*, 25 (1/2): 88-100.

[11] R.M. Titmuss (1950), Note on LSE interview, TP (AO).

[12] TP (AO).

[13] R.M.Titmuss to E.Younghusband, and E.Younghusband to R. M.Titmuss, 27 June 1951,TP (AO).

[14] R.M.Titmuss to E.Younghusband, 6 July 1951,TP (AO).

[15] YP, Diaries 1949-58, MSS.463/EY/J32-42.

[16] Hartshorn, A. (1982) *Milestone in education for social work: The Carnegie Experiment 1954–1958*, London:The Carnegie United Kingdom Trust, p 68.

[17] YP Tapes, transcript.

[18] Proposal for a 'School of Social Work',TP (LSE),TITMUSS/4/599.

[19] R.M.Titmuss (n.d.), Note attached to proposal for an 'Institute of Applied Social Studies',TP (LSE),TITMUSS/4/599.

[20] H. Roberts to E.Younghusband, 10 May 1953,YP, MSS.463/EY/P1121-1175.

[21] Stewart, J. (2006) 'Psychiatric social work in inter-war Britain: child guidance, American ideas, American philanthropy', *Michael Quarterly* 3: 78-91.

[22] Fisher, R.M. (n.d.) 'Charlotte Towle', CTP, Box 13, Folder 9,

[23] Jones, K. (1984) *Eileen Younghusband: A biography*, London: Bedford Square Press, pp 58-9.

[24] R.M.Titmuss (1958, lecture given 1951) 'Social administration in a changing society', in *Essays on 'the welfare state'*.

[25] 'Ewing destroys F.S.A. Pamphlet', *Greensburg Daily Tribune*, 16 April 1951.

[26] Committee on Un-American Acts (1949) 'Review of the Scientific and Cultural Conference for World Peace', Washington DC: US House of Representatives.

[27] E.Younghusband to C.Towle, 21 July 1954, CTP.

[28] E. Younghusband to R.M. Titmuss, 24 October 1953, TP (LSE), TITMUSS/4/601.

[29] A. Carr-Saunders to R.M. Titmuss, 2 February 1954, TP (LSE), TITMUSS/4/602.

[30] 'Obituary, Baroness Seear', *Independent*, 24 April 1997.

[31] CI, no 7, p 4.

[32] Wootton, B. (1959) *Social science and social pathology*, London: George Allen & Unwin Ltd, p 273.

[33] Titmuss, R.M. (1959) 'Perfectionism and pessimism: a review article', *Case Conference*, 6 (5):119-24, atp 24.

[34] Correspondence between R.M.Titmuss and B.Wootton and K. McDougall, December 1959–February 1960, TP (AO).

[35] Keith-Lucas, A. (1953) 'The political theory implicit in social casework theory', *The American Political Science Review*, 47 (4): 1076-91.

[36] CTP, Box 4, Folder 6.

[37] Urwick, E.J. (1930) *The principle of reciprocity in social life and action*, Charles Loch Memorial Lecture, London: Charity Organisation Society.

[38] C.Towle to E.Younghusband, 18 January 1956, YP, MSS.463/EY/P1291-1338.

[39] R.M.Titmuss to E.Younghusband, 2 June 1955, YP, MSS.463/EY/P1246-1290.

[40] D. Donnison, Interview, 17 April 2013.

[41] C.Towle to E.Younghusband, 18–19 May 1957, YP, MSS.463/EY/P1339-1601.

[42] Jones (1984), p 63.

[43] C.Towle to E.Younghusband, 23 June 1957, YP, MSS.463/EY/P1339-1601.

[44] R. Parker, Interview, 27 November 2013.

[45] Jones (1984), p 62. The origin of these terms as applied to participants in the LSE Affair is unclear.

[46] K. Elliott to E. Younghusband, 23 June 1957, YP, MSS.463/EY/ P1339-1601; D. Donnison to R.M.Titmuss, 10 May 1957, TP (LSE), TITMUSS/4/602.

[47] D. Donnison to R.M.Titmuss, 17 January 1957, TP (LSE), TITMUSS/4/606.

[48] K. McDougall to R.M.Titmuss, 21 January 1957, TP (LSE), TITMUSS/4/606.

[49] K. Russell to E.Younghusband, 19 February 1957, YP, MSS.463/EY/P1339-1601.

[50] 'Helen' to E.Younghusband, 21 February 1957, YP, MSS.463/EY/ P1339-1601.

[51] C.Towle to E.Younghusband 10 June 1957, YP, MSS.463/EY/ P1339-1601.

[52] D.N. Lowe to R.M.Titmuss, 21 February 1957, YP, MSS.463/EY/ P1339-1601.

[53] D. Donnison, Personal communication.

[54] S. Clement Brown, reported in undated document, TP (LSE), TITMUSS/4/606.

[55] R.M. Braithwaite and others to R.M.Titmuss, 26 February 1957, TP (LSE), TITMUSS/4/606.

[56] G.S. Prince to R.M.Titmuss, 26 February 1957, TP (LSE), TITMUSS/4/606.

[57] 'Jane' to E. Younghusband, 22 February 1957, YP, MSS.463/EY/ P1339-1601. David Donnison confirms this view (see D. Donnison, LSE HDSP, 2013, p 9).

[58] Undated document by R.M. Titmuss, TP (LSE), TITMUSS/4/602.

[59] D.N. Lowe to E. Younghusband, 15 April 1957, YP, MSS.463/EY/ P1339-1601.

[60] D.N. Lowe to C. Towle, 17 April 1957, YP, MSS.463/EY/ P1339-1601.

[61] R.M. Titmuss to E. Younghusband, 4 March 1957, YP, MSS.463/EY/ P1339-1601.

[62] R.M. Titmuss to E. Younghusband, 22 March 1957, YP, MSS.463/EY/ P1339-1601.

[63] R. M. Titmuss to C. Towle, 21 February 1957; C. Towle to E. Younghusband, 11 March 1957, YP, MSS.463/EY/ P1339-1601.

[64] C. Towle to R.M. Titmuss, 21 March 1957, YP, MSS.463/EY/ P1339-1601.

[65] C. Towle, Note (n.d.) attached to copy of C. Towle letter to R.M. Titmuss, 21 March 1957, sent by C. Towle to E. Younghusband, YP, MSS.463/EY/ P1339-1601.

[66] C. Towle to S. Caine, 27 March 1957, CTP, Box 3, Folder 13.

[67] CI, no 24, p 27.

[68] E. Younghusband to R.M. Titmuss, 20 March 1957, TP (LSE), TITMUSS/4/602.

[69] D. Donnison to R.M. Titmuss, 10 May 1957, TP (LSE), TITMUSS/4/602.

[70] C. Towle to E. Younghusband, 18–19 May 1957, YP, MSS.463/EY/ P1339-1601.

[71] C. Towle to E. Younghusband, 18–19 May 1957, YP, MSS.463/EY/ P1339-1601.

[72] C. Towle to E. Younghusband, 23 June 1957, YP, MSS.463/EY/ P1339-1601.

[73] D. Donnison (1965) 'Taking decisions in a university', in D. Donnison, V. Chapman, M. Meacher, A. Sears and K. Urwin, *Social policy and administration revisited*, London: George Allen & Unwin Ltd, pp 253-85.

[74] C. Towle to E. Younghusband, 18 January 1956, YP, MSS.463/EY/ P1291-1338.

[75] C. Towle, Diary for 1955, CTP, Box 20.

[76] C. Towle to E. Younghusband, 23 June 1957, YP, MSS.463/EY/ P1339-1601.

[77] K. Elliott to E. Younghusband, 23 June 1957, YP, MSS.463/EY/ P1339-1601.

[78] E.Younghusband to S. Caine, 2 May 1957,YP, MSS.463/EY/P1339-1601.

[79] D. Donnison to E.Younghusband, 15 May 1957,YP, MSS.463/EY/P1339-1601.

[80] Platt, J. (1991) 'Anglo–American contacts in the development of research methods before 1945', in M. Bulmer, K. Bales and K.K. Sklar (eds) *The social survey in historical perspective 1880–1940*, Cambridge: Cambridge University Press, pp 340–58.

[81] YP Tapes, transcript.

[82] Z. Butrym, Interview, 5 September 2013.

[83] R. Pinker, Interview, 18 September 2013.

[84] Dahrendorf, R. (1995) *LSE: A history of the London School of Economics and Political Science 1895–1995*, Oxford: Oxford University Press, p 384.

[85] R.M.Titmuss to L. Farrer-Brown, 26 September 1957,TP (AO).

[86] I. Shaw (in press) 'Sociology and social work: in praise of limestone?', in J. Holmwood and J. Scott (eds) *The Palgrave handbook of sociology in Britain*, London: Palgrave, pp 123–54.

[87] Jones, K. (1984) *Eileen Younghusband: A biography*, London: Bedford Square Press, p 70.

Chapter 11, Post-mortem

[1] 'Noblewoman dies in wreck', *The Robesonian*, 28 May 1981.

[2] 'Martha Branscombe', www.naswfoundation.org/pioneers/b/branscombe.htm; see also http://simpsonhistory.com/notes/marthabranscomb.

[3] M. Branscombe to E. Younghusband, 9 April 1954, YP, MSS.463/EY/P1097-1120.

[4] Freedman, E. (1979) 'Separatism as strategy: female institution building and American feminism, 1870–1930', *Feminist Studies*, 5 (3): 512–29.

[5] Gordon, L. (1992) 'Social insurance and public assistance: the influence of gender in welfare thought in the United States, 1890–1935', *American Historical Review*, 97 (1): 19–54, p 26; Gordon, L. (1996) 'Fitting Charlotte Towle into the history of welfare thought in the U.S.', paper presented at conference in honour of Charlotte Towle sponsored by the University of Chicago School of Social Service Administration.

[6] 'Tailgunner' Parkinson (1981) 'Obituary, E. Younghusband', *New Society*, 11 June.

[7] C. Towle (1946) 'Social casework in modern society', reprinted in H.H. Perlman (ed) (1969) *Helping: Charlotte Towle on social work and social casework*, Chicago: University of Chicago Press, pp 97–119, at p 100.

[8] CI, no 2, p 23.

[9] CTP, Box 12, Folder 1.

[10] Branscombe, M. (1948) 'A friend of international welfare', *Social Service Review*, 22 (4): 436-41, at p 441.

[11] Costin, L.B. (1983) *Two sisters for social justice: A biography of Grace and Edith Abbott*, Urbana and Chicago: University of Illinois Press, p 100.

[12] Shoemaker, L.M. (1998) 'Early conflicts in social work education', *Social Service Review*, 72 (2): 182-91, at p 189.

[13] Abbott, E. (1942) *Social welfare and professional education*, Chicago: University of Chicago Press, p vii.

[14] Abbott, E. (1942), pp 1-19; Titmuss, R.M. (1958) 'The university and welfare objectives' in *Commitment to welfare*.

[15] Abbott (1942), p 2.

[16] Costin (1983), p xii.

[17] Costin (1983), p 231.

[18] Perkins, F. (1954) 'My recollections of Florence Kelley', *Social Service Review*, 28 (1) 12-19.

[19] Bryan, M.L M. and Davis, A F. (1990) *100 years at Hull-House*, Bloomington, Indiana: Indiana University Press, p 61.

[20] Muncy, R. (1991) *Creating a female dominion in American reform 1890–1935*, New York: Oxford University Press, pp 47-8.

[21] Costin (1983), p viii.

[22] YP Tapes, transcript.

[23] YP Tapes.

[24] Kendall, K.A. (1989) 'Women at the helm: three extraordinary leaders', *Affilia,* 4(1): 23-32, at p 30.

[25] D. Donnison, LSE HDSP, 2013, pp 8, 18.

[26] R.M. Titmuss to S. Caine, 21 September 1960, TP (LSE), TITMUSS/3/436.

[27] Titmuss, R.M. (1962) 'Time remembered', *Link*, LSE, pp 3-7, at p 4.

[28] Plante, D. (1984) *Difficult women: A memoir of three*, London: Futura, p 142.

[29] D. Donnison, Interview, 17 April 2013.

[30] R. Parker, Interview, 27 November 2013.

[31] D. Donnison, LSE HDSP, 2013, p 18.

[32] H. Rose, Interview, 16 July 2013.

[33] Winner, A.L. (1947) 'Homosexuality in women', *The Medical Press*, 218 (10): 219-24.

[34] Saunders, C (2004) 'Winner, Dame Albertine Louisa (1907–1988)', *Oxford dictionary of national biography*, Oxford University Press.

[35] Perlman (1969), p xi.

[36] YP Tapes.

[37] YP Tapes.

[38] Fredriksen-Goldsen, K.I., Lindhorst, T., Kemp, S.P. and Walters, K.L. (2009) '"My Ever Dear": social work's "lesbian" foremothers – a call for scholarship,' *Affilia*, 24 (3): 325-36, at p 329.

[39] Faderman, L. (1992) *Odd girls and twilight lovers*, London and New York: Penguin, p 25.

[40] Davis, A.F. (1973) *American heroine: The life and legend of Jane Addams*, New York: Oxford University Press, p 89; Streitmatter, R. (2012) *Outlaw marriages: The hidden histories of fifteen extraordinary same-sex couples*, Boston: Beacon Press, Chapter 4.

[41] Di Leonardo, M. (1985) 'Warrior virgins and Boston marriages: spinsterhood in history and culture', *Feminist Issues*, 59 (2): 47-68.

[42] Muncy (1991), p 32.

[43] Jabour, A. (2012) 'Relationship and leadership: Sophonisba Breckinridge and women in social work', *Affilia*, 27 (1): 22-37, at p 28.

[44] Oldfield, S. (2001) *Doers of the world: British women humanitarians 1900–1950*, London: Continuum, pp 51-2.

[45] YP Tapes, transcript.

[46] YP Tapes, transcript.

[47] Willmott, P. (1992) *A singular woman: The life of Geraldine Aves 1898–1986*, London: Whiting & Birch Ltd.

[48] H. Roberts to E. Younghusband, 9 September 1948, YP, MSS.463/EY/P923-977.

[49] H. Roberts to E. Younghusband, 10 May 1953, YP, MSS.463/EY/P1121-1175.

[50] YP Tapes, transcript.

[51] YP Tapes.

[52] C. Towle, Diary for 1955, 27 January 1955, CTP, Box 20.

[53] Titmuss, R.M. (1958, lecture given 1956) 'Industrialization and the family', in *Essays on 'the welfare state'*.

[54] Kendall, K.A. (2006) 'Robin Huws Jones (UK) President 1976–1980', *Social Work and Society*, 4 (2): 341-50.

[55] YP Tapes, transcript.

[56] K. Russell to E. Younghusband, 19 February 1957, YP, MSS.463/EY/ P1339-1601.

[57] YP Tapes, transcript.

[58] C. Towle, Diary for 1955, CTP, Box 20.

[59] YP Tapes, transcript.

[60] Davis (1973), p 306.

[61] Stevenson, O. (2013) *Reflections on a life in social work: A personal and professional memoir*, Buckingham: Hinton House Publishers Ltd, p 48.

[62] Haight, G. S. (1961) 'Introduction' in K.A. McKenzie (1961) *Edith Simcox and George Eliot*, Oxford: Oxford University Press, pp xi–xviii, at p xv.

[63] R. Parker, Interview, 27 November 2013.

[64] Posner, W.B. (1986) *Charlotte Towle: A biography*, PhD dissertation, University of Chicago, p 314.

[65] YP Tapes.

[66] F. Mitchell, in transcript of 'Carnegie Resurrection Project' proceedings, YP, MSS.463/EY/2/9/1.

[67] S. Clement Brown, in transcript of 'Carnegie Resurrection Project' proceedings, YP, MSS.463/EY/2/9/1.

[68] Z. Butrym to A. Hartshorn, 6 December 1976; R.M. Braithwaite to A. Hartshorn, 25 April 1976; D. Donnison to A. Hartshorn, 12 April 1976; G. Aves to R.M. Braithwaite, 24 September 1976, YP, MSS.463/EY/2/9/1.

[69] G. Aves to R.M. Braithwaite, 24 September 1976, YP, MSS.463/EY/2/9/1.

[70] A. Hartshorn to K. Russell, 3 May 1976, YP, MSS.463/EY/2/9/1.

[71] R. Wright to R.M. Braithwaite, 14 July 1976, YP, MSS.463/EY/2/9/1.

[72] K. Kendall to K.C. Titmuss, 25 April 1973, TP (AO).

[73] E. Munro, Personal communication.

[74] P. Partridge to A. Titmuss, 19 December 1961, OP.

Chapter 12, The Troubles

[1] Kehoe, L. (1995) *In this dark house*, London: Penguin.

[2] Gullestad, M. (1996) 'Modernity, self, and childhood in the analysis of life stories', in M. Gullestad (ed) *Imagined childhoods*, Oslo: Scandinavian University Press, pp 1–39, at p 6.

[3] Cited in Warner, M. (1976) *Alone of all her sex: The myth and cult of the Virgin Mary*, London: Weidenfeld and Nicolson, p 45.

[4] TP (LSE), TITMUSS/ADD/2/5.

[5] Peter Thompson, cited in Sheard, S. (2013) *The passionate economist*, Bristol: Policy Press, p 219.

[6] File of CBE letters, TP (AO).

[7] R.M. Titmuss to J. Hewitt, 10 September 1965, TP (AO).

[8] P. Townsend, Diary, 21 August 1997, copy of unpublished ms given by PT to AO.

[9] P. Calvorcoressi et al, 'The turning point' (letter), *The Times*, 27 February 1968.

[10] Titmuss, R.M. (1960) *The social division of welfare*, Eleanor Rathbone Memorial Lecture, Liverpool: Liverpool University Press. Reprinted in B. Abel-Smith and K. Titmuss (eds) (1987) *The philosophy of welfare*.

[11] Supplementary Benefits Commission (1971) *Cohabitation: The administration of the relevant principles of the Ministry of Social Security Act 1966*, Report by the Supplementary Benefits Commission to the Secretary of State for Social Services, London: HMSO.

[12] Rowe, R. (2014) 'Titmuss: the dilemmas of benefits for women', Unpublished paper.

[13] Neubeck, K. (2006) *When welfare disappears: The case for economic human rights*, New York: Routledge.

[14] P. Townsend to R.M. Titmuss, 14 March 1963, TP (AO).

[15] 'Extract of interview with Peter Townsend on his "Essex Days"', Stories of Essex sociology, http://essexsociologyalumni.com/memories/tales-from-past, p 2.

[16] P. Townsend to R.M. Titmuss, 14 March 1963, TP (AO).

[17] R.M. Titmuss to P. Townsend, 17 December 1968, TP (AO).

[18] P. Townsend to R.M. Titmuss, 15 December 1971; R.M. Titmuss to P. Townsend, 7 January 1972, TP (AO).

[19] P. Townsend, Diary, 21 August 1997, copy of unpublished ms given by PT to AO.

[20] R.M. Titmuss to T. Lynes, 12 January 1971; H. Collison to R.M. Titmuss, 5 January 1971, TP (AO).

[21] T. Lynes, Personal communication.

[22] R.M. Titmuss to S. Caine, 21 September 1960, TP (LSE), TITMUSS/3/436.

[23] T. Lynes, Personal communication.

[24] T. Lynes, Personal communication.

[25] Millmow, A. (2009) 'The economist as gadfly: The last decade of Lord John Vaizey's life', paper presented at 22nd Conference of the History

of Economic Thought Society of Australia, University of Notre Dame, Fremantle, Western Australia, 14–17 July, http://www.hetsa.org.au, p 6.

[26] Millmow (2009), p 13.

[27] Millmow (2009), p 1.

[28] Vaizey, J. (1983) *In breach of promise*, London: George Weidenfeld & Nicolson Ltd, p 3.

[29] Dahrendorf, R. (1995) *LSE: A history of the London School of Economics and Political Science 1895–1995*, Oxford: Oxford University Press, p 445.

[30] Hoefferle, C.M. (2013) *British student activism in the long sixties*, New York: Routledge.

[31] Dahrendorf (1995), p 473.

[32] Kidd, H. (1969) *The trouble at L.S.E. 1966–1967*, London: Oxford University Press, p 101.

[33] 'A student is a student is a student', *The Times*, Editorial, 2 February 1967.

[34] Kidd (1969), pp 52-3.

[35] Dahrendorf (1995), p 454.

[36] Blackstone, T., Gales, K., Hadley, R. and Lewis. W. (1970) *Students in conflict: L.S.E. in 1967*, L.S.E. Research Monographs 5, London: Weidenfeld and Nicolson, pp 163-4.

[37] R.M. Titmuss to H. Kidd, 11 November 1968, TP (AO).

[38] Dahrendorf (1995), pp 464-5.

[39] W. Adams to F. Keohane, 22 January 1969, TP (AO).

[40] R. Blackburn, Interview, 11 November 2013.

[41] K.M. Slack, Memorandum to the teaching staff in the Department of Social Administration, 30 April 1969, TP (AO).

[42] Crouch, C. (1970) *The student revolt*, London: The Bodley Head, pp 84-5.

[43] R.M. Titmuss to G. Ashley, 1 May 1969, TP (AO).

[44] R.M. Titmuss to R. Blackburn, 30 April 1969, TP (AO).

[45] N. Bateson and R. Blackburn to W. Adams, 6 May 1969, TP (AO).

[46] R. Blackburn, Interview, 11 November 2013.

[47] 'LSE militants branded as thugs and wreckers of academic world', *The Times*, 30 January 1969.

[48] P. Townsend to B. Abel-Smith, R.M. Titmuss, R. Crossman, P. Shore and S. Williams, 23 May 1968, TP (AO).

[49] 'The case of two superbrains who didn't hit it off to a T', *Daily Mirror*, 28 December 1970.

[50] Blackstone et al (1970), pp 212-14, 231-2.

[51] R.M. Titmuss to D. Downes, 3 June 1969, TP (AO).

[52] W. Adams to K. Titmuss, 7 April 1973, TP (AO).

Chapter 13, Dusting his bookshelves

[1] See Thomas, E. (1998) 'Health and efficiency', in M. David and D. Woodward (eds) *Negotiating the glass ceiling: Careers of senior women in the academic world*, London: Falmer Press, pp 147-59.

[2] Wilson, E. (1980) *Only halfway to paradise*, London: Tavistock.

[3] Notes on interviews for the Institute of Community Studies, OP.

[4] Acker, J. (1997) 'My life as a feminist sociologist; or, getting the man out of my head', in B. Laslett and B. Thorne (eds) *Feminist sociology: Life histories of a movement*, New Brunswick, NJ: Rutgers University Press, pp 28-47.

[5] Titmuss, R.M. (1958, lecture given 1952) 'The position of women', in *Essays on 'the welfare state'*, London: Allen & Unwin, p 102.

[6] Titmuss (1958), p 117.

[7] Ardener, E. (1972) 'Belief and the problem of women', in J. La Fontaine (ed) *The interpretation of ritual*, Abingdon: Routledge, pp 135-58, at p 136.

[8] Lyon, E.S. (2007) 'Viola Klein: forgotten émigré intellectual, public sociologist and advocate of women', *Sociology*, 4 (5): 829-42, at p 836.

[9] Savage, M. (2010) *Identities and social change in Britain since 1940: The politics of method*, Oxford: Oxford University Press, p 93.

[10] Fenstermaker, S. (1997) 'Telling tales out of school: three short stories of a feminist sociologist', in Laslett and Thorne, pp 209-28, p 220

[11] Ingraham, C. (1994) 'The heterosexual imaginary: feminist sociology and theories of gender', *Sociological Theory*, 12 (2): 203-19, at p 213.

[12] Franklin, S. (1996) 'Introduction', in S. Franklin (ed) *The sociology of gender*, Cheltenham: Edward Elgar, p xiii.

[13] Hird, M.J. (2000) 'Gender's nature: intersexuality, transsexualism and the "sex"/"gender" binary', *Feminist Theory*, 1 (3): 347-64, at p 348.

[14] Delphy, C. (1993) 'Rethinking sex and gender', *Women's Studies International Forum*, 16 (1): 1-9.

[15] *The Oxford English Dictionary*.

[16] Rose, H. (1981) 'Re-reading Titmuss: the sexual division of welfare', *Journal of Social Policy*, 10 (4): 477-501, at p 480.

[17] 'Including the kitchen sink', *The Economist*, 8 February 1975.

[18] Oakley, A. and Mooney, B. (1975) 'What is a housewife?', *NOVA*, January: 16-23.

[19] Vincent, S. (1974) 'Kitchen stink', *New Society*, 14 November, p 433.

[20] McQuillan, D. (1974) 'The housetrap', *Hibernia*, 6 December.

[21] O'Rourke, F. (1983) 'A dirty business', *Sunday Press*, 13 November.

[22] Shapiro, L. (1974) 'A broom of one's own', *The Real Paper*.

[23] Fawkes, S. (1974) 'How Mrs Oakley learned to stop burning beefburgers and live', *Daily Express*, 4 September.

[24] Cooper, J. (1975) 'Housework', *The Sunday Times*, 9 February.

[25] Titmuss, R.M. (1958, lecture given 1952) 'The hospital and its patients', in *Essays on 'the welfare state'*, p 120.

[26] Titmuss, R.M. (1974) 'Postscript' in B. Abel-Smith and K. Titmuss (eds) *Social policy: An introduction*, London: George Allen & Unwin.

[27] 'Note from Westminster Hospital', October 1972, TP (AO).

Chapter 14, Vera's rose

[1] Mansfield, P., and Collard, J. (1988) *The beginning of the rest of your life?*, Houndmills, Basingstoke: Macmillan, p 23.

[2] http://oldroses.nl/my-roses/gallicas/charles-de-mills/.

[3] Mills, K. (2000) 'Preface', pp xii-xiii, in K. Mills (ed) *C. Wright Mills: Letters and autobiographical writings*, Berkeley: University of California Press.

[4] D. Howard to R.M. Titmuss, 12 December 1967; R. M. Titmuss to D. Howard, 3 January 1968, TP (AO).

[5] Cited in Holroyd, M. (2002) *Works on paper: The craft of biography and autobiography*, London: Abacus, p 81.

Chapter 15, This procession of educated men

[1] Nicolson, N. (2000) *Virginia Woolf*, London: Weidenfeld & Nicolson, pp 129-30.

[2] Woolf, V. (1992, originally published 1938) *A room of one's own, and Three guineas*, Oxford: Oxford University Press, pp 240-1.

[3] Woolf (1992), p 249.

[4] Shiach, M. (1992) 'Introduction' to *A room of one's own and Three guineas*, pp xii-xxxii, at p xxvii.

[5] Nicolson (2000), p 133.

[6] Walby, S. (1990) *Theorizing patriarchy*, Oxford: Blackwell, p 20.

[7] Rose, H. (1998) 'An accidental academic', in M. David and D. Woodward (eds) *Negotiating the glass ceiling: Careers of senior women in the academic world*, London, Falmer Press, pp 101-13, at pp 111-12.

[8] Cockburn, C. (1991) *In the way of women: Men's resistance to sex equality in organizations*, Houndmills, Basingstoke: Macmillan, p 6.

[9] Thorne, B. and Hochschild, A.R. (1999) 'Feeling at home at work', in B. Glassner and R. Hertz (eds) *Qualitative sociology as everyday life*, London: Sage Publications, pp 211-14.

[10] YP Tapes, transcript.

[11] D. Piachaud, p 3, S. Sainsbury, p 14, and D. Donnison, p 18, LSE HDSP, 2013.

[12] Keefe, T. (1993) 'The flawed bible', *The Times Higher*, 26 March.

[13] Crosland, M. (1992) *Simone de Beauvoir: The woman and her work*, London: Macmillan, pp 372, 359.

[14] Lyon, E.S. (2000) 'Biographical constructions of a working woman: the changing faces of Alva Myrdal', *European Journal of Social Theory*, 3 (4): 407-28, at p 417.

[15] Ekerwald, H. (2000) 'Alva Myrdal: making the private public', *Acta Sociologica*, 43: 342-52; Holmwood, J. (2000) 'Three pillars of welfare state theory: T.H. Marshall, Karl Polanyi and Alva Myrdal in defence of the national welfare state', *European Journal of Social Theory*, 3 (1): 23-50.

[16] Lionel Trilling, cited in Matthews, A. (1992) 'Rage in a tenured position', *The New York Times*, 8 November.

[17] Jacobs, S.P. (2006) 'Denied tenure, Skocpol alleged sexual discrimination', *The Harvard Crimson*, 5 June.

[18] Banks, O. (1999) 'Some reflections on gender, sociology and women's history', *Women's History Review*, 8 (3):401-10.

[19] YP Tapes, transcript.

[20] Halsey, A.H. (2004) *A history of sociology in Britain*, Oxford: Oxford University Press, p 88.

[21] Parsons, T. and Bales, R.F. (1956) *Family, socialization and interaction process*, London: Routledge and Kegan Paul.

[22] T. Blackstone, Interview, 19 April 2013, and Personal communication.

[23] Oakley, A. (1974) *The sociology of housework*, Oxford: Martin Robertson, Chapter 1, "The invisible woman: sexism in sociology'.

[24] Platt, J. (2007) 'The women's movement and British journal articles, 1950–2004', *Sociology*, 4 (5): 961-75.

[25] Platt (2007), pp 962, 972.

[26] Oakley, A. (2004) 'Epilogue in eight essays: Ann Oakley', in Halsey, pp 214–17.

[27] Halsey (2004), pp 170–1.

[28] Banks (1999), p 408.

[29] Rose (1998), p 113.

[30] M. Stacey to B. Wootton, 14 May 1967, Girton College Personal Papers, Wootton 1/2/5.

[31] Stacey, M. (1998) 'A flying start', in David and Woodward, pp 83–100, p.98.

[32] T. Blackstone, Personal communication.

[33] Tizard, B. (2010) *Home is where one starts from*, Edinburgh: WP Books.

[34] Bagilhole, B. (1993) 'How to keep a good woman down: an investigation of the role of institutional factors in the process of discrimination against women academics', *British Journal of Sociology of Education*, 14 (3): 261–74, at p 269.

[35] 'Unique unit where men are in minority', *The Times Higher*, 15 January 1993, p 21.

[36] See www.ioe.ac.uk/ssru/; https://eppi.ioe.ac.uk; /www.annoakley.co.uk

[37] Blackstone, T. (1987) 'Education and careers for women and girls: the broken chain', *Policy Studies*, 8 (2): 1–18.

[38] Equality Challenge Unit (2012) *Equality in higher education: Statistical report. Part 1: staff*.

[39] Rich, A. (1980) *On lies, secrets, and silence*, London: Virago, p 136.

[40] Chakrabortty, A. (2014) 'Meet the new breed of fat cat: the university vice-chancellor', *The Guardian*, 3 March.

[41] Barone, C. (2011) 'Some things never change: gender segregation in higher education across eight nations and three decades', *Sociology of Education*, 84 (2): 157–76.

[42] Russ, J. (1998) *What are we fighting for? Sex, race, class, and the future of feminism*, New York: St Martin's Press, p 203.

[43] Bagilhole (1993), p 270.

[44] Davies, C. and Holloway, P. (1995) 'Troubling transformations: gender regimes and organizational culture in the academy', in L. Morley and V. Walsh (eds) *Feminist academics: Creative agents for change*, London: Taylor & Francis, pp 7–21, at p 15.

[45] Bernstein, B. (1984) 'A note on the position of funded research staff', Internal Institute of Education memorandum, 25 January.

[46] Woolf (1992), p 204.

[47] Nicolson (2000), p 111.

Chapter 16, Telling stories

[1] Stevenson, O. (2013) *Reflections on a life in social work: A personal and professional memoir*, Buckingham: Hinton House Publishers Ltd, p 2.

[2] Russ, J. (1998) *What are we fighting for? Sex, race, class, and the future of feminism*, New York: St Martin's Press, p xiv.

[3] Wright Mills, C. (1959) *The sociological imagination*, New York: Oxford University Press, p 226.

[4] See e.g. Cook, B.W. (1979) 'Female support networks and political activism', in N.F. Cott and E.H. Pleck (eds) *A heritage of her own*, New York: Simon & Schuster, pp 412-44; Faderman, L. (1985) *Surpassing the love of men*, London: Women's Press; Smith-Rosenberg, C. (1975) 'The female world of love and ritual: relations between women in nineteenth-century America', *Signs*, 1 (1): 1-30; Stanley, L. (1992) 'Romantic friendship? Some issues in researching lesbian history and biography', *Women's History Review*, 1 (2): 193-216.

[5] Bellow, G. (2013) *Saul Bellow's heart: A son's memoir*, London: Bloomsbury, p 223.

[6] www.english-heritage.org.uk/content/imported-docs/p-t/blue-plaques-selection-criteria.pdf.

[7] Bellow (2013), p 3.

[8] R. Pinker, Personal communication.

[9] P. Townsend, Diary, 21 August 1997, copy of unpublished ms given by PT to AO.

[10] Kincaid, J. (1984) 'Richard Titmuss', in P. Barker (ed) *Founders of the welfare state*, Aldershot.: Gower Publishing Co., pp 114-20; Reisman, D. (2001) *Richard Titmuss: Welfare and society*, Houndmills: Palgrave; Welshman, J. (2004) 'The unknown Titmuss', *Journal of Social Policy*, 33 (2): 223-47.

[11] R.M. Titmuss to H. Wilson, 14 October 1972; H. Wilson to R.M. Titmuss, 14 November 1972, TP (AO).

[12] T. Blackstone, Interview, 19 April 2013.

[13] CI, no 14, p 33.

[14] TP (LSE), TITMUSS/ADD/2/5.

[15] Fontaine, P. (2002) 'Blood, politics, and social science: Richard Titmuss and the Institute of Economic Affairs, 1957–1973', *Isis*, 93:401-434.

[16] Maitland, F.W. (1906) *The life and letters of Leslie Stephen*, London: Duckworth.

[17] Annan, N.G. (1977) *Leslie Stephen*, New York: Arno Press, pp 94-5.

[18]   Myrdal, J. (1971, trans. C. Swanson) *Childhood*, Chicago, IL: LakeView Press; Myrdal, J. (1994, trans. A. Bernstein) *Another world: An autobiographical novel*, Chicago: Ravenswood Books.

[19]   Bok, S. (1991) *Alva Myrdal: A daughter's memoir*, Reading, MA: Addison-Wesley.

[20]   Fölster, K. (1992) *De tre löven. En myrdalsk efterskrift*, Stockholm: Bonnier.

[21]   Heilbrun, C.G. (1997) *The last gift of time: Life beyond sixty*, New York: Ballantine Books, pp 119-20.

[22]   Evans, M. (2009) 'Can women be intellectuals?', in C. Fleck, A. Hess and E.S. Lyon (eds) *Intellectuals and their publics*, Farnham, Surrey: Ashgate, pp 29-40, at p 34.

[23]   Holroyd, M. (2003) *Works on paper*, London: Abacus, p 11.

[24]   Bryan, M.L.M. (2011) 'The Jane Addams Papers: a project in scholarly reconstruction', *Peace and Change*, 36 (1): 80-89, at p 82.

[25]   R. Huws-Jones to G. Ryan, 6 October 1988, YP, MSS.463/EY/2/3/6.

[26]   Glennerster, H. (2014) *Richard Titmuss: forty years on*, CASE Paper 180, p 3.

[27]   Gough, I. (1979) *The political economy of the welfare state*, London: Macmillan; Kincaid (1984); Mishra, R. (1984) *The welfare state in crisis*, London: Macmillan; Wilding, P. (1976) 'Richard Titmuss and social welfare', *Social and Economic Administration*, 10 (3):147-66.

[28]   Deacon, A. (1993) 'Richard Titmuss: 20 years on', *Journal of Social Policy*, 22(2): 235-42; Wilding, P. (1995) 'Titmuss' in V. George and R. Page (eds) *Modern thinkers on welfare*, Hemel Hempstead: Prentice-Hall/Harvester Wheatsheaf.

[29]   Rose, H. (1981) 'Re-reading Titmuss: the sexual division of welfare', *Journal of Social Policy*, 10 (4): 477-501.

[30]   Mann, K. (2009) 'Remembering and rethinking the social division of welfare: 50 years on', *Journal of Social Policy*, 38 (1): 1-18, at p 11.

[31]   Thane, P. (1996) *Foundations of the welfare state*, Harlow: Addison Wesley Longman Ltd, p 246; Welshman, J. (1999) 'Evacuation, hygiene, and social policy: The Our Towns Report of 1943', *The Historical Journal*, 42 (3): 781-807.

[32]   Welshman (2004).

[33]   Reisman, D. (2005) *Democracy and exchange*, Cheltenham: Edward Elgar, Chapter 11.

[34]   Harris, J. (1992) 'Political thought and the welfare state 1870–1940', *Past and Present*, 135: 116-41, at p 137.

[35]   Kincaid (1984).

[36] Offer, J. (1999) 'Idealist thought, social policy and the rediscovery of informal care', *Journal of Sociology*, 50 (3) :467–88; Rose (1981).

[37] Rose, H. (1998) 'An accidental academic', in M. David and D. Woodward (eds) *Negotiating the glass ceiling: Careers of senior women in the academic world*, London, Falmer Press, pp101–113, p107.

[38] D. Piachaud, LSE HDSP, 2013, p 11.

[39] Donnison, D. (2000) 'The academic contribution to social reform', *Social Policy & Administration*, 34 (1) :26–43.

[40] J. LeGrand, LSE HDSP, 2013, p 15.

[41] Reisman (2005), p 294.

[42] David, M.E. (2003) *Personal and political: Feminisms, sociology and family lives*, Stoke on Trent: Trentham Books, p 78.

[43] Pioneers of qualitative social research, UK Data Service, http://ukdataservice.ac.uk/teaching-resources/pioneers.aspx.

[44] Eliot, G. (1872) *Middlemarch*, London: Blackwood, p 226.

[45] Costin, L.B. (1983) *Two sisters for social justice: A biography of Grace and Edith Abbott*, Urbana and Chicago, IL: University of Illinois Press, pp 31–2.

[46] Mackenzie, N. and MacKenzie, J. (eds) (2000) *The diaries of Beatrice Webb*, London: Virago, in association with LSE, p 73, entry for 28 May 1886.

[47] Muncy, R. (1991) *Creating a female dominion in American reform 1890–1935*, New York: Oxford University Press, p 77.

[48] Deegan, M.J. (1997) 'Hull-House maps and papers: the birth of Chicago sociology', in K. Plummer (ed) *The Chicago School: Critical assessments, vol 11 Theory, history and foundations*, Routledge: London, pp 5–19, p 13.

[49] Addams, J. (1930) *The second twenty years at Hull-House*, New York: Macmillan, p 405.

[50] Oakley, A. (2000) *Experiments in knowing: Gender and method in the social sciences*, Cambridge: Polity Press, Chapter 3.

[51] Oakley, A. (2000) 'Paradigm wars: some thoughts on a personal and public trajectory', *International Journal of Social Research Methodology*, 2 (3): 247–54.

[52] Elias, N. (1994) *Reflections on a life*, Cambridge: Polity Press, pp 73–4.

[53] Towle, C. (1969, originally published 1961) 'Social work: cause and function', in H.H. Perlman (ed) *Helping: Charlotte Towle on social work and social casework*, Chicago: University of Chicago Press, pp 278–99, at p 280.

[54] Webb, B. (1971, originally published 1926) *My apprenticeship*, London: Longmans, Green and Co, p 291.

[55] Parker, R. (1972) 'Social ills and public remedies', in W.A. Robson (ed) *Man and the social sciences*, London: LSE and George Allen and Unwin Ltd, pp 113–29.

[56] CI, no 7, p 7.

[57] Platt, J. (1996) *A history of sociological research methods in America 1920–1960*, Cambridge: Cambridge University Press, p 264.

[58] Coghan, C.L. (2005) '"Please don't think of me as a sociologist": Sophonisba Preston Breckinridge and the early Chicago school', *The American Sociologist*, April: 3-22.

[59] Urwick, E.J. (1930) *The principle of reciprocity in social life and action*, Charles Loch Memorial Lecture, London: Charity Organisation Society, p 14.

[60] Rose (1981), p 479.

[61] D. Downes, LSE HDSP, 2013, p 22.

[62] T. Blackstone, Interview, 19 April 2013.

[63] D. Piachaud, p 8, and S. Sainsbury, p 15, LSE HDSP, 2013.

[64] Dahrendorf, R. (1995) *LSE: A history of the London School of Economics and Political Science 1895–1995*, Oxford: Oxford University Press, p 385.

[65] Lewis, J. (1995) *The voluntary sector, the State and social work in Britain*, Aldershot, Hants.: Edward Elgar.

[66] Yeo, E.J. (1996) *The contest for social science: Relations and representation of gender and class*, London: Rivers Oram Press, p 297.

[67] Willmott, P. (1985) 'The Institute of Community Studies', in M. Bulmer (ed) *Essays on the history of British sociological research*, Cambridge: Cambridge University Press, pp 137-50.

[68] Titmuss, R.M. (1968, lecture given 1964) 'The relationship between schools of social work, social research and social policy', in *Commitment to welfare*.

[69] Urwick (1930).

[70] K.C. Titmuss to A. Hartshorn, 11 October 1982, TP (AO).

[71] H. Glennerster, Personal communication.

[72] Wisselgren, P. (2009) 'Women as public intellectuals: Kerstin Hesselgren and Alva Myrdal', in Fleck et al (2009), pp 225-41.

[73] Savage, M. (2010) *Identities and social change in Britain since 1940: The politics of method*, Oxford: Oxford University Press, p 123.

Richard Titmuss and Ann Oakley: main publications

Richard Titmuss

(1938) *Poverty and population*, London: Macmillan

(1942, with K. Titmuss) *Parents revolt*, London: Secker & Warburg.

(1943) *Birth, poverty and wealth*, London: Hamish Hamilton.

(1950) *Problems of social policy*, London: HMSO.

(1952) The position of women, Millicent Fawcett Lecture, reprinted in *Essays on 'the welfare state'*.

(1955) The social division of welfare, Eleanor Rathbone Memorial lecture, reprinted in *Essays on 'the welfare state'*.

(1956) Abel-Smith, B. and Titmuss, R.M. *The cost of the National Health Service in England and Wales*, Cambridge: Cambridge University Press.

(1958) *Essays on 'the welfare state'*, London: Allen & Unwin

(1962) *Income distribution and social change*, London: Allen & Unwin.

(1968) *Commitment to welfare*, London: Allen & Unwin.

(1970) *The gift relationship*, London: Allen and Unwin.

(1961, with B. Abel-Smith and T. Lynes) *Social policies and population growth in Mauritius*, London: Methuen.

Posthumous publications:

(1974) Abel-Smith, B. and Titmuss, K. (eds) *Social policy: An introduction*, London: George Allen & Unwin.

(1987) Abel-Smith, B. and Titmuss, K. (eds) *The philosophy of welfare: Selected writings of Richard M. Titmuss*, London: Allen & Unwin.

Ann Oakley

(1972) *Sex, gender and society*, London: Temple Smith (new edition 2015, Farnham: Ashgate).

(1974) *Housewife*, London: Allen Lane.

(1974) *The sociology of housework*, London: Martin Robertson.

(1979) *Becoming a mother*, Oxford: Martin Robertson (later retitled *From here to maternity*).

(1980) *Women confined: Towards a sociology of childbirth*, Oxford: Martin Robertson.

(1981) *Subject women*, Oxford: Martin Robertson.

(1984) *The captured womb: A history of the medical care of pregnant women*, Oxford: Basil Blackwell.

(1984) *Taking it like a woman*, London: Jonathan Cape.

(1986) *Telling the truth about Jerusalem*, Oxford: Basil Blackwell.

(1992) *Social support and motherhood: The natural history of a research project*, Oxford: Basil Blackwell.

(1993) *Essays on women, medicine and health*, Edinburgh: Edinburgh University Press.

(2000) *Experiments in knowing: Gender and method in the social sciences*, Cambridge: Polity Press.

(2002) *Gender on planet earth*, Cambridge: Polity Press.

(2007) *Fracture*, Bristol: Policy Press.

(2011) *A critical woman: Barbara Wootton, social science and public policy in the twentieth century*, London: Bloomsbury Academic.

Ann Oakley, publications on Richard Titmuss

(1987) 'Social welfare and the position of women', Titmuss Memorial Lecture, Hebrew University of Jerusalem, Thomas Coram Research Unit Occasional Paper No 5.

(1991) 'Eugenics, social medicine and the career of Richard Titmuss in Britain 1935-50', *British Journal of Sociology*, 42 (2):165-94.

(1996) *Man and wife: Richard and Kay Titmuss, my parents' early years*, London: HarperCollins.

(1997, edited with J. Ashton) *The gift relationship by Richard M. Titmuss*, London: LSE Books.

(2001, edited with P. Alcock, H. Glennerster and A. Sinfield), *Welfare and wellbeing: Richard Titmuss's contribution to social policy*, Bristol: Policy Press.

(2004, edited with J. Barker) *Private complaints and public health: Richard Titmuss on the National Health Service*, Bristol: Policy Press.

Additional bibliography (books referred to in the text not listed in the endnotes)

Addams, J. (1895) *Hull-House maps and papers*, New York: Hull-House Association.

Blauner, R. (1964) *Alienation and freedom: The factory worker and his industry*, Chicago: Chicago University Press.

Dahrendorf, R. (1959) *Class and class conflict in industrial society*, London: Routledge and Kegan Paul.

de Beauvour, S. (1949, trans. Y. Moyse and R. Senhouse) *She came to stay*, London: Secker & Warburg.

De Schweinitz, K. (1961) *England's road to social security*, New York: A.S. Barnes & Co.

Engels, F (1969) *The condition of the working class in England*, Panther.

Firestone, S. (1972) *The dialectic of sex*, London: Paladin.

Friedan, B. (1963) *The feminine mystique*, London: Victor Gollancz.

Greer, G. (1990) *Daddy, we hardly knew you*, London: Penguin.

Greer, G. (1971) *The female eunuch*, London: Paladin.

Haire, D.B. (1972) *The cultural warping of childbirth*, International Childbirth Education Association.

Hamilton, G. (1940) *The theory and practice of social casework*, New York: Columbia University Press.

Jephcott, P. (1971) *Homes in high flats: Some of the human problems involved in multi-storey housing*, Edinburgh: Oliver and Boyd.

Lundberg, F. and Farnham, M.F.L. (1947) *Modern woman: The lost sex*, New York: Harper & Bros.

Luria, A.R. (1969) *The mind of a mnemonist: A little book about a vast memory*, London: Jonathan Cape.

Maushart, S. (1999) *The mask of motherhood: How becoming a mother changes everything and why we pretend it doesn't*, London: Pandora.

Millett, K. (1971) *Sexual politics*, London: Rupert Hart-Davis.

Mitchell, J. (1966) 'Women: the longest revolution', *New Left Review*, no 40, pp 11-37.

Myrdal, G. (1944) *An American dilemma*, New York: Harper and Row.

Myrdal, A. and Klein, V. (1956) *Women's two roles: Home and work*, London: Routledge and Kegan Paul.

Oakley, A. (1975) 'Sex discrimination legislation', *British Journal of Law and Society*, 2 (2): 211-17.

Rathbone, E.F. (1944) *The disinherited family*, London: Arnold.

Richmond, M.E.(1917) *Social diagnosis*, New York: The Free Press.

Sartre, J.-P. (1969, trans. H. E. Barnes) *Being and nothingness*, London: Methuen.

Smith, J. (1989) *Misogynies*, London: Faber.

Spender, D. (1980) *Man-made language*, London: Routledge and Kegan Paul.

Styron, W. (1976) *Sophie's choice*, London: Jonathan Cape.

Styron, W. (1992) *Darkness visible: A memoir of madness*, London: Pan.

Towle, C. (1945) *Common human needs*, Federal Security Agency.

Townsend, P. (1962) *The last refuge: A survey of institutions and homes for the aged in England and Wales*, London: Routledge & K. Paul.

Vaizey, J. (1958) *The costs of education*, London: Allen & Unwin.

Vaizey, J. (1959) *Scenes from institutional life*, London: Faber & Faber.

Woolf, V. (1993) *The crowded dance of modern life*, London: Penguin.

Wootton, B.(1967) *In a world I never made*, London: George Allen & Unwin.

Young, M. and Willmott, P. (1957) *Family and kinship in East London*, London: Routledge & Kegan Paul.

Young, M. and Willmott, P. (1973) *The symmetrical family: A study of work and leisure in the London region*, London: Routledge & Kegan Paul.

Younghusband Report (1959) *Report of the Working Party on Social Workers in the Local Authority Health and Welfare Services*, London: HMSO.

Index

NOTE: Family relationships in parentheses refer to the author, Ann Oakley.